S0-ARL-267

DISCOVERING HISTORY IN CHINA
American Historical Writing on the Recent Chinese Past

Studies of the East Asian Institute, Columbia University

DISCOVERING HISTORY IN CHINA

American Historical Writing on the Recent Chinese Past

PAUL A. COHEN

Columbia University Press
New York 1984

The Andrew W. Mellon Foundation, through a special grant, has assisted the Press in publishing this volume. The author and publisher acknowledge the generous support given them by the National Endowment for the Humanities. Research leading to this book was funded by a 1980-81 grant, and publication has been assisted by a matching grant from the Endowment.

Library of Congress Cataloging in Publication Data

Cohen, Paul A.
Discovering history in China.

Includes bibliographical references and index.
1. China—History—19th century—Historiography.
2. China—History—20th century—Historiography.
I. Title.
DS755.C63 1984 951'.0072'073 83-20868
ISBN 0-231-05810-1 (alk. paper)

Columbia University Press
New York Guildford, Surrey

Printed in the United States of America

Clothbound editions of Columbia University Press books are Smyth-sewn and printed on permanent and durable acid-free paper

For Joanna, Nathaniel, Lisa, and Emily

Contents

Preface

People who are not historians sometimes think of history as the facts about the past. Historians are supposed to know otherwise. The facts are there, to be sure, but they are infinite in number and speak, if at all, in conflicting, often unintelligible, voices. It is the task of the historian to reach back into this incoherent babel of facts, choose the ones that are important, and figure out what it is they say.

This is not an easy job. Although we have rules of evidence to help keep us honest, a large subjective element necessarily enters into all historical scholarship. Which facts we choose and which meanings we invest them with are deeply influenced by the questions we ask and the assumptions we operate under, and these questions and assumptions, in turn, reflect the concerns that are uppermost in our minds at any given moment. As times change and concerns shift, the questions and assumptions reflecting them also change. Thus, it is often said, each generation of historians must rewrite the history written by the preceding generation.

The concept of generation is, however, an ambiguous one. In corporate terms, every historian belongs to a particular generational cohort, and there is a tendency within the historical profession to associate generational cohorts (scholars, for example, trained at Harvard in the 1950s under John King Fairbank) with particular approaches or stages in a field's evolution (the "Harvard school" of China historiography). In individual terms, however, all historians, in the course of their productive years, also move through a succession of generational changes. The corporate generation to which each of us belongs is a powerful force, and it places real constraints on our capacity for intellectual movement. But the constraints are partial, not absolute. For one thing, individuals differ from the outset. People of the same age trained during the same time period by the same mentor, although sharing certain assumptions, never replicate each other exactly; indeed, as a close reading of the following pages will amply demonstrate, they may vary substantially in historical approach. For another thing, as we grow older, biologically and psychologically, and as the world we live in changes, sometimes in quite drastic ways, inevitably we are affected by these internal and external shifts, even those among us of stubbornly conservative bent whose bedrock assumptions appear to remain least disturbed.

Both of these generational perspectives—the corporate phases marking the development of a field and the individual phases experienced by historians as they respond to the changes going on about (and within) them—are reflected in the present book. The book is a critical appraisal of some of the major approaches that, since World War II, have shaped American writing on recent Chinese history. By "recent" I mean, in general, the nineteenth and twentieth centuries, a span of time often referred to as the modern era. For reasons that will become plain, I have developed serious misgivings about the application of the term "modern" to Chinese history, even for purely nominal purposes, and where possible have used labels like "recent" or "post-1800" instead. I have found it impossible, however, to avoid using the term entirely, as so many of the writers I discuss themselves divide Chinese history up into modern and traditional (or premodern) segments.

Aside from being an exploration of American historiography on China—and, as such, bearing directly on the intellectual dimension of Sino-American relations more broadly framed—the book also marks a point in the inner evolution of one historian. The decision to write it, taken shortly after I reached my fortieth year, was a direct outgrowth of intellectual problems with which I had been struggling for some time. These problems were partly biographical, partly historical in genesis. When my first book, *China and Christianity,* came out, I had only recently been launched on my career as a teacher, and my main preoccupations were in some ways more personal and professional than intellectual. Between the time of the book's germination as a seminar paper in my third year of graduate school (1957–1958) and its publication in 1963, nothing very earthshaking had happened in the world at large—nothing, at least, that shook my small piece of the earth. Unchallenged from without, the assumptions I had when I began the book were more or less the ones I had when I finished it. Coming from a nonacademic background and not quite believing that writers of books were real people, I was primarily concerned with proving to myself that I could indeed be a historian, which meant, in essence, producing a work of scholarship that measured up to the standards of craftsmanship set by the historical profession.

It was 1974 when my second book, *Between Tradition and Modernity,* appeared. I was surer of myself now as a historian and felt that it was a good book—better, from the point of view of craft, than the first. But I worried about whether it was "right." Right, that is, in terms of the internal coherence of the book's intellectual design and the validity of the assumptions that informed it. Unlike the period from 1957 to 1963, the years from 1964 to 1973, during which I was at work on this second book, were troubled, tumultuous years in America. What the Great Depression had done for an earlier generation, Vietnam, Cambodia, the Club of Rome report on the limits of growth, and Watergate did for mine. There was a difference, however. Where the Depression years had aroused a deep sense of concern over how American wealth was distributed and American society structured, the successive crises of the 1960s and early 1970s, by highlighting the contradiction between the destructive capability of American technology and the moral opaqueness of those Americans who had ultimate control over its use, raised questions about the very course of "modern" historical development. After Vietnam, there could be no more easy assumptions about the goodness of American power, no more easy equating of being "modern" with being "civilized."

Between Tradition and Modernity was about a Chinese reformer, Wang T'ao, who lived on the cultural frontier between China and the West in the latter half of the nineteenth century and thought and wrote about the Sino–Western encounter extensively. The problem I faced in trying to understand Wang was that the assumptions concerning "China" and "the West," "modernity" and "tradition," that I had when I started the book were severely jarred in the course of the decade that it took me to complete it. I was aware of this difficulty and at a number of points in the text discussed the problematic character particularly of the tradition–modernity polarity. I even toyed with the idea of entitling the book *Beyond*—rather than *Between—Tradition and Modernity*. But in the end, although Wang T'ao may have been "beyond," I remained "between." The thrust of my thinking pushed in one direction, but the concepts that still framed it were pulling me in another, with the result that the underlying intellectual framework of the book was marked by a certain tension.

After completing the Wang T'ao book and gaining some distance from it, my discomfort came to a head and I realized that the only way to deal with it was to confront directly the overarching conceptual frameworks or paradigms that, it seemed to me, had dominated postwar American writing on nineteenth- and twentieth-century Chinese history. (As will shortly be noted, I had already made a preliminary stab in this direction in 1970.) Although in terms of motivation there was bound to be a strong personal component to such a confrontation, the end product, I hoped, would also be of use to colleagues and students. The field of recent Chinese history had been relatively free of self-critical historiographical writing until the late 1960s. Beginning around that time, in the

Bulletin of Concerned Asian Scholars (and later in the quarterly journal *Modern China,* which began publishing in 1975), a more critical perspective had gradually developed. I welcomed this critical perspective and felt that its effects on a field that had grown overly sleepy in its thinking were salutary. I did not, however, always agree with the specific criticisms leveled. Moreover, even when I wanted to agree I often found the empirical data gathered in support of the criticisms to be inadequate or the criticisms themselves to be too unqualified or simplistic or extreme to be persuasive. Torn between uneasiness over parts of the new critical perspective and equal uneasiness over much that the critics were criticizing, I aspired to present a historiographical overview that, if less iconoclastic than some of the critiques that had thus far been offered, would at least have the merit of clarifying the central issues involved.

Although the work of many friends and colleagues is subjected to scrutiny in this book, there is not one from whom I have not learned something. Indeed, to several of them, above all John King Fairbank, whom I was privileged to have as a teacher, and Joseph R. Levenson, whom I knew only slightly but admired from afar, I feel an immense intellectual debt. Indebtedness among historians is a peculiar thing, however. We don't simply, in mechanical fashion, inherit a body of knowledge, add something to it, and pass it on. We also question, test, and shake here and there the intellectual scaffolding surrounding our predecessors' work, in the full, ironic knowledge that someone else is going to come along and give the scaffolding surrounding our own work a good shake, too, that no historian, in short, is ever permitted the final word.

But criticism is one thing; unfairness is another. I take the matter of unfairness very seriously and have worried about it a good deal in the writing of these pages. I have tried to be balanced in my judgments and, in pointing out deficiencies in an individual's work or an overall approach, have spelled out as clearly as possible the premises on which my criticism is based. Still, a certain amount of distortion is inevitable when one attempts to present someone else's writing as confirmation of one's own analytical perspective. Something of the ebb and flow of people's ideas in time is bound to get lost; the contrapuntal themes and qualifications, even the redeeming inconsistencies, that texture any scholar's work are apt to recede from view. Thus, in portraying John Fairbank and Joseph Levenson as leading exponents of the dominant approaches of American historiography in the 1950s and 1960s, it is easily forgotten that Fairbank, in the course of a career spanning more than fifty years, has approached China from a number of different perspectives—he never, in any case, was remiss in welcoming scholarship rooted in premises other than his own—and that Levenson, although prevented by a tragic death in 1969 from responding to the new currents of interpretation just then emerging, had a mind that was far too searching and subtle to be permanently confined by any one framework of assumptions.

If perfect balance has not been possible in the treatment of individuals, I have not sought it in respect to subject matter. This is a highly—some will say shamelessly—selective book. It lays somewhat more stress on the nineteenth century, as this period is absolutely crucial for two of the intellectual paradigms—impact–response and tradition–modernity—to be examined. The book is also selective in the scholarly writings it covers and the particular topics and problems it addresses, reflecting intellectual concerns that have been paramount in the mind of one historian but surely not all. I assume that some of my colleagues will have a quite different agenda of concerns and that if they were to attempt a book like this it would come out looking very different. I hope they will make the attempt.

Although embodying common themes and forming a coherent whole, the four chapters into which the book is divided may also be read as independent, self-contained essays. Chapters 2 to 4 were written expressly for this volume. The first chapter, dealing with the impact–response paradigm, consists of an updated and heavily recast version of a piece originally published some years ago.* The working plan of chapter 1 differs somewhat from that of the other chapters in that it weighs the impact–response approach against actual historical cases, whereas chapters 2 to 4 concentrate more directly on analysis of the scholarly writings of American historians. Although I did not plan it as such, there is somewhat greater emphasis in chapter 1 on political history, in chapter 2 on intellectual history, in chapter 3 on economic history, and in the concluding chapter on social history. These are only emphases, however; all of the chapters, for example, deal to some extent with problems of political history.

Since my aim in this book is to identify and analyze critically the assumptions that have pervaded *American* historiography, other major historiographical traditions dealing with nineteenth- and twentieth-century China—Chinese, Japanese, European, Soviet—are largely omitted from the discussion. This is in no way to discount the immense influence that historians working in other traditions—above all those of China and Japan—have exerted on American scholarship. This influence, however, has been filtered and shaped by American concerns and preoccupations. And it is the manner in which these latter have generated a peculiarly American historiography that is my central interest.

There is an important premise here that needs to be explicated. Among the several factors governing the evolution of any field of historical inquiry, the political, intellectual, and cultural milieu within which the historian lives and works is, in my view, primary; everything else is secondary. Certainly, all historical fields undergo a process of internal development, as new techniques are discovered, language training and competence improve, knowledge is accumulated, and entrée is gained to archival and other sources of data that previously were either unknown or inaccessible. But while this internal

*As "Ch'ing China: Confrontation with the West, 1850-1900," in James B. Crowley, ed., *Modern East Asia: Essays in Interpretation* (New York: Harcourt, Brace, and World, 1970), pp. 29–61.

development is an essential precondition for a field's growth, it does not determine the direction and pattern of growth. The approaches followed, the basic questions asked, will still be principally shaped by the sociocultural environment of the historian. Similarly, with respect to the potential influence of alternative historiographical traditions, the influence is likely to be strongest in the areas of empirical data, research techniques, and strategies for investigating discrete, well-defined historical problems, weakest in the realm of overall conceptual approach. Japanese and mainland Chinese historians, under the sway of Marxist historiography, were paying close attention to socioeconomic causation for years before American historians got around to taking such causation seriously. When they finally did, toward the end of the 1960s, it was a reflection of important shifts taking place in the United States, not of anything new happening in China or Japan.

Consistent with this general point of view, the great preponderance of historians whose writings are brought under scrutiny in this book are from America. An occasional exception is, however, made in the case of scholars who, though not themselves American, are heavily involved in an American professional milieu, periodically attend conferences and share journal space with American historians, and regularly collaborate with them in scholarly publication. However individually creative these writers may be, they do not, in my view, constitute a radically distinct historiographical tradition. A slightly different case is presented by historians of Chinese origin resident in the United States. Such historians, in terms of both numbers and influence, form an important part of the Chinese history field in America. With very few exceptions, those of them whose work is discussed in these pages, in addition to teaching in this country, received all or part of their training here and do most of their scholarly writing in English. Their inclusion in any account of American historiography is, therefore, not merely justified but imperative.

A word or two, finally, on mechanical matters. Since I view this book not as a comprehensive "review of the literature" but as an interpretive discussion of the major approaches that have shaped American historical writing on the recent Chinese past, I have resisted the inclusion of a bibliography. Full publication information is, however, supplied in the notes to each chapter on a source's first citation in that chapter. With respect to the transcription of Chinese words, although increasing numbers of publications in the China field are changing over to the *pinyin* system, I have retained the Wade-Giles system here. The reason, quite simply, is that this is a book about other books, the vast majority of which themselves employ the older system. Since there are numerous direct quotations from these writings in the text, if I were to switch in my own prose to the newer system it would be needlessly confusing to all but the most specialized of readers, who alone could be trusted to know that Tz'u-hsi and Cixi were not two different ladies.

Because there are as many experts on the subject matter of this book as people familiar with American scholarship on nineteenth- and twentieth-century Chinese history, I was able, at every step along the way, to lean heavily on the advice and criticism of other scholars. Among these, my greatest debt is to Merle Goldman, Philip Kuhn, Lillian Li, Andrew Nathan, James Polachek, Mary Rankin, Henry Rosemont, and James Sheridan, all of whom read the manuscript with unusual attentiveness and took the trouble to write out lengthy comments for my use. I also want to thank Paul Evans, John Fairbank, Noriko Kamachi, Jonathan Ocko, John Schrecker, and Benjamin Schwartz, for their suggestions and admonitions on a wide range of matters.

I benefited from audience questions and comments when the main themes of chapter 2 were presented in lectures at Whitman College and the University of Washington. Helpful discussion and criticism of portions of the manuscript also came from colleagues at Wellesley and Harvard and from participants in a conference on Chinese society in the late Ch'ing and early republican periods, held at Fudan University in Shanghai in August 1981.

I am indebted to the National Endowment for the Humanities and to Wellesley College for grant support during the 1980–81 academic year. For support of an entirely different nature, involving a rare combination of warm encouragement, sound counsel, and invaluable practical assistance, I am delighted at last to have the opportunity to express my deep gratitude to Dorothy Borg.

Finally, I want to thank my children, to whom this book is lovingly dedicated, not for anything in particular but for everything contributed over the years to making my life a richer and fuller one.

DISCOVERING HISTORY IN CHINA
American Historical Writing on the Recent Chinese Past

How can mankind move upward except by standing on the shoulders and faces of the older generation?

JOHN KING FAIRBANK

No one has the norm of norms.

JOSEPH R. LEVENSON

Introduction

THE SUPREME problem for American students of Chinese history, particularly in its post-Western impact phase, has been one of ethnocentric distortion. One source of this problem is the obvious fact that the West—our West—has played a direct and vitally important part in recent Chinese history. Another source, somewhat less obvious, is that the Chinese themselves, both Marxist and non-Marxist, in reconstructing their own history, have depended heavily on vocabulary, concepts, and analytical frameworks borrowed from the West, thus depriving Western historians of compelling insider-produced alternatives to our own outsider perspectives. These perspectives have, until very recently, tended to distort Chinese history either by exaggerating the role of the West or, more subtly, by misconstruing this role. The great challenge for Western historians is not the impossible one of eliminating all ethnocentric distortion; it is the possible one of reducing such distortion to a minimum and in the process freeing ourselves to see Chinese history in new, less Western-centered ways.

Up through World War II, American writing tended to stress those aspects of the recent Chinese past with which the West itself had been most immediately concerned: the Opium War, the Taiping uprising, Sino–foreign trade, treaty port life and institutions, the Boxers, Sun Yat-sen, diplomatic relations, the missionary enterprise, Japanese aggression, and so on. This emphasis on the more Western-related facets of Chinese history was partly a consequence of the inability of most American scholars to handle Chinese sources and the inaccessibility, in any case, of important collections of these sources. It was also a result of an intellectual bias that equated *modern* with *Western* and *Western* with *important*. For many Americans of this era, even educated ones, Westernized China and modern China were indistinguishable.

This was the amateur phase of American writing on China. Much of the work was in the hands of missionaries, diplomats, customs officials, and the like, people with little formal training as scholars and none as historians of China. Then, in the two decades following World War II, building on the foundation laid by a tiny handful of trained historians who had studied in China in the 1930s, a new generation of American China specialists came into being, and the level of sophistication of American study of Chinese history underwent a quantum leap forward. A true professional field was, for the first time, now constituted. As language training improved, partly owing to the impetus of the war, and more and more scholarship came to be based on a solid ground of Chinese documentation, an entire new world gradually became accessible to Americans. We began to get inside China, to see how the Chinese themselves felt about their recent past.

The emphasis, nevertheless, was still to an overwhelming extent on the shaping role of the Western intrusion. There were exceptions. One thinks, in particular, of the early studies of Ping-ti Ho on population (1959) and social mobility (1962) and of the excellent pioneering work on nineteenth-century social, political, and military history done by Chung-li Chang, Kung-chuan Hsiao, Franz Michael, and other participants in the Modern Chinese History Project at the University of Washington in the 1950s and 1960s.[1] In the field as a whole, however, the great preponderance of scholarly work during this period was structured either in terms of the Western challenge and how this challenge had been met or in terms of the impact of modernization—Western-carried and Western-defined—on China's traditional culture and society.

These two allied approaches came under sharp attack in the late 1960s. The basis for the attack, however, was not that the role of the West had been overstated but rather that the impact–response and modernization approaches seemed to present Western expansion in positive terms and Chinese resistance to the West in negative language. The critics, strongly influenced by classical theories of imperialism and the application of these theories to China by American and Chinese writers in the 1930s and 1940s, found fault with what they saw as an excessive emphasis by American historians upon studies of internal Chinese developments, an emphasis that seemed to them to imply that China's problems in the past century and a half had stemmed mainly from weaknesses or deficiencies in Chinese society and culture. In place of this, they called for case studies of Western imperialism, with a view to showing the negative, stunting effects that imperialism had had on Chinese development. Back we were told to go again to the Opium War, the unequal treaties, the treaty ports, and the Boxers. Only now, with a radically different perspective in mind, we were asked to explore the ways in which Western involvement in China had inhibited and distorted the natural forward movement of Chinese history.

In the pages that follow, these three conceptual frameworks—impact–response, modernization, and imperialism—will each be brought under critical scrutiny. On the most general level, my main point will be that all three, in one way or another, introduce Western-centric distortions into our understanding of nineteenth- and twentieth-century China. The impact–response framework, by focusing on China's response to the "Western challenge," encourages a tendency to interpret developments that were not simply or primarily responses to the West as if they were; it also prompts historians to define aspects of recent Chinese history that had no obvious connections with the Western presence as unimportant—or, alternatively, as important *only* insofar as they shed light on China's response to the West.

The modernization, or tradition–modernity approach, with deep roots in nineteenth-century Western attitudes toward culture, change, China, and the West, sins in imposing on Chinese history an external—and parochially Western—definition of what change is and what kinds of change are important. Implicitly, if not explicitly, it concentrates more on asking of Chinese history questions posed by modern Western history—whether, for example, China could have generated on its own a modern scientific tradition and an industrial revolution or why it didn't—and less on asking questions posed by Chinese history itself. The underlying assumption is that modern Western history is the norm, with the corollary assumption that there is something peculiar or abnormal about China requiring special explanation.

The imperialism approach, at least in its more sweeping formulations, is vulnerable on a number of counts. Sometimes it falls into the ahistorical trap of *assuming* for Chinese history a "natural" or "normal" course of development with which Western (and later Japanese) imperialism interfered. At other times, it sees China as being stalled in nondevelopment and thus in dire need of a jolt from without. In these circumstances, the proponents of the approach don't quite know what to do with the West. The West, to some, seems necessary in order to "activate" Chinese history. Yet, to all, the West is consistently seen as a baleful influence, as the source of everything—or nearly everything—that went wrong in China in the last 150 years.

Before going any further, let me attempt to clarify a number of matters that may already be puzzling or confusing some readers. First, my real quibble in this book is not with the disciplined, descriptive application of terms like *imperialism, impact, response,* or even *modern* to specific, precisely delimited processes or phenomena that have emerged in the past century or so of Chinese history; what I object to is the use of these concepts as broad, overarching intellectual constructs purporting to tell us what was important—and by implication not important—about an entire period of historical time.

More specifically, in finding fault with the heavily Western-centric character of the major paradigms that have guided postwar American writing on nineteenth- and twentieth-century Chinese history, I do not mean to suggest quixotically that, in my judgment, the West was of little consequence in this history. My aim, instead, is to expose critically modes of addressing recent Chinese history that *predefine* the West's importance and then go on to demonstrate it. We are dealing here, in other words, with two things: the ideas American historians carry in their heads with respect to the role of the West in nineteenth- and twentieth-century China, and the West's actual historical role. My argument is not that the West's actual historical role was unimportant but rather that it has been blown out of proportion in comparison with other factors and misstated, and that both the overstatement and misstatement have been a consequence largely of the conceptual paradigms with which Americans have approached China.

The overstatement has been particularly egregious with respect to the nineteenth century; the misstatement, I think, runs through the entire period. The impact–response and modernization paradigms are structured in such a way as to select out principally those phases of the historical process that either promote or retard "progress," "development," and "modernity"; the imperialism paradigm is so structured as to select out mainly those factors that promote or retard the "revolution," which, in turn, is assumed to be the essential precondition for "progress," "development," and "modernity." All three paradigms are thus burdened by Western-inspired assumptions about how history *should* go and built-in questions—equally Western-inspired—about why it does or does not go as it should. Like all approaches of a highly teleological nature, they are fundamentally circular in that they end up finding in a vast and complex historical reality precisely what they set out to look for.

Finally, in repudiating the old Western picture of a static, unchanging China as being a reflection of parochial assumptions concerning the sorts of change that are significant, I have no intention of insinuating into Chinese history an equally parochial, equally Western-centric, equally counterhistorical set of assumptions, to wit, that change *as such* is good, that the more change a society experiences the "better" it is, and that therefore, to even the score with the West, China *must* be seen as a vigorous and dynamic society, alive with change of every sort. I most emphatically do not believe that change per se is good; I believe that some change is good and some bad. As a historian, on the other hand, I take it as an article of faith (convinced, of course, that it is more than faith) that all societies undergo change all the time and that the degree to which such change is deemed significant, is "noticed," is ultimately a relative matter, dependent upon what a particular historian living in a particular society at a particular time happens to regard as important.

This, it seems to me, is the nub of the issue. In each of the analytic frameworks examined in the first three chapters of this book, a particular yardstick is used to determine what kind of change is important. Because this kind of change did not in fact take place in China prior to the arrival of the West or—and this is a very different matter—because it was believed by the Westerners who designed the yardstick to have been *incapable* of taking place in the West's absence, when the yardstick is applied to China we discover, not surprisingly, a society that is unchanging or at best only trivially changing.[2] There are two problems with this perception. First, because Westerners on the whole and Americans in particular happen to place a high cultural valuation on change, or at least certain forms of it, the vision of a nonchanging or trivially changing China is implicitly condescending. The other—and much more serious—problem is that the perception is almost certainly incorrect.

This last point is developed at length in the final chapter of the book, which delineates some of the more recent trends in American China historiography, in particular the move away from the impact–response and tradition–modernity paradigms toward a more China-centered approach to Chinese history, and summarizes the implications of the new orientation. This new orientation has been part of a broader shift in American historical scholarship, visible in recent work on Africa, the Muslim Middle East, and other non-Western areas, as well as China. Details of timing and circumstance have varied from case to case, but in each instance the general direction of movement has been the same: away from an external—often "colonial history"—perspective toward a more internal approach characterized by a vigorous effort to see the history of any given non-Western society in its own terms and from its own point of view rather than as an extension—actual or conceptual—of Western history.[3]

In the case of China, this shift began to occur around 1970 or just before, precisely at the time, ironically, that some members of the profession were reviving the old imperialism paradigm, with its pronounced Western-centric bias, to attack the influence of modernization theory on American scholarship. The irony reflects a fundamental contradiction that came to light during the Vietnam War and has been confirmed and reconfirmed since. Vietnam, from one perspective, represented the apotheosis of American imperialism—the unleashing of enormous destructive power against a nation far smaller, poorer, and weaker than our own. It was natural, in these circumstances, for American historians, appalled and deeply ashamed by their country's behavior in the war, to see imperialism with new eyes, as key to the problems experienced by China and other Asian countries over the preceding century.

But Vietnam also took Americans beyond imperialism. Like the Arab oil embargo of 1973 and the Iranian hostage crisis of 1979–1981, it confronted us with the limits of our power, the very real constraints upon our capacity to bend the world to American purposes. This second meaning of Vietnam also, in my judgment, had a profound impact on American historians of China. By exposing the myth of American global supremacy—political, moral, cultural—it freed American historians, perhaps for the first time, to abandon Western norms and measures of significance and to move toward a more genuinely *other*-centered historiography, a historiography rooted in the historical experience not of the West but of China.

CHAPTER ONE

The Problem with "China's Response to the West"

AMERICAN INTERPRETATIONS of Chinese history from the Opium War (1839–1842) to the Boxer uprising (1899–1900) tended, in the 1950s and 1960s, to lean heavily on the concepts "Western impact" and "Chinese response." This conceptual framework rested on the assumption that, for much of the nineteenth century, the confrontation with the West was the most significant influence on events in China. A further assumption, implicit in the phrasing of the concepts, was that it was the West that played the truly *active* role in this period of Chinese history, a much more passive or *reactive* part being taken by China.

One of the strongest evocations of the paramount importance of the Western impact was made by Ssu-yü Teng and John K. Fairbank in the introduction to their influential book, *China's Response to the West* (1954):

> Since China is the largest unitary mass of humanity, with the oldest continuous history, its overrunning by the West in the past century was bound to create a continuing and violent intellectual revolution, the end of which we have not yet seen. . . . Throughout this century of the "unequal treaties," the ancient society of China was

brought into closer and closer contact with the then dominant and expanding society of Western Europe and America. This Western contact, lent impetus by the industrial revolution, had the most disastrous effect upon the old Chinese society. In every sphere of social activity the old order was challenged, attacked, undermined, or overwhelmed by a complex series of processes—political, economic, social, ideological, cultural—which were set in motion within China as a result of this penetration of an alien and more powerful society. The massive structure of traditional China was torn apart. . . . The old order was changed within the space of three generations.[1]

"Western impact" and "Eastern response" are also core concepts in one of the most frequently reprinted and widely distributed textbooks of the postwar era, *The Far East: A History of the Western Impact and the Eastern Response,* by Paul H. Clyde and Burton F. Beers. "Throughout the past 150 years," Clyde and Beers wrote in the 1966 edition of their work,

Eastern Asia has been the stage for a revolution perhaps unequalled in all history in the breadth and depth of its penetration. It has involved two great movements. The first was the expansion of Western civilization in all its aspects and power into the old and traditional societies of Middle and Eastern Asia. This movement, which began in the early nineteenth century and is usually called the "Impact of the West," had all but conquered Asia in terms of political power by the beginning of the twentieth century. By that time, however, the second aspect of this revolution was well under way. The response of Asia to the Western impact was at first faltering, uneven, and uncharted, but by the end of World War II it had gathered an irresistible momentum. The result in mid-twentieth century was a new Eastern Asia.[2]

Although the Clyde–Beers text applies the impact–response paradigm to the entire sweep of recent Chinese history, most applications have focused on the nineteenth century. The classic example is found in *A History of East Asian Civilization,* coauthored by John K. Fairbank, Edwin O. Reischauer, and Albert M. Craig. The treatment of nineteenth-century China in the second volume of this text (1965), principally the responsibility of Fairbank, centers on the question: "Why did China not respond to foreign encroachment earlier and more vigorously?" Because this is the key question, a number of imbalances or distortions emerge in Fairbank's account. First, on a purely quantitative level, disproportionate attention (roughly 75 percent of overall coverage) is paid to Western-related facets of the history of the period. Second, because these Western-related facets are seen largely through the prism of the impact–response approach, their historical import is stated in insufficiently complex terms: developments that were, in significant measure, responses to internal factors are overinterpreted as responses to the foreign impact. And third, Fairbank's need to account for China's "unresponsiveness to the Western challenge" forces him repeatedly to characterize—one might almost say caricaturize—the non-Western-related aspects of nineteenth-century China (state, society, economy, thought) in terms of their "remarkable inertia."[3]

Although the impact–response approach, as a framework for serious scholarly analysis, had its heyday in the 1950s and 1960s, its influence on textbooks and other undergraduate teaching materials continues unabated. In some cases, as in *China's Response to the West,* this is because the original work has never been revised.[4] In other cases, as in the Clyde–Beers and Fairbank–Reischauer–Craig texts or another widely used textbook, *The Far East in the Modern World* by Franz Michael and George Taylor, revised editions have periodically appeared but without altering the overall conceptual framework of the first edition.[5] One way or another, we are thus faced with a lag between the latest trends of scholarly research and the picture of Chinese history with which beginning students are presented.

The main trouble with this picture is not that it is "wrong" but that its intellectual reach is not clearly spelled out and delimited. Much as, in the field of physics, developments over the past century, though not disproving Newton's laws, have shown these laws to have a limited range of applicability, the impact–response approach to late Ch'ing (1644–1912) history can account for some things, but it cannot, as in the instances noted above, tell the whole story.[6]

THE IMPACT–RESPONSE FRAMEWORK: SOME PROBLEMS

In addition to the general question of scale of applicability, there are a number of more specific problems pertaining to the impact–response approach. One such is the tendency, when speaking of the "Western impact," to ignore the enigmatic and contradictory nature of the modern West. Most of us, while properly humbled by the superficiality of our understanding of "non-Western" societies, think of the West, which is home ground, as a known quantity. Yet, "when we turn our attention back to the modern West itself," as Benjamin Schwartz has observed, "this deceptive clarity disappears. We are aware that the best minds of the nineteenth and twentieth centuries have been deeply divided in their agonizing efforts to grasp the inner meaning of modern Western development. . . . We undoubtedly 'know' infinitely more about the West [than about any given non-Western society], but the West remains as problematic as ever."[7]

One reason why it remains so problematic is that the modern West has changed greatly over time. The West that China encountered during the Opium War and the West that exerted such great influence on Chinese intellectual and political life in the 1920s and 1930s were both the "modern West." But there were vast differences between the two. It is a truism, easily forgotten, that the West, in its modern phase, has not stood still.

Also easily forgotten is the fact that "the West" is a relative concept only. Without an "East" or a "non-West" to compare it with, it would quite simply not exist; there would be no word for it in our vocabulary. If the concept of the West did not exist, of course, the spatial variations within the geographical area now subsumed under "the West" would loom much larger in our minds. The differences between France and America might seem just as great as those between China and the West. We may also suppose, to carry the point to its logical conclusion, that if America were the only country in the world, it would be known neither as America nor as a country, and our awareness of difference would be focused entirely upon the internal variations within "American" culture.

It is easier, when we think in this vein, to grasp the notion that the "total West" never had an impact on other societies. Shanghai in the late nineteenth century seemed "Western" in contrast to an indubitably Chinese hinterland, but Shanghai—its administrative institutions dominated by colonial Britain, its economy heavily commercialized, its population overwhelmingly Chinese—was no more a microcosmic representation of Western culture than New York City is of the culture of North America. Similarly, in viewing the first half of the twentieth century, when virtually every strain of Western thought at one time or another found an advocate in Chinese intellectual circles, it would be absurd to think in terms of an impact of the total culture of the West. Even when Chinese talked of "all-out Westernization," what they really had in mind was not the mechanical substitution of Western society and culture for Chinese but the transformation of China in line with a highly selective vision of what the West was all about. Hu Shih (1891–1962) wanted China to adopt Western science and democracy, not Western Christianity; his conception of science and democracy, moreover, was distinctly Deweyan, not generically Western.

The "West" that countries like China encountered was only part of a whole. Even this part, moreover, was metamorphosed in the process of encounter. A man who left the West to do missionary work in China in the nineteenth century was probably not a very typical Westerner to begin with. After living in China for a while, he surely became even less typical. In learning Chinese and adopting certain Chinese customs, he interacted with his new environment, and a process of hybridization set in. No longer a Westerner pure and simple, he became a Westerner-in-China. Although the Chinese with whom he came in contact continued to view him as a foreigner—which of course he still was—their perception of his foreignness was colored by *his* response to *Chinese* foreignness. It is not enough, therefore, to explain what took place simply in terms of a Western impact and a Chinese response; there was also a Western response to a Chinese impact.

A similar hybridization occurred in the realm of ideas. Ideas, unlike people, cannot actively respond to situations. But they are, at least in part, defined by situations, for they have meaning only in the minds of people and the meaning a given idea has for a given person will be richly conditioned by the circumstances of its presentation. It makes little sense, then, to talk of direct Chinese responses to such Western ideas as national sovereignty, Christianity, and progress. Before these ideas could evoke responses, they had to be communicated, and they could be communicated only by being filtered through Chinese language and thought patterns. (The reference here is not, of course, to that minority of Chinese who in the twentieth century had direct access to Western languages.) Inevitably this resulted in distortion of the original ideas. (For example, "liberty" or "freedom" was translated *tzu-yu,* which literally means "from the self" and has connotations of license or lawlessness.) And it was to the distorted native version rather than to the foreign original that most Chinese responded.[8]

The initial Western impact was subject to another sort of distortion when it was Chinese-carried. In some cases, as in the relationships between merchants and compradors or missionaries and converts, the West's impact was more or less immediate and direct. But in others it was not. When Christianity was purveyed by Chinese rebels or Western-style institutions were championed by Chinese reformers, the impact of the West was at one or more removes from its source. As this happened, it became hopelessly entangled in the web of Chinese personalities and politics, and it is highly questionable whether, from this point on, the conventional impact–response framework of analysis remains useful. The Ch'ing government's response to the Taiping insurgency and the responses of conservatives and moderate reformers to the reform movement of 1898 were elicited as much by familiar challenges of rebellion and reform as by the unfamiliar challenge of the West. It would be extremely misleading to characterize them simply as responses to the West.

One more trap that is easily fallen into is the tendency to lapse into excessive abstraction in discussing the "Chinese response." China, as a geographical entity, is continental in size and exhibits a staggering range of ethnic, linguistic, and regional variation. Within any given region there has always been a great gulf between the world view and life pattern of the elites and those of the masses. Even within each of these two broad social divisions, as in any grouping of human beings anywhere, attitudes and behavior have been governed by personality, character, age, sex, and the particular constellation of a given individual's social, religious, economic, and political relationships. The term *Chinese response,* therefore, can serve at best as shorthand for a very complex historical situation. On one level, to be sure, all natives of China—men and women, city dwellers and peasants, rich people and poor, Cantonese and Hunanese—were participants in a common cultural order that can properly be labeled Chinese. But on another level the experiences of these people were not common at all. Each subgroup's point of entry into the larger Chinese culture was different, and this differentness gave shape to the ways in which they responded to situations. When we refer to such responses as Chinese, therefore, we are engaging in a kind of adding up and averaging that can at best lead to a homogenized perception of historical reality; at worst, in moving recklessly from the particular to the general, we risk distorting this reality altogether.

In brief, the story of China's response to the West in the last century is nothing if not complicated. Much that happened in this era, although historically important, was unrelated, or only marginally related, to the Western impact. And much else that happened was directly or indirectly shaped by this impact but cannot be viewed simply, or even in some instances principally, as a "response" to it, in the sense of a conscious effort to deal with the new problems it created. Examples of the former category of historical activity will be looked at in chapter 4. Here I should like to explore the latter category, with a view to demonstrating the limitations of the impact–response approach as a guide to historical understanding, even in situations in which one might expect it to be most applicable.

WESTERN-RELATED ASPECTS OF LATE CH'ING HISTORY

REBELLION

In terms of immediate effect on the position of the Ch'ing dynasty and the lives of tens of millions of ordinary Chinese subjects, the most noteworthy development in China in the middle of the last century was not the nettling behavior of small enclaves of Westerners pocketed here and there along the seacoast. The big story was internal unrest. Aside from numerous local revolts, there were four rebellions of major proportions: a Muslim rebellion in Yunnan (1855–1873), another Muslim rebellion in the northwest (1862–1873), the Nien (1853–1868), and the Taiping (1850–1864). Of these, by far the most important uprising was the Taiping. It was also the most destructive, leaving large portions of the Lower Yangtze Valley region completely devastated and an estimated twenty to forty million Chinese dead. The Taipings were the only one of the mid-century rebel movements to be significantly affected by the Western intrusion. Whether they may profitably be viewed in the larger framework of "China's response to the West," as suggested in a number of textbook treatments,[9] however, is another matter. Let us take a closer look at the movement's history and general character.

The spawning ground for the Taiping movement was south China, where conditions favorable to rebellion were probably riper than anyplace else in the empire. The south was the last part of China to be brought under Manchu rule in the seventeenth century, and it remained one of the least secure links in the Ch'ing power structure. By the end of the eighteenth century it was subject to severe pressures from overpopulation and tenancy. On top of all this, it was in south China that the disruptive effects of Sino–foreign trade and the Opium War were most pronounced. Changing trade patterns (for example, the shift of foreign trade away from Canton to other ports after the war) and the spread of piracy and smuggling into the interior encouraged social dislocation, while British defeat of the Manchus activated Cantonese xenophobia and helped to give it an anti-Manchu focus. Whatever may be said of the superficiality of the Western impact elsewhere in China prior to 1850, in the far south it was real and profound.

The man who was to become the founder and early leader of the Taiping movement, Hung Hsiu-ch'üan, was born in south China, about thirty miles from Canton, in 1814. Significantly, Hung belonged to an ethnic minority—the Hakkas, or "guests"—which, although it had migrated south centuries before, was still segregated from the surrounding society by its distinctive language and customs. The brightest in a family of five children, Hung was given enough schooling to permit him to compete in the government examinations held in Canton. Each time he took the examinations, however, he failed. Once after this happened, he suffered a mental collapse and was confined to bed for forty days, during which time he later claimed to have had visions. In 1843, after failing the examinations once again, he read a Christian tract that had been given him some years before and for the first time understood the meaning of his visions. Hung became convinced that he was the younger brother of Jesus, that he had been divinely charged to rid the world of demons and idols and to institute on earth the Kingdom of Heaven.

Hung Hsiu-ch'üan and a friend, also an unsuccessful examination candidate, now began to lead proselytizing forays in Kwangtung and Kwangsi. With their followers, who consisted mainly of discontented peasants and secret society members, they formed a loose grouping known as the Society of God-Worshipers. By the late 1840s local unrest and famine forced the society to organize for military protection against banditry. They themselves, however, were not readily distinguishable from bandits, and in the unsettled conditions then prevailing in south China, they soon found themselves engaged in pitched battle with imperial troops. One thing led to another, and in January 1851 they raised the standard of antidynastic revolt, Hung taking the title of Heavenly King (*t'ien-wang*) and the new order being christened the Heavenly Kingdom of Great Peace (T'ai-p'ing t'ien-kuo).

The Taiping rebels soon pressed north, piling success on success against the hapless imperial forces, until they reached the Yangtze River. They then turned eastward and in March 1853 established their capital in Nanking, which remained the political center of the movement until its collapse in 1864. In the course of their northward march in the early 1850s, the Taipings grew from a smallish provincial rebellion into a movement that, in terms of its human and physical resources, was huge in scale. Although the chief arena of rebel control remained in east central China, in fifteen years of fighting most of China's provinces were affected. A northern expedition in the mid-1850s reached the environs of Tientsin before being turned back, and in the early 1860s, as the center of rebel strength shifted toward the coast, Shanghai was threatened on a number of occasions.

In the view of many American scholars, the most revolutionary aspects of the Taiping movement were its ideology and organizational structure.[10] Taiping ideology was a bizarre alchemy of evangelical Christianity, primitive communism, sexual puritanism, and Confucian utopianism. The rebels' advanced social and economic doctrines (which included security and protection for the aged, the handicapped, the widowed, and the orphaned) were built around the idea of the brotherhood and equality of all mankind, a corollary to the belief in the fatherhood of God. Women were to be treated as full equals of men, being permitted to fight in the army, take the government examinations (though the evidence on this point is somewhat tenuous), and hold office. The feminism of the Taipings was further evidenced in their proscription of footbinding, prostitution, and polygamy and in their injunction that land be allotted equitably without distinction as to sex. All private property was abolished, and movable goods were supposed to be placed in common treasuries for redistribution on the basis of need.

The political goal of the Taipings was to overthrow the Ch'ing and establish a new dynasty—new in kind as well as in name. The model for their political-military organization was taken from the *Chou li* (Rites of Chou), a Chinese classical text believed to describe the administrative system of the early Chou period. At the top of the rebels' political structure was the Heavenly King, Hung Hsiu-ch'üan, who, theoretically at least, was supreme in both the spiritual and temporal realms. Hung was surrounded initially by five other "kings" (*wang*), each of whom had full civil and military power within his territorial jurisdiction. Beneath the top leadership was a hierarchy of lesser military commanders who served concurrently as the military officers, civil administrators, and religious leaders of their units. The resulting organization, which was largely the creation of Hung's chief lieutenant Yang Hsiu-ch'ing (d. 1856), has been characterized by Franz Michael as "totalitarian" and, in Michael's view, provided for "a system of total control of all life by the state which had no parallel in Chinese history."[11]

From this brief overview it is clear that the Taiping uprising would have been a very different affair had it not been for the presence of the West. China's defeat in the Opium War and the disruptive influence of foreign trade in south China contributed to the general dislocation out of which the rebellion emerged. The revolutionary challenge to the existing social and political order posed by the rebels' ideology was generated, at least in part, by Protestant Christianity. One of the top rebel leaders in the last years of the insurrection, Hung Jen-kan (1822–1864), was directly exposed to Western culture.

Moreover, the suppression of the uprising in the early 1860s was materially assisted (above all in Kiangsu province) by British and French troops, Western-led mercenaries (most notably the "Ever Victorious Army"), and Western-supplied modern arms.

Yet, for all this, the Taiping movement cannot be viewed in any significant sense as a response to the West. It was not directed against the West. It was not, as is sometimes claimed in the popular literature, an attempt to catapult China into "the modern world."[12] Nor could the movement be characterized, except marginally, as an effort to cope with the West or problems the West had created. Rather, it was a Western-influenced variation on a theme that was played in widely scattered parts of China from approximately 1850 to 1870 in response to conditions that by and large predated the impact of the West. It cannot be too much emphasized that, as Mary Wright wrote:

> In the mid-nineteenth century, the struggles for the control of China were internal struggles. The Western impact, for all its seminal importance, was at the time still scarcely felt, and the foreign presence was seen as a local irritant, confined to five ports on the southeastern fringes of the Chinese Empire.[13]

The movement did, on the other hand, exert an important influence on China's response to the West. First, the insurgents' link with Christianity and the inability of a disunited missionary movement to dissociate itself convincingly from the uprising tarnished the Western religion's image in China. Second, the new sources of regional and local power that came into being in the course of the suppression of the insurgency weakened the central power permanently and thereby hampered the dynasty's subsequent efforts to respond creatively to the Western presence. Finally, the sheer magnitude of the problems created by the Taiping and other mid-century uprisings, together with the deceptively familiar character of these problems, drew Chinese leaders inward at the very moment when their Japanese counterparts were devoting full attention to the challenge of the West. The "slowness" of China's response, in other words, was due not just to the *nature* of Chinese society but also to the extraordinary historical circumstances facing this society in the middle of the last century. Internal matters were of greatest urgency. The West could wait.

REFORM

In the middle decades of the nineteenth century, the major question facing Chinese leaders was "Whither the Ch'ing?" By 1900 it had become "Whither China?" The story of the reform efforts that were made in the intervening period can be told in terms of the transition from the first question to the second.

In relating this story, however, we must take special care to resist the facile assumption that reform was a mere subcategory of Sino–Western relations—something that came into existence in the wake of, and had meaning only in reference to, a Western impact. Chinese reform thought and activity in the late Ch'ing, although increasingly influenced by the West, were also part of a longstanding reformist tradition, which, in its origins, its style, and even much of its content, owed little or nothing to foreign inspiration.[14]

Reform-minded Chinese began to respond to the West as early as the Opium War. But it was not until the 1870s and 1880s that the problem of the West finally assumed paramount importance—and even then for only a tiny minority of scholars and officials. In the decade or so prior to the 1870s, the principal concern of most Chinese reformers was the problem of domestic rebellion. Indeed, it was widely supposed during the T'ung-chih period (1862–1874) that, if the ills that had made rebellion possible could be removed, the problem of the West would take care of itself. The West, after all, would never have become a problem to begin with if China's house had been in better order.

In the fall of 1860 things could not have looked bleaker for the Manchus. British and French troops, following their victory in the "Second Opium War," had destroyed the Summer

Palace and occupied Peking. The Hsien-feng Emperor had fled to Jehol with his entourage. The Taiping movement, which had seemed in the late 1850s to be fading rapidly, had gained a new lease on life with the advent to power of such leaders as Li Hsiu-ch'eng (d. 1864) and Hung Jen-kan. Everything considered, the Ch'ing dynasty appeared to be on the verge of collapse.

And yet, miraculously, it did not collapse. The death of Hsien-feng in 1861 paved the way for a new era at court. Chinese and Manchus both rallied to the support of the throne, and the top posts in the bureaucracy were staffed in the ensuing decade with an unusually gifted array of officials. The foreigners, after forcing through a new set of treaties, evacuated the capital and returned south, demonstrating that they were not hungry for Chinese territory. Most important, and partly as a result of these other factors, the tide finally turned against the Taipings, and by 1862 the fate of the insurgency was sealed.

The T'ung-chih reign was classified by the Chinese as a restoration (*chung-hsing*), suggesting an eleventh-hour attempt by the dynasty to revitalize its severely shaken institutional foundations and regain popular and gentry support. There had been several other restorations in Chinese history. The novel feature of this one was the presence of the West, which forces us to consider the question: To what extent was the T'ung-chih Restoration a response to the West?

To answer this question, something needs to be said of the reforms proposed and implemented in the 1860s. By and large these were restorative rather than innovative in character. In the sphere of civil government, for example, while the importance of selecting men of talent for official posts was generally recognized, "talent" continued to be defined in the older sense of omnicompetence rather than specialized ability, and most Chinese remained convinced that, as long as the bureaucracy was staffed by men of talent, institutional changes would be unnecessary. Similarly, when it came to reviving a seriously disrupted examination system, the best that critics could offer was the conventional suggestion that more emphasis be placed on substance and less on calligraphy and style. Nothing was done to update the subject matter of the examinations to cover the various branches of Western learning.

In the economic field, too, as Mary Wright has ably shown, the overriding emphasis in the proposed reforms was on restoration of the antebellum economy.[15] In agriculture, efforts were made to reduce imperial expenditures, increase the area of land under cultivation, repair waterworks, and the like. But the growing problem of tenantry, above all the need for agrarian rent reduction, was left unheeded.[16] Moreover, it was still taken for granted that agriculture was the only truly important sector of the economy, and no one objected to high taxation of such nonagricultural activities as commerce. Further evidence of the backward-looking orientation of Restoration economic thought was the great resistance to the introduction of railway and telegraph systems. No Chinese of any consequence shared the foreign view that an expansion of Sino–Western trade offered China her best hope of prosperity and growth. The very concept of economic growth eluded the understanding of Restoration leaders.

There were two important areas in which Restoration officials accepted the need for innovation along Western lines. The first was the reorganization of China's military. The Taiping challenge had bared the hopeless decay of the dynasty's regular military units, and the recent display of British and French power dramatically highlighted the benefits of Western military methods and technology. In response, Restoration leaders, with Western technical aid, founded modern arsenals and shipyards and made a significant effort to streamline China's fighting forces and introduce more effective methods of training. Thus began the "self-strengthening" (*tzu-ch'iang*) movement, the aim of which was to provide for China's long-term security.

The other important change made in the Restoration period was in the field of foreign relations. China's old system, based on tribute, was revived for dealing with Asian countries. But for the Western nations a new institution was created, the Tsung-li ko-kuo shih-wu ya-men (Office for General Management of Foreign Affairs). From its inception in 1861 the Tsungli Yamen had to grapple with enormous problems, for in addition to shouldering the usual burdens of a foreign office, it had to master the intricacies of an entirely strange system of international relations and somehow justify its acquiescence in this system to an unsympathetic Chinese public. Measured against its problems, the achievements of the Yamen by the end of the 1860s were considerable.

Significantly, in both of these areas of innovation there were extenuating circumstances that made the changes appear less drastic. Learning from the West in the military sphere was only a variation on a well-worn Chinese theme. At various points in their long history, the Chinese had been able to accept being tutored in the arts of war by "barbarians." The creation of a new institution for dealing with the Western countries was more genuinely innovative, but here also there was a catch—namely, that it was conceived only as a temporary step. Prince Kung (1833–1898) and his associates, in their memorial urging the establishment of the Tsungli Yamen, had clearly specified: "As soon as the military campaigns are concluded and the affairs of the various countries are simplified, the new office will be abolished and its functions will . . . revert to the Grand Council for management so as to accord with the old system."[17]

Thus, even in those areas in which the Restoration leaders innovated, the generally noninnovative character of the period was underscored. Chinese reformers, with very few exceptions, were still far from the point where they could attach a positive valuation to fundamental change.

Mary Wright assesses the T'ung-chih Restoration in the following terms:

> This last of the great restorations of Chinese history was at the same time the first, and the most nearly successful, of a series of efforts to modify the Chinese state to a point where it could function effectively in the modern world without revolutionary changes in traditional Chinese values or in the institutions that embodied them.

One of Wright's major theses is that "the Restoration failed because the requirements of modernization ran counter to the requirements of Confucian stability."[18]

Two questions may be raised with regard to this thesis. First, did the Restoration in fact fail?[19] Second, assuming that it did, was it, as Wright suggests, because of the conflicting claims of modernization and Confucianism? These questions have an immediate bearing on the broader issue of the extent to which the Restoration reform program was a response to the West, for the areas in which it most clearly was—the diplomatic, the military, and the commercial—were just those areas where, in Wright's view, the Restoration was "the *most* and not the *least* successful."[20] On the other hand, the areas in which the T'ung-chih reformers were possibly least successful—the restoration of effective civil government, the reestablishment of local control, and the rehabilitation of the economy—were the very areas in which they were least concerned with the Western challenge. The frustration of Restoration efforts in the domestic arena, it could thus be argued, was due less to any fundamental incompatibility between modernization and the establishment of a stable Confucian order than to the refusal (or inability) of most Chinese reformers of this period to see the *relevance* of modernization to what in their eyes were essentially old and familiar problems. The center of gravity of Chinese thinking in the 1860s still lay within.

One might also go a step further and question the viability of the very terms in which Wright's argument is set. First, it is not at all clear that "Confucian stability" is the best way to describe the primary operative goal of Chinese elites during this era. Undoubtedly it was so for important segments of the elite. But the work of Philip Kuhn and James Polachek suggests that during the Taiping insurgency a substantial extension of gentry power took place at the local level and that the beneficiaries of this new power were intent upon keeping, if not furthering, it in the post-Taiping period, even if this placed them in direct conflict with other Restoration objectives.[21] Second, to the extent that for some elites (or for all elites in some respects), "stability" remained an overriding concern, it may be questioned whether "modernization" as such was perceived as the main threat. (One of the central themes of the T'ung-chih Restoration, let us not forget, was the use of selective modernization to *bolster* the old order.) Rather, I would argue, the main threat was radical change.

The case of the famous T'ung-chih reformer Feng Kuei-fen (1809–1874) is particularly instructive in this regard. Feng, while living in Shanghai in 1860–1861, composed forty essays on "statecraft," which he entitled *Chiao-pin-lu k'ang-i* (Essays of protest from Feng Kuei-fen's studio). In these essays, he vigorously attacked such flagrant abuses of Ch'ing administration as low official salaries, the Byzantine complexity of administrative procedures, the rule of avoidance (which prohibited officials from serving in their native provinces), the sale of offices, tax inequities, and the subbureaucracy of despised yamen (government office) clerks and runners. Feng's solutions to these problems, inspired by the writings of his intellectual idol, Ku Yen-wu (1613–1682)—and also, Polachek would insist, by the social, political, and economic interests of the gentry class, which Feng represented—would have, if implemented, revolutionized the nature of Chinese local administration by replacing yamen clerks with lower degree-holders (*sheng-yuan*), providing for the election of village headmen by paper ballot, extending the terms of office of district magistrates, and establishing a network of submagistrates to lighten the impossible workload of the magistrates proper.[22]

Although some of Feng's ideas (particularly the provision for elections) may have been influenced by the West, such a connection has not been conclusively established. Feng himself, in any event, insisted, as Kuhn points out, that every one of his proposals could reasonably be deduced from China's own traditions of political reformism.[23]

The example of Feng Kuei-fen is illuminating in two important respects. First, it directly challenges a set of assumptions, firmly held by American historians in the 1950s and 1960s, to the effect that fundamental change in the Chinese system was in essence the same thing as "modernization" and that such change, being contingent upon absorption of Western ideas and institutional models, could not be generated from within the Confucian intellectual world itself. (These assumptions are more closely scrutinized in chapter 2.) Second, the cautiousness with which Feng treated his own proposals and the even greater cautiousness with which his compatriots responded to them highlight the tremendous resistance, not to modernization but to radical change, that prevailed in Feng's time and for many years after. Feng himself never committed the *Chiao-pin-lu k'ang-i* to print. His sons published the more innocuous of the essays after his death. The complete text did not appear until 1885.[24] And it was only during the radical reform movement of the late 1890s that, under instructions from the Kuang-hsu Emperor himself, the *K'ang-i* was widely circulated and studied among Chinese officials.

It is sometimes maintained that one of the major reasons for the failure of the Taipings, or, conversely, for the success of the imperial forces in vanquishing them, was the Christianized ideology of the insurgents. "No rebellion," Joseph Levenson wrote, "was ever more rebelled against."[25] Because of the anti-Confucian implications of Taiping ideology, the argument runs, many Chinese scholars and officials who in other circumstances might have supported an uprising against the Manchus chose instead to cast their lot with the dynasty. The fate of Confucianism hung in the balance, and that was a much more important issue than Sino–Manchu intramural rivalry. The logical end product of this line of reasoning is that the whole Restoration effort to reestablish the foundations of Confucian society (assuming one acknowledges that there was such an effort) was precisely what I have suggested it was not: a massive, if negatively stated, response to the impact of the West.[26]

This is a beguiling thesis but not a terribly convincing one. It rests on several assumptions that should be brought out clearly: first, that alienation of elite Chinese from their Manchu rulers was still a significant force two hundred years after the founding of the dynasty;[27] second, that Chinese scholars, gentry, and officials, despite their vested interest in order and security, would have flocked to the Taiping banner in sizable numbers had the ideology of the rebels been more in keeping with Confucian precepts (in passing it may be noted that in the last years of the rebellion there was actually a considerable degree of "re-Confucianization" of rebel ideology, partly owing to the efforts of Hung Jen-kan); third, that it was the Western origin of this ideology rather than its general heterodox (non-Confucian) nature that was decisive; and fourth, that the *ideological* threat represented by the Taipings, regardless of its cultural origin, was more crucial in the eyes of contemporaries than the sheer physical destructiveness of the movement. Since none of these assumptions has yet been proved (and there is a fair amount of evidence in support of their opposites), it would seem unwise to go too far in viewing Restoration behavior as having been principally conditioned by the challenge of the West.

Technically, the T'ung-chih Restoration ended with the death of the T'ung-chih Emperor in 1874. When it actually ended depends on what one believes it to have been in the first place. Mary Wright, assigning considerable weight to the Restoration effort to devise a viable framework for Sino–Western relations, feels that the Tientsin Massacre and the rejection of the Alcock Convention in 1870 marked the beginning of the end.[28] If, shifting the emphasis somewhat, one were to attach primary importance to the tone and character of the reform thought of the period—its inward- and backward-looking orientation—one could argue that "restorationism" as a response to China's difficulties continued to attract adherents well into the succeeding Kuang-hsu reign (1875–1908). As late as the 1890s there were still Chinese who minimized the Western threat and believed that China's problems could best be solved by the time-honored methods of the past.

Still, it was a measure of the change that had taken place that such persons were now viewed as obscurantists. Certainly, they no longer stood in the mainstream of Chinese reform thought. In the two decades from the end of the T'ung-chih period to the outbreak of the Sino-Japanese War (1894), China was free of large-scale internal unrest. But the penetration of Westerners and of Western influence, instead of abating, became more intense than ever. In response to this, the central preoccupation of growing numbers of reform-minded Chinese shifted to the challenge of the West, and there emerged among them a heightened recognition of the need for change patterned after the Western example.

Here, if anywhere, it would appear, we have a clear-cut example of a genuine Chinese response to the West. Such, certainly, is the picture of late nineteenth-century reform presented in the most influential scholarship of the 1950s and 1960s.[29] The question, I submit, is not whether the picture is right or wrong but whether it is sufficiently complex. I shall return to this question later in this chapter and again in chapter 4. For now, let me briefly characterize the reform thought and activity of the late nineteenth century, seen as a response to the Western impact.

Although more and more Chinese in the last decades of the century saw a need for change along Western lines, the acceptance of such change as a positive good was slower in developing. Reformers therefore often felt obliged to camouflage their advocacy of Western-oriented change in a variety of intellectual disguises designed to make the changes appear innocuous. How much this intellectual masking was dictated by the psychological requirements of the reformers themselves and how much by the political need to deflect the criticism of their opponents is a puzzle intellectual historians are still working out.

Many of the most common justifications for reform were outgrowths of a kind of Chinese thinking known as *pen-mo: pen* (literally, "root") meaning the beginning, the fundamental, the essential; and *mo* (literally, "branch") meaning the end, the incidental, the nonessential. The best-known illustration of this was the *t'i-yung* formula, immortalized in

1898 by Chang Chih-tung (1837–1909) in the famous phrase, "Chung-hsueh wei t'i, Hsi-hsueh wei yung" ("Chinese learning for the essential principles, Western learning for the practical applications"). The purpose of *t'i-yung* thinking, which became particularly prevalent in the late 1890s, was to justify the acceptance of "Western learning," with all its practical benefits, while at the same time reasserting the sanctity and ultimate worth of Chinese civilization. For *t'i* and *yung* some Chinese substituted *tao* (ultimate values) and *ch'i* (technical contrivances). But the meaning was at bottom the same. The dilemma inherent in all such thinking, according to the analysis of Joseph Levenson, was that it ended up in a kind of intellectual zero-sum game. As more and more of the Western "model" was accepted by Chinese reformers, as the content of *yung* (or *ch'i*) expanded from ships and guns to science and mathematics, then to industrialization, and finally to modern schooling, *t'i* (or *tao*) inevitably shrank, and the Chinese found themselves in the impossible position of trying to preserve a civilization by subjecting it to fundamental change.[30]

Another justification for reform, one that flourished in the period just before and after the reform movement of 1898, was the argument that Western learning originated in China. This was an updated version of the *hua-hu* thesis propounded by Chinese centuries earlier as an apology for the acceptance of Buddhism. (Buddhism, it was maintained, was an Indianized form of Chinese Taoism and therefore could be followed by Chinese without shame.) It was widely claimed, for example, that Western military technology, science, mathematics, and Christianity were originally derived from the writings of the Warring States philosopher Mo-tzu. The functions of this line of reasoning were several: First, it provided a sanction for Western-inspired changes without doing damage to Chinese cultural pride; second, it reassured the Chinese that, as a race, they were not intellectually inferior to the Westerners; and, third, it suited the general Chinese predilection for appealing to antiquity.[31] On the other hand, the sudden respectability accorded the heterodox, non-Confucian Mo-tzu reflected a shift of the greatest importance that was taking place in the last years of the nineteenth century. Nationalism was rapidly becoming the chief stimulus behind Chinese reform thought. The key fact about Mo-tzu was that he was Chinese.

This same transition was mirrored in the evolution of yet another sanction for change: the goal of establishing a wealthy and powerful Chinese state. The preoccupation with wealth (*fu*) and power (*ch'iang*)—enshrined in the slogan, "Enrich the state and strengthen its military power" ("fu-kuo ch'iang-ping")—was a Legalist contribution to Chinese political thought and represented a distinct alternative to the usual Confucian (and Restoration) emphasis on frugal government and popular welfare. There was, however, a less orthodox strain of Chinese political economy which maintained that the goals of wealth and power were quite compatible with ultimate Confucian values. This train of thought began to appear with growing frequency in the 1870s and 1880s, as increasing numbers of Chinese became convinced that the Chinese state would have to be greatly strengthened if the Confucian values they cherished were to be saved from extinction. The danger of this kind of thinking was that the means—the creation of a wealthy and powerful China—would eventually supplant the end—the preservation of Confucian civilization. When wealth and power became goals to which all other values were subordinated, the ground was laid for a thoroughgoing nationalism. This was precisely the point reached, in the mid-1890s, by Yen Fu (1853–1921), the famous translator of Western social and political thought.[32] And in the ensuing decade, hundreds of other Chinese flocked to join Yen.

All the justifications for reform so far discussed were aimed at maintaining the Confucian order intact. None affirmed the possibility—certainly not the desirability—of a fundamental change of this order. There was, however, one current of reform thought that did do this, by attempting to find sanctions for change within the Confucian tradition itself. As early as 1880, the pioneer journalist Wang T'ao (1828–1897) wrote that if Confucius were alive in the nineteenth century he would unhesitatingly give his support not only to the introduction of Western technology and industry but to the general cause of reform. Wang's view of Confucius as a would-be reformer provided a justification for particular changes; implicitly, it also introduced into Confucianism a more affirmative attitude toward change in general.[33]

Much more influential and systematic than the ideas of Wang T'ao were those of K'ang Yu-wei (1858–1927), a leading figure in the reform movement of 1898. K'ang rejected as spurious the interpretations of the classics then current and insisted that the only authentic interpretation was that of the "New Text" school. In the doctrines of this school he claimed to discover philosophical grounds not only for viewing Confucius as an architect of new institutions (in itself a revolutionary stand) but for treating history as an evolutionary process. Influenced by recent Western thought, K'ang pushed the New Text interpretation far beyond the limits of contemporary Confucian acceptability and ended up with nothing less than a full-dress presentation of the modern Western concept of progress.[34]

Reinterpreting Confucianism in order to provide a positive sanction for innovation represented a significant alternative to such negative sanctions as the *t'i-yung* formula. But it still failed to solve the basic problem of how China could change fundamentally and remain Confucian at the same time. The other sanctions pretended that Confucianism need not be changed at all. The sanction developed by K'ang Yu-wei rested on the equally questionable premise that true Confucianism had always been open to change. In either case, Confucianism as it had been known receded into the shadows, and by 1900 the path was cleared for an intellectual revolution of unprecedented scale.

To argue that Confucianism, as it had been known, receded from view is not, however, to argue that Confucianism died. Nor is it to accept the premise that Confucianism, in all of its dimensions, was in fact wholly incompatible with meaningful change. It is easy, when faced with this problem, to lapse into a kind of retrospective determinism that, starting from the conscious rejection of Confucianism in the May Fourth period, sees all modifications of Confucianism in the immediately preceding decades as leading inexorably to this conclusion. One antidote to such reasoning is to remind ourselves that radical changes in Confucian doctrine had taken place before in Chinese history without bringing an end to the tradition. It is very possible that neither Han nor Sung Confucianism would have been recognizable to Confucius, but this did not keep their adherents from seeing themselves as authentic followers of the Sage. Similarly, in the case before us, there is probably no way of determining whether the liberties K'ang Yu-wei took with Confucianism were fatal to it in any objective sense. What we can say, with some certainty, is that K'ang continued to regard himself as a Confucian and that many Chinese who in subsequent years did *not* regard themselves consciously as Confucians continued to be influenced, unconsciously, by Confucian values and modes of thinking.

To what extent did the growing intellectual acceptance of Western-style reform in the late nineteenth century find expression in action? How much innovation was there in fact? As early as the T'ung-chih reign, a small number of reform-minded Chinese saw that "modernization" would have to go well beyond the level of "ships and guns."[35] Feng Kuei-fen, one of the first writers to use the classical phrase *tzu-ch'iang* (self-strengthening) specifically in reference to the Western threat, recognized that foreign military superiority was rooted in the West's advanced knowledge of mathematics and urged that Chinese study both the mathematics and the natural sciences of the "barbarian." Feng's plea for the translation of Western books led to the founding of a translation bureau and foreign languages school in Shanghai in the 1860s.

Wang T'ao was another writer who, at a relatively early date, perceived the difference between the new barbarian and the old. Appalled by the provincialism of China's knowledge of the rest of the world, he conceived a plan in the late 1860s to write a history of France. This book was completed in 1871 and was followed two years later by another on the Franco-Prussian War. Both Feng Kuei-fen and Wang T'ao lived for varying periods of time in Shanghai (Wang T'ao also lived in Europe and Hong Kong), where direct exposure to Westerners and to Western ways helped them transcend the insularity of their contemporaries.

During the 1870s and 1880s much was done to improve the state of China's knowledge of the West. More books were either written or translated (often by missionaries). Modern newspapers, with up-to-date coverage of world affairs, began publication in port cities like Shanghai and Hong Kong. Young Chinese were sent to the United States and Europe to study, and in 1876 China for the first time appointed diplomatic representatives to the major world capitals.

Reform efforts were also made in the economic and military fields. The transformation of China's army and navy, begun during the T'ung-chih period, went on apace. Mining, textile, and other new industrial enterprises were initiated, often with Western technical assistance. In 1881 the first telegraph line was opened between Shanghai and Tientsin, and a short railroad was completed.

The Chinese seemed to be making visible progress in the direction of "self-strengthening." Yet, if there was ever any real basis for optimism, it was cruelly shattered by China's humiliating defeat in the Sino-Japanese War of 1894–1895 and the ensuing intensification of Western imperialist activity. Now, for the first time, an acute feeling of shame enveloped significant numbers of Chinese and stimulated them to contemplate a much more extensive reform effort. Between 1895 and 1898 reform-oriented newspapers and periodicals sprang up in many places, and societies for the discussion of reform were founded. When the Kuang-hsu Emperor himself became sympathetic to the need for far-reaching reform, the stage was set for the hectic, drama-filled summer months of 1898.

The reform movement of 1898 began on June 11, the date of the emperor's first reform decree. It ended abruptly on September 21 with the resumption of tutelage over Kuang-hsu by his aunt, the empress dowager (Tz'u-hsi).[36] During this period, often referred to as the Hundred Days, reform decrees on a vast array of matters were issued by the throne. With K'ang Yu-wei's prodding, the young emperor took as his models not the sage kings of Chinese antiquity but such reform-minded monarchs as the Meiji Emperor and Russia's Peter the Great.[37] Orders were sent down for the remodeling of the examination system and the establishment of new-style schools; the modernization of the army, navy, police, and postal systems; the revision of China's laws; the elimination of superfluous officials and posts from the bureaucracy; the promotion of commerce, agriculture, mining, and industry; and so forth.

Although most if not all of these reforms had been proposed at one time or another by Wang T'ao, Cheng Kuan-ying (1842–1923), an intellectually disposed comprador, and others, collectively considered they went far beyond all previous efforts. This was the first massive assault on China's outmoded institutional structure and, equally significant, the first time such an assault had been launched from the top.

And yet, when the dust had settled, it was clear that little had been accomplished. Only in a few provinces (most notably, Hunan, which had a governor sympathetic to reform) was any real effort made to carry out the emperor's decrees. In the rest of the empire reactions ranged from passive bewilderment to stubborn resistance. Many officials who might have been willing to carry out the reforms did not understand them, and many who understood their import only too well vigorously resisted implementing them. Manchus were piqued at the fact that the reformers closest to the emperor were mostly Chinese. Conservatives were fearful of reform in general. Moderates were afraid that reform would enhance the political influence of K'ang Yu-wei and his group, whom they detested. And many in the bureaucracy, though perhaps not opposed to reform as such, were apprehensive lest this or that particular reform jeopardize their personal futures as bureaucrats. All in all, it can be said of the reformers of 1898 that if they were long on good intentions, they were abysmally short on the practical political wisdom and experience needed to put their good intentions into effect. This applied above all to the Kuang-hsu Emperor who, as Luke Kwong persuasively argues, had no coherent reform program of his own and was a disaster as a political leader.[38]

The picture of late nineteenth-century Chinese reformism that emerges from the foregoing account defines the reform process, in large measure, as a response to new problems created for China by the West and by an increasingly Westernized Japan. Not only is reform, in this picture, closely tied to the Western challenge, it is also presented as a predominantly intellectual problem in which the main issues are: How can China be made stronger and, in pursuit of this goal, how much of the Western "model" can she afford to adopt without threatening her cultural identity?

That Chinese reform efforts in the last three decades of the nineteenth century were *related* to the impact of the West is beyond dispute. The question is, is it enough to view them simply as responses to this impact? Or were they also, in varying degree, Western-influenced responses to internal Chinese challenges? A similar set of questions may be asked with respect to antireform activity. Was such activity grounded exclusively in antipathy to change and/or the West? Or was it also conditioned in important ways by the Chinese political environment?

In addressing these questions, it is important to note at the outset that the reform efforts here summarized were, for the most part, national in focus. Provincial- and local-level reform initiatives, particularly the latter, offered a quite different picture. Local reform activity, unlike that at the central and provincial levels, was in the hands of nonbureaucratic elites. It was much smaller in scale and therefore more readily capable of quick results.[39] Also, insofar as it was reflective of local interests and problems, it was unlikely to be undertaken in response to the West, though in coastal provinces like Chekiang—and by the end of the Ch'ing even in provinces of the interior—it came to be influenced by Western ideas and methods.[40]

At the provincial and national levels the West was more clearly a factor. But the part it played was seldom straightforward and simple. Students of nineteenth-century Japanese history have shown that Japan's "response to the West" and Japanese responses to internal Japanese political conditions were subtly and inseparably linked. Thus, in the late *bakumatsu* (1853–1868) period the *jōi* slogan, literally meaning "expel the barbarian," was used as "a stick to beat the *bakufu* [shogunate]" by samurai who, it turned out, not only had no intention of expelling the barbarian but were actually quite receptive to certain kinds of Western influence.[41] Similarly, the efforts of Chōshū and Satsuma leaders, on the eve of the Meiji Restoration, to introduce Western science and weaponry into their respective *han* (feudal domains) were as much *han* responses to the impending struggle between the *bakufu* and the throne as Japanese responses to the West.

A number of studies suggest that a comparable phenomenon existed on the Chinese side. Stanley Spector, for example, compares the two great "regional" leaders, Tseng Kuo-fan (1811–1872) and Li Hung-chang (1823–1901), in the following terms:

> While Tseng's protestations of loyalty to Confucian civilization and the Ch'ing dynasty may seem to indicate that he strengthened his own forces in order that he might better serve his imperial masters, the same cannot be said for Li Hung-chang. When Li Hung-chang spoke of self-strengthening, he discussed generalities; when he engaged in self-strengthening, he was strengthening himself.[42]

In short, what seemed to be a simple response by Li to the Western challenge was also, at least in part, a response to internal Chinese power rivalries. Ultimately, the problem of Li Hung-chang may have been just as important to Li as the problem of the West.[43]

In other instances Chinese took stands *against* Western-influenced innovation not because they were flatly opposed to such innovation (though many of course were) but because they found the circumstances surrounding the innovation to be in one way or another politically unacceptable. A prime example of this, already noted, was the antireform sentiment of 1898, much of which appears to have been aroused less by fear of reform than by hostility to K'ang Yu-wei. An example of a somewhat different sort was supplied by the purchase and dismantling of the foreign-constructed Woosung Railway by Shen Pao-chen (1820–1879) in 1876–1877. Although this action, superficially considered, might seem to have been inspired by conservative opposition to Western technology, recent research argues that Shen's true motives were of a more patriotic character. Having served as director of the Foochow Navy Yard during the late 1860s and early 1870s, Shen did not have to prove his credentials as a self-strengthener. The problem with the Woosung Railway was that it had been built by foreign merchants without Chinese authorization.[44]

On the popular level as well, there is evidence that opposition to reform was only partly grounded in simple fear of innovation. The burden of financing the intensified reform efforts of the late nineteenth and early twentieth centuries fell disproportionately on the shoulders of the peasantry and urban poor, Joseph Esherick argues, but "the fruits of the reforms remained inaccessible to all but the small reformist elite which directly participated in the reform institutions." Popular antireform violence was the result.[45]

Were Chinese reform efforts in the late nineteenth century slow and ineffective? Did they fail? The obvious answer to both questions is, of course, yes. And this is the verdict rendered by Fairbank and others, who have viewed Chinese reformism in the perspective of China's inadequate response to the Western challenge.[46] But there are also less obvious answers. Scholars, even while inveighing against historical determinism, find it difficult to write history without acquiescing in the very thing they denounce. Thus, China loses to Japan in 1895, reform loses to "reaction" in 1898, and historians, ever uncomfortable with immediate and accidental causes, seek long-term explanations for the two events. The more we seek, the more we find that there were grave shortcomings in the Chinese reform effort prior to the Sino-Japanese War. And the more these shortcomings come to monopolize our attention—as they must, given the questions asked—the more the events of the 1890s appear inevitable. One way of counteracting this sort of distortion is to focus less on the discrete instances of "failure" of the 1890s and more on broader, long-term processes of change beginning in the last decades of the nineteenth century and extending into the twentieth.[47] This is the direction in which numbers of Chinese historians—and some Americans—have been moving in recent years, and in the process they have arrived at a substantially more favorable assessment of late nineteenth-century reform activity.[48]

A similarly misleading perspective is occasioned by the widespread tendency to contrast China's response to the Western challenge to that of Japan.[49] Such comparison is invaluable in disclosing the more salient differences between Chinese and Japanese societies, but it can have the unfortunate side effect of masking over some very fundamental similarities. For example, both China and Japan in the late nineteenth century had unusually high rates of male literacy for preindustrial societies, and in both countries the social benefits of literacy had long been universally recognized. Again, although the government of Meiji Japan was much more effective than that of late Ch'ing China in amassing state power, both countries (China even more than Japan) enjoyed long experience with centralized bureaucratic rule, and both were able, partly for this very reason, to avoid being dominated politically by the West. The point is a simple one. If China and Japan alone are compared in respect to effectiveness and rapidity of response to the "challenge of modernity,"[50] Japan must necessarily come off well, China poorly. But if the comparative perspective is considerably widened and the performances of China and Japan are measured against those of the rest of the nations of the world, we are liable to find, as recent scholarship suggests, that both Japan *and* China come off relatively well.

REACTION

Reformism in late Ch'ing China, whether restorative or innovative in impulse, was basically an elitist phenomenon. Reaction—which is here taken to mean uncompromising resistance to the West or to foreign encroachment—was, like rebellion, a form of behavior involving both the masses and the elites. Intellectually, reaction appeared as a noisy, intemperate strain in the writing of China's educated strata. But it also had a more physical side, as dramatized in the endless succession of antimissionary outbreaks that punctuated the second half of the nineteenth century. When violence and disorder became sufficiently large-scale, as happened in the Boxer uprising of 1899–1900, distinctions between reaction and rebellion were in danger of being lost.

In the 1870s and 1880s, as we have seen, a significant effort was made by reform-oriented scholar-officials to meet the West on its own terms. Other scholar-officials during the same period, however, took an aggressively anti-Western stand, embodied most typically in the political force known as *ch'ing-i*. Literally meaning "pure talk or discussion" and sometimes freely translated as "public opinion," the term *ch'ing-i* had been used in the Later Han dynasty to describe the criticisms of disenfranchised Confucian literati against a government increasingly dominated by eunuchs and empresses' relatives. It was used again during the Southern Sung, when China lay under threat of "barbarian" invasion, to characterize that segment of opinion which vehemently opposed a policy of appeasement. In all periods, *ch'ing-i* manifested itself as a militant defense of Confucian doctrinal and moral purity aimed at those power holders whose actions in one way or another threatened to undermine the Confucian order.

Unlike public opinion in modern Western countries, the usual vehicles for the expression of *ch'ing-i* in the nineteenth century were not newspapers and public speeches but social gatherings, poems, folk songs, essays, and above all official memorials. In the 1870s and 1880s the main guns of *ch'ing-i* attack were trained on the growing trend toward limited accommodation of the West, as evidenced in the activities of the self-strengthening movement and in the policy of yielding to foreign military pressure. A harbinger of things to come had been the denunciation and recall in 1851 of the Fukien governor, Hsu Chi-yü (1795–1873), whose book *Ying-huan chih-lueh* (A brief survey of the maritime circuit), first published shortly before, was one of the earliest Chinese attempts to gather together information on the West. Hsu was attacked because he had not been sufficiently tough in his relations with foreigners, although, ironically, his book revealed a considerable strain of antiforeign sentiment.[51]

In the 1870s the most celebrated instance of *ch'ing-i* excoriation was the assault on Kuo Sung-tao (1818–1891). Kuo, though deeply immersed in the Confucian tradition, was one of the first to recognize (in the early 1860s) the fundamental differences between the barbarian tribes China had previously encountered and the new barbarians from the West. Realizing the impossibility of defeating the Western countries militarily, he urged that Westerners be treated with fairness and sincerity and insisted on the need to resolve conflicts with the West through diplomatic rather than military means. Kuo's first run-in with *ch'ing-i* vitriol came as a result of his impeachment of the governor of Yunnan in connection with the Margary affair of 1875. Although his hidden intent was, by having the governor charged with the relatively minor offense of dereliction of duty, to prevent his being subject to the much graver accusation of connivance in the murder of a British consular officer, the literati failed to detect this and condemned Kuo as a traitor. The attack on Kuo was especially savage in his native city of Changsha, Hunan, where his impending voyage to England as the head of a Chinese apology mission was satirized in 1876 in the following couplet:

> Outstanding among his associates,
> Elevated above his peers,
> Yet ostracized in the nation of Yao and Shun.
> Unable to serve men,
> Why able to serve devils?
> Of what use to leave his fatherland and mother country![52]

Under unbearable social pressure, Kuo Sung-tao tried to

beg off going to England. But the throne insisted, and he left Shanghai late in 1876. In England, where he was accredited as China's first envoy to the Court of St. James, Kuo continued to feel the sting of *ch'ing-i*. When the diary of his mission, in which he had some favorable things to say about the West, was published by the Tsungli Yamen, it aroused such savage criticism that the court had to order its suppression. On finally returning to China, moreover, Kuo was so fearful of attack in Peking that he went straight home to Hunan, where, his public career in a shambles, he spent the rest of his life in self-imposed obscurity.

Proponents of *ch'ing-i* in the 1870s and early 1880s did not stop at the vilification of those who saw some worth in Western civilization. Even the limited objective of adopting Western military technology was vehemently rejected by some. Reviving a tradition that had its roots in the Southern Sung and that Schwartz has described as "muscular Confucianism," these men maintained that what was needed to expel the barbarian was not the cunning gadgetry of the West but an aroused Chinese population. As one *ch'ing-i* die-hard put it, "The superiority of China over foreign lands lies not in reliance on equipment but in the steadfastness of the minds of the people."[53]

The natural corollary to *ch'ing-i* deprecation of Western military strength was *ch'ing-i* bellicosity in situations when war with the West threatened. In the summer of 1870, when the Tientsin Massacre brought China and France to the verge of war, Tseng Kuo-fan was so severely criticized by *ch'ing-i* stalwarts for his policy of accommodation that the throne had to transfer him from his post as Chihli governor-general. Again, during the Sino–Russian controversy over Ili in 1879–1880 and the Sino–French conflict of 1884–1885, the enunciators of *ch'ing-i* took militant prowar stands. Now it was the "appeasement" course of Li Hung-chang that came in for the brunt of the attack; but as before, *ch'ing-i* proved itself a political force to be reckoned with.

Ch'ing-i, as an intellectual phenomenon, was manifestly a

response to the West. But it was also something more. The key point is that, for all its surface concern with the West, it was predominantly a Chinese affair, involving the responses of certain Chinese to the actions and policies of other Chinese. By its very nature, *ch'ing-i* had to be intramural: one demanded Confucian purity not of barbarians but of Confucians.

Furthermore, as we have seen, *ch'ing-i* was not, in any case, *just* an intellectual phenomenon. It was also—some would say principally—a powerful political instrument. "Officials who attracted attention by their rigorous Confucianism," Lloyd Eastman writes, "were often promoted to higher posts. And charges that a political opponent had disregarded Confucian ritual, disrespected the emperor, or was a sycophant of the foreigners frequently sufficed to remove the object of attack from imperial favor."[54] Under these circumstances, there was always the temptation, especially among lower- and middle-level officials with little administrative power, to use *ch'ing-i* to further what were essentially selfish and parochial interests. And as Eastman shows, in the complex balance of political forces prevailing in China in the late nineteenth century, the throne too could manipulate the expression of *ch'ing-i* for the purpose of gaining political leverage against such powerful provincial officials as Li Hung-chang. Thus, it would appear that in at least one important respect *ch'ing-i* preoccupation with Western culture ran parallel to Taiping preoccupation with Western religion. In both instances, the West was made to serve as an unwitting accomplice in the playing out of dramas that would have been staged, in one form or another, even in the West's absence.

The strongly instrumentalist nature of *ch'ing-i* concern with the West and the deeply political character of the *ch'ing-i* phenomenon as a whole are underscored by the fact that during the 1880s substantial numbers of *ch'ing-i* adherents underwent what appears to have been a sharp reversal of opinion with respect to borrowing from the West, such that by 1898 many of the leading reformers (including K'ang Yu-wei) were men with strong *ch'ing-i* affiliations. As John Schrecker and more recently Mary Rankin have pointed out, the old picture of the *ch'ing-i* type as irrevocably conservative, xenophobic, and obstructionist simply does not hold up. Some *ch'ing-i* partisans remained militantly anti-Western and lined up with the Boxer movement in 1900. But others became enthusiastic Westernizers, and still others, though hardly warming to the West culturally, became intrigued by the role the West's parliamentary institution might play in restructuring Chinese government and increasing their own capacity to influence policy. What all *ch'ing-i* elements shared by the end of the nineteenth century, aside from the desire for greater access to power, was an acute sense that the world—their world—was falling apart and that something radical had to be done to save it.[55]

Another manifestation of Chinese reaction in the last century—the hostility to missionaries and converts—seems, at first glance, to have been more unequivocally a response to the Western presence. Even here, however, when the response is understood not just in intellectual and psychological terms but in the context of the social and political forces operating on the local scene, a more complicated motivational picture comes into focus.

During the period from 1860 (the year in which missionaries were first permitted to reside and preach in the Chinese interior under treaty protection) to 1900, antimissionary activity in China was extremely widespread.[56] There were several hundred incidents important enough to need top-level diplomatic handling, while the number of cases that were settled locally probably ran into the thousands. Moreover, aside from incidents as such—the burning down of churches, the destruction of missionary and convert homes, the killing and injuring of Christians both Chinese and foreign—there were times when portions of the empire were deluged with inflammatory anti-Christian pamphlets and handbills.

The sources of anti-Christian feeling were many and complex. Aside from such intangibles as a virile tradition of ethnocentrism, which had been vented long before against

Indian Buddhism and, since the seventeenth century, had been focused increasingly on Western Christianity, there were a variety of more tangible grounds for Chinese hostility. In part, the mere presence of the missionary made him an object of attack. Missionaries were the first foreigners to leave the treaty ports and venture into the interior, and for a long time they were virtually the only foreigners whose day-to-day labors carried them to the farthest reaches of the Chinese empire. For many Chinese in the last century, therefore, the missionary stood as a uniquely visible symbol against which opposition to foreign intrusion could be directed.

In part, too, the missionary was attacked because the manner in which he made his presence felt after 1860 seemed almost calculated to offend. By indignantly waging battle against the notion that China was the sole fountainhead of civilization and, more particularly, by his assault on many facets of Chinese culture per se, the missionary directly undermined the cultural hegemony of the gentry class. Also, in countless ways he posed a threat to the gentry's accustomed monopoly of social leadership. Missionaries were the only persons at the local level, aside from the gentry, who were permitted to communicate with the authorities as social equals; in addition, they enjoyed an extraterritorial status that gave them greater immunity to Chinese laws than the gentry had ever possessed.

More important, perhaps, than any of these concrete invasions of the gentry's established prerogatives was the fact that the missionary was a teacher. He was educated, at least to the extent that he could read and write; he preached in public; and, especially if he was a Protestant missionary, he wrote and distributed a prodigious amount of literature. The effect of this on the literati was aptly summarized by a leading Protestant missionary:

> It is impossible not to displease them. To preach is to insult them, for in the very act you assume the position of a teacher. To publish a book on religion or science is to insult them, for in doing that you take for granted that China is not the depository of all truth and

knowledge. . . . To propound progress is to insult them, for therein you intimate that China has not reached the very acme of civilisation, and that you stand on a higher platform than they.[57]

Although it was the avowed policy of the Chinese government after 1860 that the new treaties were to be strictly adhered to, this policy could be carried out in practice only with the wholehearted cooperation of the provincial and local authorities. Unfortunately, such cooperation was seldom forthcoming, partly because the officials, themselves members of the gentry class, shared in the general opposition of this class to Christianity. But there were also a number of more specific factors. For one thing, in a severely understaffed bureaucracy that ruled as much by persuasion as by force, the official was highly dependent on the active cooperation of the local gentry. If he energetically attempted to implement the treaty provisions concerning missionary activities, in direct defiance of gentry sentiment, he ran the risk of alienating this class and destroying his future effectiveness as an official.

Another factor was the missionary's exploitation of his privileged status and the resulting challenge to the prestige and authority of the official. Sometimes this challenge was a direct consequence of the missionary's treaty rights, as when missionaries who suffered injury or property damage obtained satisfaction from the Chinese government. In other cases missionaries made their power felt on the local scene by abusing their treaty rights or by using them with a minimum of discretion. Both Catholics and Protestants regularly accepted the application of force on their behalf to obtain redress. Catholic missionaries routinely demanded, as restitution for injuries suffered in antimissionary riots, buildings (such as literati halls and temples) that had been erected with public funds and were of symbolic importance to the Chinese. Most serious of all, in the view of Chinese officials, missionaries after 1860 frequently intervened in local legal proceedings either on behalf of converts or in order to win converts.

Although many missionaries of the last century felt that the general populace was not unalterably opposed to the spread of

Christianity, the unpleasant truth is that the participants in, if not the instigators of, antimissionary disturbances were largely drawn from this group. Nor do we have to search far for reasons. Missionary attacks on ancestor worship and "idolatrous" folk festivals offended all Chinese, not merely the elites, and missionary demands for compensation following antimissionary outbreaks often had to be met by impoverished commoners in the localities concerned. Ordinary Chinese were further irritated by the pretentious behavior many of their fellow countrymen exhibited after becoming converts, and they were bewildered and frightened by the strange ways of the foreigners in their midst.

Even when the populace of a given locale had concrete grievances against the Christians, however, these grievances usually had to be articulated before they could be translated into action. Often, antimissionary incidents were not spontaneous but were planned in advance and, to some extent, organized. Here the role of the gentry and official classes became crucial. The gentry, primarily through the distribution of inflammatory anti-Christian tracts and posters, were able, on the one hand, to create an explosive climate of rumor and suspicion concerning the activities of the foreigner and, on the other, to activate suspicions, fears, and resentments that the non-Christian populace accumulated on its own through immediate contact with the missionary and his followers. In this way an interplay of forces was built up that, given the necessary spark, could and often did lead to violence.

The officials' part in this process sometimes paralleled the gentry's, but usually it was more indirect and passive. The officials gave the gentry almost complete liberty to carry on their propagandist and organizational activities and rarely took action against them when antimissionary incidents occurred. They thereby furnished the gentry with an operating framework relatively free of obstacles or risks.

Still, wherever the sympathies of officials may have lain, the fact remains that after 1860 antimissionary incidents were a source of acute embarrassment for the Chinese government at all levels. At the local and provincial levels, if the incidents were serious enough, officials could be demoted or otherwise punished. At the level of the central government, there was always the possibility that foreign force would be applied, resulting in humiliation and loss of prestige for the dynasty.

This raises some nice questions: If antimissionary activity posed such grave problems for the Chinese authorities, how sure can we be that, in the period from 1860 to 1900, the primary motive for active opposition to the missionaries was invariably antimissionary feeling and never antiofficial or antidynastic feeling? Was antiforeignism, to put it somewhat differently, always "authentic"? Or was it sometimes politically inspired? Certainly, there were more than enough grounds for the kindling of genuine antiforeign sentiment in nineteenth-century China. But it does not follow that, given the proper context, antiforeignism could not be manipulated for political purposes.

To illustrate, there is evidence that the Yangtze Valley riots of 1891 were fomented in part by disgruntled secret society members whose aim was less to do injury to Christians than to bring down the dynasty by forcing it into conflict with the Western powers. The initial phase of the Boxer movement, in which White Lotus sectarians played an important (if somewhat confusing) role, may have been guided by a similar impulse: early in 1899, the Boxers made much of the slogan, "Overthrow the Ch'ing, destroy the foreigner."

Conversely, the authorities themselves, in some instances, deliberately identified with extreme antiforeign stands, not so much because they themselves were extremely antiforeign (though such was often the case) but because this was the only way to prevent popular antiforeign feeling from being turned against them. This happened in Canton in the 1840s. It may also have been a factor in the official and dynastic responses to the Boxers.

Political antiforeignism was more directly a response to Chinese political conditions than to the West. What about authentic antiforeignism? This is a hard question to answer, for there were several varieties of Chinese antiforeignism in the second half of the nineteenth century, derived from different emotional sources but all equally authentic. First, there was the anger-centered antiforeignism experienced by all classes; second, there was the fear-centered antiforeignism of the uneducated strata, perhaps more properly described as xenophobia; third, there was the contempt-centered antiforeignism of the educated, based on their overwhelming sense of Chinese cultural superiority; and, finally, there was the shame-centered antiforeignism of a small but growing number of protonationalistic Chinese, who were more averse to Western political encroachment than cultural influence and tended to favor reform along Western lines over wholesale rejection of the West.

In the last case, antiforeignism was manifestly one aspect of an overall Chinese response to problems posed by the West qua West. In the other three cases, however, the situation was more ambiguous. Anger-centered antiforeignism may be seen as a natural human (rather than culturally Chinese) reaction to genuine inequities created on the local scene by missionary and convert behavior; contempt-centered antiforeignism (the sort often evoked by *ch'ing-i*) was more a Chinese response to a non-Chinese (but not specifically Western) cultural threat; and popular xenophobia (of the kind vented in antimissionary disturbances) was at least in part a local response (Cantonese or Szechwanese, rather than Chinese) to the presence of strangers who just happened to be Western.[58] Obviously, to lump all of these manifestations of antiforeignism together and label them simply "Chinese responses to the West" does scant justice to the historical complexities involved. Aside from the difference between "political" and "authentic" antiforeignism, an important distinction is to be made between varieties of antiforeignism that could have emerged at any juncture in Chinese history and varieties that were linked to a specifically Western impact.

Generalizing still further, it may be argued that even where antiforeignism (of whatever kind) was the most visible manifestation of Chinese behavior, the underlying causes of this behavior were often to be found elsewhere. Sometimes these causes were of a deep structural nature, building silently over long stretches of time and reflective of the most basic material conditions in a particular section of the country. Sometimes they had a more temporary and contingent character. Not infrequently, as in the uprising of the Boxers in western Shantung at the turn of the century, they were a product of both sorts of causation.

If we view the Boxer movement, as is commonly done, as a kind of last spasm of Chinese resistance to foreign encroachment in the late nineteenth century, it makes perfect sense to treat it as a response to the West. There are other perspectives from which the Boxers may be viewed, however, that are equally persuasive. One, suggested by the French scholar Marianne Bastid-Bruguière, in a masterful survey of late Ch'ing social change, sees the Boxers as a particular expression of a more general breakdown of the agrarian order in post-Taiping China. This breakdown was characterized, in the first instance, by progressive rural impoverishment caused by accelerating demographic expansion (especially in the North China plain), disruption within the handicraft industries, rising taxes and rents, and a variety of other factors. The breakdown was aggravated, at one social extreme, by a growing rural subproletariat—"a population completely destitute, with no fixed livelihood, often with no regular place of residence, hardest hit by famines, natural disasters and epidemics"—and, at the other extreme, by the exodus of landlords from the countryside to the towns and cities, resulting in a deterioration of landlord–tenant relationships. The growth of an unemployed population of uprooted elements and social rejects, together with the crumbling of traditional social structures and economic safeguards, encouraged an enhanced role for secret societies (*hui-tang*), which provided the new subproletariat with some measure of protection and security, in return for which the societies gained access to a ready supply of easily mobilized manpower for their political activities.

This complex process of rural deterioration was accompanied, in the period between the suppression of the mid-century rebellions and the end of the dynasty, by a high level of popular turbulence, which accelerated from about 1890 on. Bastid-Bruguière does not believe that this unrest can be described as a manifestation of peasant war or class conflict in the strict sense. Many of the disturbances were directed against Christian missions, foreigners, Manchus, or modern technology rather than landlords or tax collectors, and the social origins of the participants were extremely heterogeneous, including not infrequently leaders from the privileged classes. Nonetheless, she insists on the underlying social and economic basis of the turbulence, even when directed against foreigners, and points out that riots against foreign missions at the end of the Ch'ing were invariably preceded by "agricultural calamity or local economic disaster." This was true of the Chungking riots of 1886, which took place against a backdrop of sharp rises in the local price of rice; it was true of the 1891 disturbances in the Yangtze Valley, which followed upon several years of flooding and scarcity; and it was, above all, true of the Boxer insurrection, which erupted in the wake of a succession of natural disasters, famines, and requisitions in western Shantung between 1895 and 1898.

Although Bastid-Bruguière's account deals with the Boxers as such only in passing, it shows how, in spite of their idiosyncratic character, the Boxers exemplified broad patterns of social change that were spreading throughout agrarian China in the last half-century of the imperial era. Joseph Esherick, in a recent examination of the origins of the Boxer movement, supplies a perspective that, although much closer to the ground than Bastid-Bruguière's, incorporates many of the same themes. In scrutinizing the three areas of western Shantung that were of key importance in the early stages of the insurrection, Esherick pays special attention to the social and economic factors affecting the local balance of forces in each area and shows how the intrusion of a new system of authority—

the Catholic church—into western Shantung aggravated tensions that had already been building for other reasons and imparted to the Boxer movement, as it evolved, its specifically antiforeign and anti-Christian cast.

Bastid-Bruguière notes, in general, that Chinese uprisings against the Western presence after 1870 tended to take place in areas where the number of Westerners was small and foreign economic operations were at a low level or nonexistent. Esherick, with specific reference to the Boxers, makes much the same point, arguing that if the Boxer uprising had been a consequence of Western economic aggression, it should by all rights have originated in Kwangtung or Kiangsu or, if in Shantung, in the eastern coastal region, where foreign economic activity was extensive, rather than in the western part of the province, where it was conspicuously absent. The point is not that either Bastid-Bruguière or Esherick wishes to minimize in any way the antiforeign, anti-Christian, or anti-imperialist orientation of the Boxer movement. Rather, they do not see this orientation as being causally related to foreign economic inroads. Even more pertinent for our purposes, they do not see it as a psychological or intellectual response on the part of the Chinese populace to the impact of the West. It would appear, rather, that both scholars view the anti-Western animus of the Boxers principally as a function of a rapidly deteriorating rural situation in China—the resultant of a complex mix of social, economic, and political factors influenced in diverse and often indirect ways by the intrusion of a new foreign agency.[59]

A CORRECTIVE TO THE IMPACT–RESPONSE APPROACH

In the broadest sense, the problem with the impact–response approach is that it predefines what is important about nineteenth-century Chinese history in terms of a set of questions prompted by the Sino–Western encounter. More specifically, it fosters several kinds of distortion: It discourages serious inquiry into those facets of the history of the period that were unrelated, or at best remotely related, to the Western presence; it is prone to interpret Western-related aspects of nineteenth-century China as "Chinese responses to the Western challenge" when they were partly—in some cases principally—responses to indigenous forces; and, finally, insofar as the emphasis is on conscious "responses," the approach is naturally drawn toward intellectual, cultural, and psychological modes of explanation at the expense of social, political, and economic ones.[60]

As a corrective to these distortions, it may be useful to think of Chinese history in the nineteenth century as being comprised of several distinct zones. The outermost zone (outermost, that is, in a geographical and/or cultural sense) would consist of those facets of late Ch'ing history that were most clearly and unambiguously responses to or consequences of the Western presence. In this zone would be included such diverse phenomena as treaty ports, modern arsenals and shipyards, journalists like Wang T'ao, Christian converts, institutions like the Tsungli Yamen and the Maritime Customs Service, and the dispatch of Chinese students and envoys abroad. It is here that the conventional impact–response paradigm seems most clearly applicable. But it must be used with all caution. A Chinese might convert to Christianity as a result of his being convinced, on doctrinal grounds, of that religion's superior merit—a clear response to the West. But he might also convert in order to gain leverage against an adversary in a lawsuit—not so clearly a response to the West.

Next, there would be an intermediate zone embracing aspects of the period that were activated or given shape and direction, but were not actually brought into being, by the West. The Taiping movement, the T'ung-chih Restoration, some self-strengthening efforts, bureaucratic and court politics, antiforeignism, and social and economic tensions between urban and rural China are the kinds of things that might be included here. Again, we have a very heterogeneous assortment. In some instances (expressions of shame-centered antiforeignism, for example), the impact–response framework of analysis may still work tolerably well. In other instances (such as politically inspired antiforeignism or self-strengthening activity undertaken to augment personal power), modes of behavior that appear to be simple responses to the West turn out, on closer inspection, also to be responses to internal political challenges. In still other cases (the Taiping movement being the most notable), even the semblance of a response to the West is largely absent: The response is to a Chinese situation, in some respects (such as population pressure) unprecedented in nature, and the West's role is largely confined to that of an influencing agent. These examples all seem to suggest that in a Chinese setting a "pure" response to the West was virtually an impossibility. Perhaps it would be safer and more productive to think in terms of Western-influenced responses to Western-influenced situations, the degree of Western influence at both ends varying from case to case.

Finally, located in the innermost zone would be those facets of late Ch'ing culture and society that not only were not products of the Western presence but were, for the longest time period and to the highest degree, left undisturbed by this presence. Alongside such slow-changing cultural attributes as language and writing, we would find in this zone indigenous forms of intellectual, religious, and aesthetic expression; the style and pattern of life in agrarian China; and time-honored social, economic, and political conventions and institutions. Once having graduated beyond the assumption that important changes in nineteenth-century China had to be directly or indirectly induced by the West, we would also be in a position to seek out and identify, within this innermost zone, patterns of secular change that were taking place in Chinese society and culture and that contributed, possibly in decisive ways, to the history of the late Ch'ing.

The contents of these zones were fluid, and among the zones there was frequent interaction. The relative importance of any given zone, moreover, might change appreciably over time. We must be wary, however, of assuming that, as the outermost zone of Western-influenced change grew in importance during the last decades of the Ch'ing, the innermost zone of indigenous change inevitably shrank. History is not a seesaw, and there is no reason for supposing that, even if it were, Western-inspired and Chinese-inspired change would necessarily be situated on the seesaw's opposite ends, equidistant from an imaginary center.[61]

Viewed from this perspective, the main problem for the student of the Sino–Western encounter in the last century is to place this encounter in a larger context of Chinese cultural and social change, so that the interconnections between Western-related and non-Western-related varieties of change can be identified and analyzed. The concept of a "Western impact" conveys nicely the sense of an initial collision, but it says little about the complex chain of effects set in motion by the collision. Conversely, the concept of a "Chinese response" will not take us very far if we insist on linking it too closely to an initial Western impact. If we are going to retain these concepts at all, it is imperative that we address ourselves to a much more elaborate web of impacts and responses—Chinese *and* Western in each instance. Only then will we arrive at a surer understanding of the transformations that overtook China in the nineteenth century and the part taken by the West in effecting these transformations.

CHAPTER TWO

Moving Beyond "Tradition and Modernity"

For some years now a major change has been in progress in American writing on the recent Chinese past. The old picture of a stagnant, slumbering, unchanging China, waiting to be delivered from its unfortunate condition of historylessness by a dynamic, restlessly changing, historyful West, has at last begun to recede. China is, indeed, being liberated. It is being liberated, however, not from itself but from us, not from an *actual* state of changelessness but from an externally imposed perception of changelessness derived from a particular—and heavily parochial—definition of what change is and what kinds of change are important.

This basic shift in American scholarship has been closely allied with another shift that has begun to take place in the conceptual realm. I refer to the increasing disenchantment that has emerged with respect to modernization theory as a framework for approaching recent Chinese history. The literature on modernization theory is enormous, and I make no pretense here to a comprehensive treatment of it. What I am particularly interested in is that aspect of the theory that divides societies into "traditional" and "modern" phases of evolution. It is this tradition–modernity dyad, rather than modernization theory in its more elaborated form, that has cast the greatest spell over American historians of China.[1] Virtually all such historians in the 1950s and 1960s used the terms *traditional* and *modern* to subdivide China's long history (*modern* usually referring to the period of significant contact with the modern West), and even now, although the way in which these terms are used has changed substantially, they are still very much in evidence in scholarly writing. Few individuals have become so sensitive to their capacity for historical mischief as to call for their complete abandonment.[2]

Modernization theory, as a corpus of societal analysis, first assumed explicit shape in the years following World War II. Against the backdrop of the Cold War, it served the ideological need of Western—primarily American—social scientists to counter the Marxist-Leninist explanation of "backwardness" or "underdevelopment." It also provided a coherent intellectual explanation of the processes whereby "traditional" societies became "modern"—or, as the editors of a series on the "modernization of traditional societies" phrased it, "the way quiet places have come alive."[3]

Although the proximate origins of modernization theory were the conditions of the postwar world, in its most fundamental assumptions about non-Western cultures and the nature of change in such "quiet places," it drew heavily on a cluster of ideas that were widely current among Western intellectuals of the last century. This nineteenth-century connection has occasionally been noted in general discussions of modernization theory.[4] It has been largely overlooked, however, by American students of China, who have been more prone to emphasize and take pride in the ways in which postwar historical scholarship has moved beyond the assumptions of the Victorian era.

THE NINETEENTH-CENTURY WESTERN VIEW OF CHINA

Although these assumptions were held with reference to the non-West in general, I will discuss them here mainly as they were reflected in commentary on China. One almost invariable ingredient in such commentary was the image of China as a static, unchanging society, a society in a state of perpetual repose. Just prior to the beginning of the nineteenth century, the French mathematician-philosopher Condorcet wrote of the "human mind . . . condemned to shameful stagnation in those vast empires whose uninterrupted existence has dishonoured Asia for so long." Johann Gottfried von Herder, around the same time, pronounced that in Europe alone was human life genuinely historical, whereas in China, India, and among the natives of America there was no true historical progress but only a static unchanging civilization. Playing a variation on the same theme, Hegel, some years later, entered the judgment, "We have before us the oldest state and yet no past . . . a state which exists today as we know it to have been in ancient times. To that extent China has no history." The historian Ranke described China as being in a state of "eternal standstill," and John Stuart Mill referred in his writings to what he called "Chinese stationariness."[5]

A particularly nasty example of this kind of thinking, on the American side, was supplied by Ralph Waldo Emerson in a notebook entry of 1824:

> The closer contemplation we condescend to bestow, the more disgustful is that booby nation. The Chinese Empire enjoys precisely a Mummy's reputation, that of having preserved to a hair for 3 or 4,000 years the ugliest features in the world. . . . Even miserable Africa can say I have hewn the wood and drawn the water to promote the civilization of other lands. But China, reverend dullness! hoary ideot!, all she can say at the convocation of nations must be— "I made the tea."[6]

The view of China as unchanging was nothing new. It had enjoyed wide currency prior to the nineteenth century also. What was new was the negative judgment placed upon China's alleged immobility. For numbers of writers prior to the French Revolution, the stable, changeless quality of Chinese society had been regarded as a definite mark in its favor, a condition worthy of Western admiration and respect. (Oliver

Goldsmith, in *The Citizen of the World,* for example, described "an Empire which has thus continued invariably the same for such a long succession of ages" as "something so peculiarly great that I am naturally led to despise all other nations on the comparison."[7]) However, from the late eighteenth century, the industrial revolution brought what appeared to be a widening gap between European and Chinese material standards, and as Europeans began to identify "civilization" with a high level of material culture, China, whose technical skill and material abundance had once been the envy of the West, came to be identified as a backward society.

This new picture of China was reinforced by important intellectual shifts that were taking place in Europe. In the economic sphere there was a strong reaction against mercantilist constraints and an increased tendency to espouse the principles of free trade and laissez faire; the political arena saw a growing revulsion (at least in some quarters) for despotism, enlightened or any other kind; more generally, Europeans became wedded to the values of progress, dynamic movement, and change in all spheres of life. As this new world view came more and more to be equated with being "enlightened," China, with its annoying restrictions on trade, its autocratic government, and its apparent resistance to change of any sort, took on the aspect, for many Westerners, of an obsolescent society doomed to languish in the stagnant waters of barbarism until energized and transformed by a dynamic, cosmopolitan, and cosmopolitanizing West.

In the *Communist Manifesto* (1848), Marx and Engels expressed the prevailing vision of the nineteenth-century West with admirable succinctness:

The bourgeoisie, by the rapid improvement of all instruments of production, by the immensely facilitated means of communication, draws all, even the most barbarian, nations into civilization. The cheap prices of its commodities are the heavy artillery with which it batters down all Chinese walls, with which it forces the barbarians' intensely obstinate hatred of foreigners to capitulate. It compels all nations, on pain of extinction, to adopt the bourgeois mode of production; it compels them to introduce what it calls civilization into their midst, *i.e.*, to become bourgeois themselves. In a word, it creates a world after its own image.[8]

If Marx and Engels displayed a touch (and it was only a touch) of ambivalence with respect to the credentials of the Western bourgeoisie to be considered civilized, there was little hesitation in their judgment of the Chinese as barbarians or in their assumption that China, like the rest of the "underdeveloped" world, would be made over in the image of the modern West. "The oldest and most unshattered Empire on this earth," Marx wrote in 1850,

has been pushed, in eight years, by the cotton ball of the English bourgeois toward the brink of a social upheaval that must have most profound consequences for civilisation. When our European reactionaries, on their next flight through Asia, will have finally reached the Chinese Wall, the gates that lead to the seat of primeval reaction and conservatism—who knows, perhaps they will read the following inscription on the Wall:

République Chinoise
Liberté, Égalité, Fraternité![9]

JOSEPH LEVENSON AND THE HISTORIOGRAPHY OF THE 1950s AND 1960s

The assumptions underlying the nineteenth-century Western perception of China exerted a powerful shaping influence on American historiography in the period from World War II through the late 1960s. This nineteenth-century drag effect is nowhere more dramatically evidenced than in the writings of Joseph R. Levenson, a man who addressed the issues of modernization and cultural change more persistently, imaginatively, and, for many of his readers, persuasively than perhaps any other American historian of China in the immediate postwar decades. Today, the younger generation of China historians pays little heed to Levenson, but in the 1950s and 1960s he was a compelling presence—someone with whom one felt one had to come to terms.

When Levenson's major works began to come out, in the early 1950s,[10] the Chinese Communists had only recently come to power, the dust of revolution had not yet settled, and Cold War attitudes and assumptions cast a heavy pall over American scholarly thinking. Levenson's mind, however, was far too complex to be framed by the battles of the Cold War, and although he was much concerned with "placing" Chinese communism historically, this concern was subsidiary to the larger aim of elucidating the process by which, in his view, one of the great civilizations of world history had, in the face of the modern Western invasion, disintegrated, passing (as he would have phrased it) into history, to be replaced by a new and fully modern Chinese culture. His analysis of this momentous process was filled with insights that will be of lasting value, if not in terms of the answers he supplied or the data he gathered, at least in terms of the issues he posed and the ways in which he posed them. No historian, however, can entirely elude the prevailing assumptions of his time, and it is both ironic and telling that Levenson, for all his originality as a thinker and despite persistent and strenuous efforts to counter the parochialism of American Sinology,[11] approached Chinese history from a perspective that, in its understanding of the imperatives of modernization, bore the clear stamp of the nineteenth century and epitomized the parochial core of the thinking of an entire generation of American historians.

Where this nineteenth-century parochialism was least apparent was in respect to the proposition that the West embodied civilization and China barbarism.[12] The inroads of cultural relativism in twentieth-century America have been substantial. And even though, at the level of deepest feeling, it has still been possible in adversarial situations for Americans to slip back into an exaggerated we–they dichotomization in which "we" stands for civilization and "they" for the opposite (World War II affords one example, the more recent Iranian hostage crisis another[13]), it has also been possible, as Vietnam showed, for such feelings to become inverted and for self-hatred—"we are the barbarians, not they"—to take the place of self-love. Moreover, ranged against those incorrigible spirits who, even after Vietnam, still believe that a high level of technological development is the sine qua non of civilization, there are increasing numbers of Americans who, newly sensitized to the destructive potential of modern technology (in industry as well as war), have begun to wonder whether technological capacity per se is as important a characteristic of the civilized condition as what a culture does with this capacity.

American historians of China did not, in any case, need Vietnam—we already had the Opium War—to develop empathic feelings with regard to China's cultural heritage. Chinese iconoclasts of the May Fourth generation, in the years after World War I, might, with the writer Lu Hsun (1881–1936), revile their own heritage as one of extreme barbarism, but no serious American student of this heritage in the twentieth century would think in such terms, much less employ such language. Certainly Levenson, for his part, displayed feelings of profound admiration for Chinese civilization. It was not this civilization itself, but the refusal of modern Chinese conservatives to acknowledge its death, that aroused his impatience.

With respect to the nineteenth-century notion that Chinese culture was unchanging, that it existed in a kind of steady state or equilibrium, on the other hand, Levenson and other American historians of the 1950s and 1960s were far more equivocal in their thinking. To be sure, there was a strong predisposition to believe that China's culture, like that of the West, was dynamic and changing in nature, and the contrary judgment of our forebears was repudiated as offensive and hopelessly ethnocentric. Yet this generalized profession of faith frequently did not square with concrete statements about "traditional China," which tended still to be framed in terms of unchanging or insignificantly changing categories, structures, and patterns. Students of the pre-Western impact phase of Chinese history did, it is true, make a strenuous and increasingly successful effort to get inside China and began to depict a culture pulsating with energy and change. By and large, however, historians of the period of Sino–Western confrontation, because they had one eye trained on the West, tended to approach China with a more parochial picture of the shape of change, judging it to be relatively unchanging when measured against the enormous transformations experienced in the West (and Japan) in modern times.

To speak of change as having "shape" is, of course, to speak in metaphorical language. The point, which is an important one, is that change is not just something that happens "out there." It is not just "past events." It is also, and perhaps predominantly, something that historians determine or "shape," on the basis of what they happen to be looking for in the events of the past. The "facts," E. H. Carr reminds us, "are like fish swimming about in a vast and sometimes inaccessible ocean; . . . what the historian catches will depend . . . mainly on what part of the ocean he chooses to fish in and what tackle he chooses to use—these two factors being, of course, determined by the kind of fish he wants to catch."[14] If, to put it more prosaically, the historian is looking for A, he is not likely to find B or C, for even though he may encounter B or C, he won't recognize them as significant.

That the Chinese past, when seen from the vantage point of the Sino–Western encounter, still tended in the 1950s and 1960s to be perceived as *relatively* unchanging, is clearly documented in the two volumes of *A History of East Asian Civilization* (1960, 1965), the most sophisticated and deservedly the most influential of postwar American textbooks on East Asian history. Significantly, in the first volume of this textbook, covering the period of Chinese history in which the Western intrusion had not yet become a factor, there is a great deal of emphasis on linear change.[15] It is only in the second volume, where the encounter with the West looms large, that the perception of the East Asian past as stable and minimally changing comes to the fore. The authors of this volume, John K. Fairbank, Edwin O. Reischauer, and Albert M. Craig, discuss in the opening pages the major interpretive concepts that they found helpful in organizing their data. One such concept is "change within tradition," which they describe in the following terms: "[In each East Asian country] the major traditional forms of thought and action, once established, had an inertial momentum, a tendency to continue in accepted ways. As long as their environment remained without direct Western contact, they underwent only 'change within tradition,' not transformation."[16]

The trouble with the concept "change within tradition" is that it reflects certain subjective preferences as to what kinds of change are more and less significant. There is an implicit circularity in the lines just quoted. "Transformation," it would appear, is what the West itself went through in modern times or what happens to a non-Western society when it encounters modern Western culture. To say, therefore, that "without direct Western contact, [the countries of East Asia] underwent only 'change within tradition,' not transformation," is a little like saying that these countries did not become Westernized until they underwent Westernization.[17] Fairbank, Reischauer, and Craig have obviously gone far beyond the cruder formulations of the nineteenth century, but they are still working, I would argue, within a framework that virtually compels them to lay particular stress on the more stable and abiding features of Chinese culture.[18]

Another widely used text that takes essentially the same approach is Immanuel C. Y. Hsü's *The Rise of Modern China* (1970). In the period from 1600 to 1800, Hsü tells us, "China's political system, social structure, economic institutions, and intellectual atmosphere remained substantially what they had been during the previous 2,000 years."[19]

Still another example, though from a sharply different intellectual and ideological perspective, is provided by Karl A. Wittfogel in his imposing theoretical analysis *Oriental Despotism* (1957). Wittfogel, who although bitterly anticommunist proudly traces his intellectual lineage to Marx and Engels and beyond them to the classical economists, sees "hydraulic society" (of which China is a prime example) as "the outstanding case of societal stagnation." Although originating in several ways and under favorable circumstances developing complex patterns of property and social stratification, hydraulic society, he argues, "did not abandon its basic structures except under the impact of *external* forces."[20]

Joseph Levenson, too, shared this perspective. For all his emphasis in volume 2 of *Confucian China and Its Modern Fate* on the tensions pervading Chinese culture—tensions between monarchy and bureaucracy, between Confucianism and the monarchy, and even within Confucianism itself—Levenson's vision of the Chinese past, from the establishment of the imperial-bureaucratic state in the third century B.C. until the nineteenth century, was an essentially harmonic vision in which everything (including the tensions) meshed with everything else and "a whole pattern of cultural preferences hung together, all appropriate to one another and to a specific social order."[21] So stable and harmoniously balanced was this social order that it not only could not (it would appear) generate significant change from within itself but was even proof against modification on any scale from without. Foreign influences might bring about cultural enrichment (an infusion of new "vocabulary"), but they had never, prior to modern times, been the source of fundamental transformation (a change in "language").[22]

Levenson's understanding of the impact of Buddhism, in terms of this distinction, is clear and unambiguous:

> The Indian homeland of Buddhism had not impinged on China socially; the contact was only intellectual, and while Chinese society had some throes of its own in Buddhism's early Chinese centuries, from the end of the Han to mid-T'ang, and the foreign creed seemed a serious menace then to the Confucianism appropriate to *a normally operating Chinese bureaucratic society, the revival of this normal operation confirmed Chinese Confucianism as the master of an originally Indian Buddhism, which settled into a modified but invincibly Chinese background.*[23]

In the very next sentence Levenson, his attention now riveted to the quantum changes generated in twentieth-century China by communist ideas, insists that "the old saw about China's absorbing everything . . . be buried once and for all."[24] There is more than a little irony in this insistence, given Levenson's minimal assessment of the earlier impact of Buddhism, by common judgment the most powerful foreign influence on Chinese cultural development prior to the nineteenth century. The irony, however, is less important than the strong implication in Levenson's phrasing that there was a "normal way" in which Chinese society operated and that the pivotal presence in this normal way was a highly stable entity called Confucianism. Levenson obviously knew better.[25] He knew that Confucianism's revival in the late T'ang and Sung, its reconfirmation as China's cultural overlord, was achieved at a steep price, the form of payment of which was its own very substantial transformation under Buddhist influence. Levenson's vantage point for viewing this transformation, however, prevented him from appreciating it in its full measure and prompted him, instead, to emphasize out of all proportion the regularities of past Chinese culture.[26] The reference to Buddhism's settling, finally, into "a modified but invincibly Chinese background" was but a rephrasing of the "change within tradition" concept earlier discussed.

The final component of the nineteenth-century perception of China broke down into a number of related propositions: first, that China could be jolted from its somnolent condition only by means of a major external shock;[27] second, that the modern West, and only the modern West, was capable of administering such a shock; and third, that this process, already in motion, would end in the making over of Chinese culture in the Western image.

American historians of the 1950s and 1960s would certainly not have subscribed to this characterization in all of its details. For "somnolent" (a favorite image of the nineteenth century) they would have insisted on substituting some less pejorative modifying phrase like "slow-motion" or "stable" or "gradually changing." Also, they would have been uncomfortable with the implicitly deterministic structure of the first proposition and would have greatly preferred to see it recast in descriptive terms. (As, for example, in the assertion about the countries of East Asia already quoted from the Fairbank–Reischauer–Craig text: "As long as their environment remained without direct Western contact, they underwent only 'change within tradition,' not transformation.") Prior to the middle or late 1960s, on the other hand, most American historians would have gone along with the unidirectional view of convergence embodied in the third proposition, and few would have seriously questioned the assumption that the sole or primary factor forcing the transformation of Chinese culture and society during the last century and a half has been the Western intrusion. There is a direct line of descent from Marx's prediction of 1853 that, its "isolation having come to a violent end by the medium of England," China's "dissolution must follow as surely as that of any mummy carefully preserved in a hermetically sealed coffin, whenever it is brought into contact with the open air"[28] to the declaration by Fairbank, Reischauer, and Craig that "increased contact with the technologically more advanced Occident gave the major initial impetus to the great changes in East Asia that started in the nineteenth century," when, in the face of the Western onslaught, the countries of this region "suddenly found their defenses crumbling, their economies disrupted, their governments threatened, and even their social systems undermined."[29]

Philip Kuhn's landmark study, *Rebellion and Its Enemies in Late Imperial China* (1970), begins to modify this overall line of interpretation. In an introductory discussion of the "boundaries of modern history," Kuhn notes that the prevailing view of China's transformation in modern times defines "modern" at least by implication as "that period in which the motion of history is governed primarily by forces exogenous to Chinese society and Chinese tradition." Uncomfortable with this definition, Kuhn recognizes that, before we can dispense with it, we must free ourselves from the old picture of a cyclically changing China. The central question to which he addresses himself in his introduction is, therefore, that of the nature of the changes taking place in Chinese society *prior* to the full Western onslaught. After noting the "phenomenal population rise (from 150 to 300 million during the eighteenth century); the inflation in prices (perhaps as much as 300 percent over the same period); the increasing monetization of the economy and the aggravation of economic competition in rural society," Kuhn expresses doubt as to whether changes of such character and magnitude can be viewed as cyclical and suggests as an alternative to the prevailing view the partly counterfactual hypothesis that "the West was impinging, not just upon a dynasty in decline, but upon a civilization in decline: a civilization that would soon have had to generate fresh forms of social and political organization from within itself."[30]

Joseph Levenson, too, was interested in the nature of the changes taking place in China on the eve of the nineteenth century. But Levenson's interest was less disinterested than Kuhn's, and the question he posed was more parochial. Kuhn's question, neutral and open-ended, is: What was happening in eighteenth-century China? He asks this question because he senses that the answer to it is going to be essential to a fuller understanding of how China became a modern society. Levenson's question, opening the first volume of *Confucian China and Its Modern Fate,* is: Is there any indication, in the existence of a group of materialist thinkers in seventeenth- and eighteenth-century China, "that the seemingly stable, traditionalistic Chinese society had the capacity to develop under its own power, without a catalytic intrusion of Western industrialism, into a society with a scientific temper?"[31]

The reason why Levenson's question is parochial is that, like Max Weber's inquiry into the origins of the spirit of capitalism or Levenson's own question, addressed on another occasion, concerning the roots of expansionism,[32] it is based on the assumption that the only kind of "development" that is important—and therefore worth looking for in the Chinese past—is development leading toward modernity, as defined by the Western historical experience. Of even greater moment than the parochial tone of Levenson's question is its lack of neutrality and open-endedness. The fact is, the only possible answers to his question are yes or no. And if the answer turns out to be yes, if "modern values" can indeed be located in early and mid-Ch'ing China, the whole edifice of Levenson's analysis of modern Chinese intellectual history collapses. Levenson recognized this clearly and made it very explicit in his introduction to the trilogy:

> Before one may suggest . . . that the great problem for Chinese thinkers in the last century has been the problem of reconciliation of their general intellectual avowals and their special Chinese sentiments, he must reflect on the history of early-modern, "pre-western" Chinese thought. For if that history was a history of burgeoning modern values (a growing spirit of science, for example—such a major strain in modern thought), then a later nagging doubt about Chinese continuity was unnecessary; if, on the other hand, the modern values cannot be traced to pre-western roots in Chinese history, such a doubt was unavoidable."[33]

The analogue of Levenson's question, equally loaded, and analyzed with great perceptiveness by Levenson himself, is the question posed by Chinese Communist historians: Are there indications of the emergence of embryonic capitalism in China prior to the arrival in force of the Westerner? If the answer to this question is no (which appears to have been the preference of Marx himself), patriotic Chinese historians are hard-pressed to demonstrate the autonomy of their own modern history. If the answer is yes, on the other hand, they can argue (1) that Chinese history ran a course paralleling that of the West (thus making it not derivative in character but part of a universal historical pattern), and (2) that Western imperialism, far from *introducing* capitalism (or, by extension, modern history) into China, actually impeded or distorted capitalism's normal development (a position of Leninist, not Marxist, inspiration). The Chinese Communist answer to their own question, to no one's particular surprise, has been a fairly consistent, if somewhat labored, yes.[34]

Joseph Levenson's answer to *his* question, equally predictable, is that prior to the introduction of modern values by the West, such values were nowhere to be found in Chinese thought. When, on the other hand, the West, in the nineteenth century, finally came to China for real—not just with mechanical clocks and Euclid, but with powerful ships and guns—Chinese history, in Levenson's view, was derailed. Total transformation now ensued. The old order, like Marx's mummy upon exposure to the open air, rapidly disintegrated, and out of the rubble and decay a new and wholly modern China emerged.

Levenson's account of this process varied, depending on whether he happened to be dealing (as was generally the case) with intellectual history or whether he was addressing himself (usually only in passing) to total societal change. In the former instance he tended to operate within the impact–response framework; in the latter his views reflected the influence and assumptions of American modernization theorists (in particular, it would appear, Marion Levy). But in either case, the part he assigned to the West was staggering. The West, for Levenson, was the author of China's modern transformation; it also was responsible for defining the entire *problematic* of modern Chinese history.

As an intellectual historian, Levenson was principally concerned not with the "exterior" realm of economic, political, and social change in modern China but with the "interior" realm of what Chinese thought and how they felt about the changing world in which they lived. The key theme he pursued throughout his work on intellectual history, including apparently the new trilogy on provincialism and cosmopolitanism left unfinished at his death,[35] was the distinction between value and history, between those aspects of a culture to which people give their allegiance because they believe them to be generally valid (good for all people for all time) and those aspects to which they commit themselves for reasons of a more subjective and proprietary nature. Under the influence of Morris Raphael Cohen's *Reason and Nature,* Levenson assumed that a stable society would be "one whose members would choose, on universal principles, the particular culture they inherited."[36] Such, he believed, was precisely the situation that prevailed "in the great ages of the Chinese Empire," a time when "conflict between history and value had been impossible," "when Chinese loved their civilization not only because they had inherited it from their fathers but because they were convinced that it was good."[37]

This harmonic condition was, in Levenson's view, totally shattered by the arrival of the West in the nineteenth century. Levenson characterized modern Chinese intellectual history, "the period of western influence, . . . as two reciprocal processes, the progressive abandonment of tradition by iconoclasts and the petrifaction of tradition by traditionalists." Both of these processes, he maintained, showed "a Chinese concern to establish the equivalence of China and the West." This quest for equivalence, for a new formula that would bring history ("mine") and value ("true") back into harmony and restore the psychological peace, formed "the common ground of all the new currents of Chinese thought since the Opium War." "Petty distinctions and conflicts between Chinese schools paled into insignificance before the glaring contrast of western culture to everything Chinese. Grounds for discrimination between Chinese schools were blurred when a new western alternative existed for them all, a more genuine alternative than they afforded one another." When "the West was a serious rival, Chinese rivals closed their ranks." The field of Chinese intellectual history became preempted by Sino–Western syncretisms.[38]

That the impact of the West on nineteenth- and twentieth-century Chinese intellectual history was of critical importance is undeniable. How we establish this importance is, however, a difficult methodological problem. Every conceptual approach carries with it its own logic. But where mathematicians only have to worry about whether their logic is internally consistent, the historian, in addition, has to worry about whether the logic of his approach is congruent with what actually took place in the past. When a historian fails to submit his logic to this test of congruence and instead imposes it upon the data, he substitutes reasonableness for reality and historical understanding suffers. Levenson's heavy reliance on the concept of equivalence enabled him to open up and explore areas of intellectual and psychological change, centering above all on alienation and identity, that previously had been sidestepped by students of the recent Chinese past. The profusion of insights that this approach generated was one of the great strengths of his writing. But the approach itself was flawed in a number of ways, and the flaws highlight some of the major shortcomings of the impact–response framework.

One such shortcoming is the assumption that when there is a Western impact there will necessarily be a Chinese response of corresponding magnitude. Sometimes, in Chinese history, this was indeed the case. But there were many occasions when it was not, when Western impacts that seemed (at least retrospectively) to be of major consequence evoked minimal Chinese responses or, conversely, when a small amount of impact set off a very substantial response. Where Levenson erred most egregiously was in his insistence that, starting with the Opium War, "the glaring contrast of Western culture to everything Chinese" transformed the central *problematic* of the Chinese intellectual world virtually overnight. Whether the culture of the West presented as stark a contrast to everything Chinese as Levenson thought is a debatable proposition in its own right. But the question I would pose, at this juncture, is whether, even if there were such a contrast, the contrast was apparent to any but a tiny handful of Chinese intellectuals at this early date. Awareness, moreover, even where it existed, did not necessarily translate into concern. Lin Tse-hsu (1785–1850), the imperial commissioner directed by the Manchu court in the late 1830s to solve the opium trade crisis, had plenty of contact with Westerners during his sojourn in Canton, and we know from his diary accounts that he perceived the West as being radically different from China. To my knowledge, however, there is no evidence that Lin's interior world was even mildly shaken by this awareness.[39]

The case of the mid-nineteenth-century scholar-official Tseng Kuo-fan is more complex and, for our purposes, more revealing. Levenson discusses at some length Tseng's intellectual eclecticism (which Tseng himself described as *li-hsueh* or the "philosophy of social usage"), arguing that "as a loyal Chinese, but a Chinese among westerners, he [Tseng] seemed to lose the will to dwell on intramural distinctions," that "when western conceptions were seen as alternative, the Chinese creed for a man like Tseng had to be close to all-inclusive."[40] This effort to establish a causal linkage between Tseng's syncretism and a Western challenge is perfectly plausible, and the force of Levenson's logic is overpowering. The linkage, however, has no empirical basis. Syncretism was a phenomenon with a very substantial history in Chinese intellectual life. The particular syncretic formulation that Tseng arrived at was much influenced, it appears, by earlier eclectic thinkers (such as his close friend, Liu Ch'uan-ying, who died in 1848). Moreover, there is ample evidence that the basis of Tseng's *li-hsueh* had been pretty well laid during the Peking phase of his career (1840–1852), a good part of which was spent in the Hanlin Academy, well insulated from contact with Chinese foreign affairs. During these years, as one might expect, Tseng's writings betray virtually no awareness of the impact of the West.[41]

Hao Chang goes further than this still, arguing that, prior to the 1890s, the impact of the West on Chinese intellectual life in general remained superficial. Far from becoming the dominant concern of many intellectuals, as in Japan, Western learning initially aroused little response. For such major intellectual figures of the late nineteenth century as Ch'en Li (1810–1882), Chu Tz'u-ch'i (1807–1882), Chu I-hsin (1846–

1894), and Wang K'ai-yun (1833–1916), as for the majority of the scholar-gentry in the fifty-year period after 1840, the central intellectual preoccupations remained the classical problems of the Confucian tradition. Chang further maintains—and Guy Alitto's study of the twentieth-century Confucian rural reconstructionist Liang Shu-ming (b. 1893) amply bears him out—that even after the Western impact became a major concern of Chinese intellectuals, it not only did not supplant older philosophical concerns but actually was shaped by these concerns in subtle and complex ways.[42]

Here again the contrast to Levenson is sharp. The enormous potency that Levenson invested in the Western impact caused him not only to date prematurely the point in time at which Western ideas penetrated from the periphery to the center of Chinese concern but also to exaggerate the degree to which, once such penetration occurred, earlier Chinese concerns became moribund. "Confucianism," Levenson maintained, "after so many centuries, had at last been drained of any relevance to Chinese reality . . . the Chinese tradition was disintegrating, and its heirs, to save the fragments, had to interpret them in the spirit of the Western intrusion." Levenson granted that "China in the nineties still had its many live thinkers of traditional ideas." But the ideas themselves, he insisted, were now "dead." For an idea, in order to be alive, had to have "real reference to an objective situation, and the history of China in the nineteenth century had been the story of the retreat of its ideology from objective significance to a purely subjective one."[43]

Levenson's entire sense of "problem" in recent Chinese intellectual history, in short, revolved around the shattering impact of the West, the problems of equivalence it posed, and the succession of Chinese responses it evoked. It was from this perspective that he wrote his book on the late Ch'ing reformer and publicist Liang Ch'i-ch'ao (1873–1929). Consequently, although there is some discussion in the book of the New Text influence on Liang and of his use of Mencius, Confucius, and Buddhism to buttress his intellectual claims, at no point does

Levenson attempt to anchor Liang in the Chinese intellectual world of his day. The fact is, with the arrival of the West, Levenson no longer took the inner dynamics of this world seriously. It was therefore impossible for him to conceive of an iconoclast like Liang continuing to be intellectually (as opposed to emotionally) attached to any part of it. It was equally impossible for him to imagine Liang (or any other Chinese intellectual) utilizing Western thought to help resolve problems that predated the impact of the West.

Although Levenson's overriding concern was with the "interior" realm of intellectual change, the part taken by the West in effecting such change was, in his view, essentially a subset of the larger role of the West in the "exterior" realm of China's political, economic, and social transformation in modern times. Indeed, as Levenson made clear on a number of occasions, it was precisely the fact that the Western impact was a total societal impact, not just an intellectual one, that made it possible for the intellectual dimension of this impact to have the transformative consequences it had:

> The effect of ideas in diffusion, the degree of their disarrangement of their fresh intellectual environment, depends, it seems, not on their disembodied character as abstract ideas but on how much of their mother societies they drag with them to the alien land. As long as one society is not being conclusively shaken up by another, foreign ideas may be exploited, as additional vocabulary, in a domestic intellectual situation. But when foreign-impelled social subversion is fairly under way (and that has been so in China, not in the West, and in China only in the nineteenth century and after), then foreign ideas begin to displace domestic. This change of language in a society may be described objectively as new choices made under conditions of total invasion, not of purely intellectual insinuation.[44]

In his periodic allusions to total societal change in China, Levenson assigned two roles to the West. One was as the precipitator of such change, the force ultimately responsible for the undermining of the old order. "The breakdown of traditional Chinese society," he asserted, "is the result of the western impact, the same western incursion that ruffled and finally ruined Chinese confidence in China's intellectual self-sufficiency." Again, in insisting that the continuity of Chinese history could be affirmed without explaining the Communist phase as the Confucian eternal return, Levenson wrote:

> Revulsion against the landlord system, the family system, the Confucian education has been building up for a long time in China, certainly not just since yesterday in doctrinaire directives. Though communists in power have helped such ideas along, *their sources are deep in a century and a half of unplanned western action on the earlier social structure that was offered up to the contact.*[45]

The flaw in Levenson's reasoning here is the same flaw that we have already encountered on several other occasions. The question is not whether Chinese society was in fact breaking down in the nineteenth century. Nor is it whether the intrusion of the West was one important factor in the acceleration of this breakdown. The argument is over Levenson's ready assumption that the West *alone* initiated the breakdown and remained its principal (if not exclusive) causal agent. The gathering evidence of recent years suggests that major social and economic changes were already under way in China in the eighteenth century, prior to the Western onslaught. Some of this evidence, above all the demographic, has been around for a long time and was known to Levenson. Yet Levenson (along with most other scholars of the 1950s and 1960s) was still operating in a mental world, inherited from the nineteenth century, in which it was assumed that Chinese society was immune to fundamental change from within and could therefore be transformed only as a result of a "fatal infection . . . from a foreign body."[46] Operating in this world it was difficult, if not impossible, to develop a more complex causal explanation of the transformation of Chinese society in the nineteenth and twentieth centuries.

In addition to initiating the breakdown of the old order, the West, in Levenson's view, also served as the primary shaping influence on the new Chinese order. His most explicit assertions in this regard were made in the 1950s, when the impact of modernization theory on American scholarship was in the ascendant and some of its more questionable premises had yet to be seriously challenged. Although modernization theory had originally developed, in part, as an alternative to the Marxist explanation of societal change, it perpetuated, ironically, the claim of Marx and other nineteenth-century thinkers that the industrialized West would create "a world after its own image." As S. N. Eisenstadt has written:

> Most of the studies of modernization in general and of convergence of industrial societies in particular, which developed in the fifties up to the mid-sixties, . . . stressed that the more modern or developed different societies [became], the more similar . . . they [would] become in their basic, central, institutional aspects, and the less the importance of traditional elements within them.[47]

Levenson, too, at least in his early writings, accepted the assumption of convergence, arguing that "as China industrialize[d], any distinction between its own culture and the West's . . . must become more and more blurred," that under the transforming agency of industrialization, Chinese society would become "an approximation of modern western society."[48] While it is possible that by the time of his death in 1969 he may have retreated somewhat from this stark picture of convergence—certainly he referred again and again to the distinctiveness of China's modern quest and was deeply sensitive to the Chinese need to own their own history—the whole structure of Levenson's analysis of recent Chinese history, above all the massive role that he ascribed to the West, made significant retreat contingent upon a basic rethinking of the analysis itself.

To sum up, in Levenson's perspective, modern society, as embodied in the culture of the West, acted upon Chinese culture in two ways concurrently: first, as a solvent, against which the old culture stood defenseless; and second, as a model on which a new Chinese culture was increasingly patterned. The picture of the Chinese revolution that emerged from this perspective was one that was shaped, from beginning to end, by problems posed for China by the modern West. It was, to use Levenson's own language, a revolution against the West to join the West. There was little room in this picture for a conception of the revolution as a response, in significant measure, to indigenous problems of long standing—problems that might be aggravated by the West but were not its exclusive, or even in all instances its primary, creations. Even less was there room in Levenson's picture for the possibility that past Chinese culture might contain significant features that, far from acting as barriers to China's modern transformation, might actually assist in this transformation and take an important part in directing it.

REDEFINING THE TRADITION–MODERNITY POLARITY

In his assumption that Confucianism and modernity were fundamentally incompatible and that the traditional order had to be torn down before a new modern order could be built up, Levenson was joined by many other scholars of the fifties and sixties. Among the most prominent and influential of these was Mary C. Wright, whose study, *The Last Stand of Chinese Conservatism,* first appeared in 1957. Wright's book, which deals with the T'ung-chih Restoration of 1862–1874 (see chapter 1), is a model of exacting and thorough scholarship and offers valuable insights into virtually every aspect of the Confucian state on the eve of its disintegration and final collapse. The central thesis of the book, however, has borne up less well. This thesis, which Wright returns to again and again, is that "the obstacles to [China's] successful adaptation to the modern world were not imperialist aggression, Manchu rule, mandarin stupidity, or the accidents of history, but nothing less than the constituent elements of the Confucian system itself."[49]

Albert Feuerwerker's pathbreaking study of China's early industrialization, published in 1958, makes essentially the same point. Feuerwerker is less explicit than Wright and far less inclined to ringing historical pronouncements. Throughout his account, nonetheless, traditional Chinese values and institutions are treated almost exclusively as obstacles, as "barriers" to be overcome or broken through, rather than as potential sources of support for China's economic modernization.[50]

The reasoning behind this pattern of thinking (which, it should be noted in passing, was given a powerful boost by the Chinese themselves in the early decades of the twentieth century) has been challenged in recent years by a growing body of scholarly opinion, which, in defining the relationship between "modern" and "traditional," rejects the implication that they are dichotomous, mutually antithetical conditions. With reference to Chinese history in particular, Benjamin Schwartz, in his critique of Levenson's organic or holistic view of culture, insists that "areas of experience of the past may, for good or ill, continue to have an ongoing existence in the present," that " 'Chinese past' and 'modernity' may not confront each other as impenetrable wholes."[51]

The assumption of radical discontinuity between tradition and modernity is attacked in a somewhat different fashion by Lloyd and Susanne Rudolph in their illuminating study of Indian political development, *The Modernity of Tradition* (1967). The Rudolphs see the problem as being rooted in the angle of vision of the investigator. They note that when modern societies alone are the subject of investigation, there has been an increasing tendency to stress traditional survivals, whereas when modern societies are compared with traditional societies, the traditional features of the former either disappear from view or "are pictured as residual categories that have failed to yield, because of some inefficiency in the historical process, to the imperatives of modernization." This "misunderstanding of modern society that excludes its traditional features is paralleled," in the Rudolphs' view, "by a misdiagnosis of traditional society that underestimates its modern potentialities. Those who study new nations comparatively often find only manifest and dominant values, configurations, and structures that fit a model of tradition and miss latent, deviant, or minority ones that may fit a model of modernity." The cumulative effect of all this, the Rudolphs conclude, "has been to produce an analytic gap between tradition and modernity." The two systems are seen as "mutually exclusive," "fundamentally different and incompatible." For the one to be superseded by the other, "social engineers working with new blueprints and new materials are required. Change takes on a systemic rather than adaptive character."[52]

The attack leveled by Schwartz, the Rudolphs, and many other scholars[53] against the picture of "tradition" and "modernity" as mutually exclusive, wholly incompatible systems bears enormous potential consequences for Western understanding of the recent Chinese past. The entire structure of assumptions inherited from the nineteenth century—the perception of China as barbarian and the West as civilized; of China as static and the West as dynamic; of China as incapable of self-generated change and therefore requiring for its transformation the impact of a "force from without"; the assumption that the West alone could serve as the carrier of this force; and finally, the assumption that, in the wake of the Western intrusion, "traditional" Chinese society would give way to a new and "modern" China, fashioned in the image of the West—this whole structure of assumptions is thoroughly shaken and a new and more complex model suggested for the relationship between past and present in a modernizing context.

It is surely no coincidence that precisely when the new understanding of the relationship between "tradition" and "modernity" was taking shape (it can be dated to the mid- to late 1960s), studies began to appear that, reflecting this new understanding, painted a sharply altered picture of the role of the past in recent Chinese history. In this picture, certain features of the past continue to be portrayed as antithetical to revolutionary change. Other features, however, not only are not seen as standing in the way of such change but are viewed as contributing to and even shaping it. Moreover, as a direct corollary to this, the Chinese revolution itself is seen as a response not just to new problems created by the Western intrusion but also to older problems of more internal origin. The upshot has been that the past century and a half of Chinese history has regained some of its lost autonomy, and the way has been paved for a less inflated, more cautious portrayal of the part played by the West in this history.

In some of these studies the focus, either explicitly or implicitly, has been on what the Rudolphs call the "modern potentialities" of traditional society. This is a persistent theme, for example, in the collaborative volume, *The Modernization of China* (1981), the contributors to which feel that, alongside a range of factors hindering China's modernization in the nineteenth and early twentieth centuries, there were also important features of the Chinese political, economic, social, and intellectual heritage that were ultimately conducive to modernization (though certain of them, having been in a state of decline since the mid-Ch'ing, slowed China's initial response to the foreign challenge in the nineteenth century). A similar motif is found in the work of Stuart Schram, who, even while acknowledging that China's tradition has been rocked to its foundations as a result of its encounter with the modern West, insists that two features of this tradition—a sense of history and a concern for politics as one of the principal domains of life—have prepared the Chinese "exceptionally well" for survival in the modern world. Along much the same lines, though with reference to a very different realm of human activity, Dwight Perkins argues forcefully that "traditional Chinese society appears to have nurtured within itself certain values and traits more compatible with modern economic growth than those of many other less-developed states. That is, far from being negative barriers, several principal features of Chinese society were a vital positive force once other real barriers to economic development were removed." Similar arguments are advanced by Thomas Kennedy with reference to Chinese self-strengthening efforts in the nineteenth century and by Evelyn Sakakida Rawski in connection with late Ch'ing literacy levels.[54]

In practically all of the new studies much attention is paid to problem areas in Chinese society, as defined by the Chinese themselves, to which modernization or revolution has held out some hope of solution. A notable example is Edward Friedman's book, *Backward Toward Revolution* (1974). Although ostensibly an examination of the Chinese Revolutionary Party (Chung-hua ko-ming tang), Friedman's study has important things to say about the fundamentally different ways in which the Chinese revolution was defined and experienced by radical intellectuals in urban China and by poor peasants in the vast Chinese hinterland.

For the former, straitjacketed by an uncompromisingly linear understanding of historical process, the past existed only to be overcome, destroyed, left behind. With Marx, Engels, and Lenin, Chinese intellectuals (liberals as much as Marxists) held to the modernizing faith "that change, the bigger the better, [was] the essence of revolution."[55] But for hundreds of millions of Chinese village-dwellers, Friedman argues, it was different. Operating within a frame of reference that was basically cyclical, they did not see their present misery as an inevitable consequence of the structure of the old society; on the contrary, they saw it as resulting from the breakdown of this society. Change in the abstract, in these circumstances, was the last thing Chinese peasants wanted. What they wanted from a revolution was not more disruption but less, not change toward some new and unknown future but the renewal and strengthening of older familial, religious, and communitarian bonds, a restored sense of the wholeness of life. "The point," Friedman stresses at the beginning of his book, "is not that there is nothing new under the sun, but rather that the force of living energy absorbed from the past helps create the power to transcend in a revolutionary fashion massive obstacles to a better future." Revolutions are complex mixtures of return and advance, of old and new. No mere restorations, they offer "another opportunity for the renewed community to come to grips with and try to solve the most basic problems of life."[56]

This ambiguous relationship between "tradition" and "revolution," in which tradition appears not merely as a barrier to revolution but also as a repository of assets for its facilitation, energizing, and legitimation, has also characterized some interpretations of Mao Tse-tung himself. This is particularly evident in the writings of Schram. Viewing the Sinification of Marxism as Mao's greatest theoretical and practical achievement, Schram maintains in his biography of the Chinese revolutionary that it was Mao's roots in tradition and sensitivity to "the real needs and aspirations of Chinese society in the 1920s and 1930s" that enabled him "to play the role he did."[57] Indeed, Mao eventually became persuaded—and here Schram's understanding sounds even more like Friedman's—that "in the last analysis . . . only iconoclasm from *within* the Chinese tradition, in a form immediately accessible to the Chinese people, would make it possible to dissolve and transcend the Confucian heritage." The Cultural Revolution, from this vantage point, "could be defined as one vast attempt . . . to overcome the evils inherited from the past, but to do so in original and specifically Chinese terms."[58]

Although Friedman's account of the problems to which rural revolution was addressed in twentieth-century China gives much weight to foreign imperialism, there is nothing in his analysis to suggest that the breakdown of Chinese village life was not also a result of endogenous forces—population explosion, intensifying class conflict, massive bureaucratic corruption—that predated significant foreign contact.[59] Philip Kuhn, in an article on local government in the late imperial and republican periods, is more explicit in sorting out the endogenous and exogenous aspects of change.[60] Kuhn analyzes the problems of local government in terms of three factors: control, autonomy, and mobilization. The last of these factors, insofar as it reflects the need to enlist local energies in new ways in order to promote economic growth and national power, does not appear on the scene until the late Ch'ing. However, the need to strike an appropriate balance between control and autonomy in local government is a problem that, Kuhn tells us, has plagued Chinese rulers from the Ming dynasty right through to the Communist era. The historical context within which this problem has been manifested has, of course, changed. But the problem itself has endured for centuries and, in important respects, mocks conventionally drawn distinctions between "traditional" and "modern."

These distinctions are also blurred by some of the ideas Chinese thinkers applied to the autonomy–control problem. I have in mind, in particular, the whole complex of political theory known as *feng-chien* (commonly, though inadequately, translated by the term *feudal*), which sought in one way or another to foster greater community of interest between the formal bureaucracy and the local population. Kuhn discusses the *feng-chien* tradition at length and shows how it was drawn upon by a long line of political reformers stretching from Ku Yen-wu in the early Ch'ing to Feng Kuei-fen, K'ang Yu-wei, and finally Sun Yat-sen and other Kuomintang ideologues of the twentieth century. Although by the time of K'ang and Sun clear conceptual links had been forged between the *feng-chien* tradition and Western ideas of representative government, Kuhn is at pains to point out that the reform measures proposed by a Feng Kuei-fen in the 1860s, however "modern"-seeming,[61] were entirely capable of being generated out of Feng's own intellectual inheritance. Thus, both the problems of local government in twentieth-century China and the measures proposed for remedying these problems, although affected and complicated by the Western presence, were deeply rooted in the indigenous setting.

The intricate connection between "traditional" and "modern" elements posited in Kuhn's analysis of local government[62] finds rich support in recent American interpretations of the May Fourth era. Yü-sheng Lin, in his work on the radical intellectuals of this era, has maintained that, in the priority such men as Hu Shih, Ch'en Tu-hsiu (1879–1942), and Lu Hsun gave to cultural and intellectual change over social, political, and economic change and in the totalistic character of their assault on Confucianism, they were influenced unconsciously by deep-seated modes of thinking in the very tradition they were bringing under attack.[63] Jerome Grieder strikes a similar note in the distinction he draws between the liberal and radical conceptions of "politics" in the May Fourth period:

> The radicals, those who sooner or later gravitated toward the revolutionary program of Marxist-Leninist doctrine, found there a restatement . . . of the traditional idea that human behavior is conditioned by environment. . . . Though they redefined the meaning of "environment," stripping it of its Confucian moral connotations and substituting a materialist theory of social and cultural determinism, by treating culture as a derivative of political power they echoed a traditional perception.[64]

Even the fiction writers of May Fourth, for all their much-vaunted iconoclasm, could not entirely escape the heritage against which they rebelled so hard. Like their literati forebears, Merle Goldman reminds us, they assumed that the essence of society was to be found in its culture and literature and that, as writers, they had a special responsibility to lead and guide their fellow countrymen.[65]

Recent work in the field of intellectual history has followed much the same pattern. In his book on Liang Ch'i-ch'ao, Hao Chang formulates the general proposition that "it is mainly in terms of a particular set of concerns and problems inherited from Confucian tradition that Chinese intellectuals responded to the Western impact in the late Ch'ing."[66] In the same work Chang carries this theme a step further, arguing, with later support from Don Price's book on the intelligentsia of the late Ch'ing and I-fan Ch'eng's essay on the Hunanese thinker Wang Hsien-ch'ien (1842–1918), that certain traditional value orientations—Liang's collectivism, the universalist yearnings of late Ch'ing reformers and revolutionaries, and the concept of *kung* or "public good" in the thought of Wang—came to serve (in Ch'eng's language) "not [as] obstacles to, but driving forces behind, China's modernization."[67]

One of the most articulate spokesmen for this overall point

of view has been Wm. Theodore de Bary. Taking direct issue with the perception of Neo-Confucianism as "a relentless canonization of tradition" (Max Weber) and "strait-jacket on the Chinese mind" (John Fairbank), a "dead set of values," incapable of modernizing China, de Bary insists that Neo-Confucianism does not "unfailingly serve the status quo," that it "can also stand as a critique of the existing order." Looking to the future, de Bary confidently predicts that "the new experience of the Chinese people will eventually be seen in significant part as a growth emerging from within and not simply a revolution inspired from without."[68]

Some of de Bary's key themes are developed by Thomas A. Metzger in his provocative essay, *Escape from Predicament* (1977). Metzger observes that, as long as scholars were mainly intent upon explaining China's failures in modern times, the old perceptions of traditional Chinese society—among them, that it was stagnant—persisted. As China's failures have come to be overshadowed by its successes, however, a new explanation, based on a quite different reading of Chinese tradition, has come to be required.[69] It is to this ambitious task that Metzger addresses himself.

Central to Metzger's thesis is the claim that Neo-Confucians were burdened by an intense, agonizing sense of predicament. This sense of predicament had an "inner" dimension, focusing on psychological, moral, and metaphysical quandaries; it also had an "outer" side, embracing economic and political problems. The Neo-Confucian goal was to escape from this complex of predicaments by transforming self and society. This transformative impulse was, however, continually frustrated, and as the solutions put forward by one thinker after another proved inefficacious, life for Neo-Confucians took on the dismal character of a Sisyphean struggle.

The entry of the West into this situation did not, as Fairbank, Levenson, and a host of other scholars have so often told us, herald disaster; instead, it brought release. Modernization—even revolution—represented not the destruction of traditional Chinese society but its fulfillment. For turn-of-the-century Chinese modernizers, the enormous appeal of Western methods, Metzger argues, was not just the instrumentalist promise that they would make China wealthy and strong; their appeal lay even more centrally in the fact that "they seemed useful for solving agonizing problems and realizing social ideals with which Confucians had long been preoccupied."[70] For what the West brought was

> not the concept of social and economic transformation per se but the belief that with modern technology, new techniques of political participation (whether liberal or Communist), and new forms of knowledge, the "outer" realm of economic and political problems, regarded as largely intractable since the euphoria of Wang An-shih's "new policies," could in fact be reformed. . . . As transformative action in the "outer" realm appeared ever more feasible to modern Chinese, the search for transformative power within the mind was relaxed. The "inner" predicament . . . became less acute and central, and a kind of Panglossian optimism spread over much Chinese thought.[71]

Max Weber, in his search for the source of a society's capacity to transform itself, hit upon the idea of "tension with the world"—the product of a society's recognition of the seemingly unbridgeable distance between its ideals and its actualities. China's failure to develop modern capitalism on its own was, in Weber's view, directly linked to what he perceived as the complete absence in the Confucian ethic of "any tension . . . between ethical demand and human shortcoming," resulting in a reduction of tension with the world "to an absolute minimum."[72] Weber's thesis not only provided an explanation for China's failure to generate modern capitalism; it also supplied theoretical buttressing for the popular Western image of traditional Chinese society as stagnant, as incapable of even conceiving of its own transformation, much less wishing it.[73]

Metzger, in his argument, appears to accept without hesitation the general Weberian assumption with respect to the link between psychological tension and societal change. However, in his view that Neo-Confucians, far from being oblivious to transformative impulses, literally yearned for the remaking of self and society, he departs from Weber's picture in a radical way. Equally radical is his reversal of the Levensonian picture of Confucian China and its modern fate. Where Levenson saw Confucian China as, at bottom, problem-free and judged its growing sense of problem in modern times to be the direct consequence of an overwhelming shock from without, Metzger sees a Confucian China writhing in problems—problems from which it cannot escape—until, with the coming of the West, solutions are presented that, almost magically, still the sense of problem and transform excruciating anxiety into unbounded optimism.

Weber and Levenson were, in my view, almost certainly wrong. But is Metzger right? A great deal of research will have to be done before this question can be answered. For now, I would simply like to identify two parts of his argument that strike me as being vulnerable. One is the key assumption that there was a massive sense of predicament in late imperial Confucianism. Metzger freely acknowledges, at one point, that "in saying that Neo-Confucians had a sense of predicament, we are saying something about them that they would not have said." He further maintains that the "awareness of this predicament has been filtered out of the leading modern interpretations of Neo-Confucianism."[74] Now the fact that late imperial Confucians did not make their sense of predicament explicit and that modern interpreters of Confucianism, like T'ang Chün-i (who is an important building block in Metzger's analysis), gloss over it does not in and of itself invalidate Metzger's claim that such a sense of predicament both existed and was pervasive.[75] It may well be, as he himself suggests, that the Neo-Confucian predicament was not made explicit just because it was taken for granted. Nevertheless, the possibility of distortion or exaggeration on Metzger's part does present itself, especially when we consider that, as a Weberian turned inside out, intent upon locating in the Chinese past the secret of China's modern success (much as Weber probed for the secret of its modern failure), Metzger would naturally be inclined to look for precisely what he claims to have found.[76]

The second part of Metzger's analysis that seems to me to be open to question is the mammoth role he ascribes to the West in recent Chinese history. In his insistence that the complex transformative movements of the late Ch'ing cannot be reduced to a simple contrast "between imported, transformative orientations and indigenous, stagnative ones,"[77] Metzger breaks decisively with the earlier view, bequeathed by the nineteenth century, that Chinese society was fundamentally lacking in any impulse to change. However, the notion that China was in a profound bind, a predicament, from which it could escape only with help from the West, has a faintly familiar ring. It parallels Mark Elvin's contention, in *The Pattern of the Chinese Past* (1973), that the late traditional Chinese economy was caught in a "high-level equilibrium trap" ("almost incapable of change through internally generated forces"), which it was "the historic contribution of the modern West to ease and then break" by opening "the country to the world market in the middle of the nineteenth century."[78]

What is troublesome in both of these instances is less the evidence Metzger and Elvin have marshaled in support of their interpretations (though in Metzger's case it is perilously thin and in Elvin's it has been seriously questioned)[79] than the language framing the interpretations and the assumptions underlying this language. In using words like *predicament* and *trap* to characterize Chinese society on the eve of the West's appearance, a picture is conveyed of that society as being "locked into" an intolerable situation, a situation that Metzger's and Elvin's nineteenth-century forebears would, with less squeamishness, have defined as "bad." The role of the West, in this situation, is for both Metzger and Elvin implicitly "good." By presenting China with a golden key, a means of exit equally from moral-psychological predicament and economic-technological entrapment, the West has earned the undying gratitude of all Chinese. It has made it possible for the Chinese economy to renew a pattern of growth that was arrested centuries ago, and it has provided Chinese society, for the first time, with the means of transforming itself in accordance with its own ancient goals.

The interpretations advanced by Metzger and Elvin raise Chinese historical studies in the West to a level of sophistication that was unattainable a generation ago. To the extent that they cast the West in the role of China's redeemer, however, both interpretations arouse a degree of uneasiness. The reason for this is not that either interpretation is necessarily incorrect, but that both are fully consistent with a mindset based on the imperative of Western primacy. In such circumstances, a stronger empirical case than either scholar presently makes is required to allay the suspicion that Chinese history is being pressed into the service of deeply rooted subjective value preferences.

THE RESIDUAL GRIP OF THE NINETEENTH CENTURY

The hold of the nineteenth century over American scholarship on recent Chinese history has been much weakened and in some cases substantially broken. But it still persists, at least in a vestigial way. The initial assault on this hold came with the scholarship of the 1950s and 1960s, which, reacting against the "treaty port" historiography of the prewar years, worked assiduously to get "inside" Chinese culture and present the Chinese side of the story. Insofar as this approach was guided by real (if qualified) respect for a non-Western civilization, it represented an important departure from the pejorative view of China that held sway over so much of earlier scholarship. The departure, however, was incomplete. Although much attention was now paid to what was taking place within China and for the first time a serious effort was made to understand Chinese attitudes and values, using archival sources and newly published Chinese documentary collections, this understanding was achieved in terms of a framework of assumptions that granted to Chinese society little potential for self-generated change and assigned to the West almost exclusive responsibility for China's modern transformation. Mary Wright's view of the Chinese revolution as, in the broad sense, a "revolution from without," not in any significant way the product of Chinese history,[80] was typical.

This picture was sharply modified by scholarly studies that began to appear in the 1970s (other examples of which are discussed in chapter 4). Although these studies point in a number of different directions, they agree for the most part in seeing China's indigenous society not as an inert body acted upon by an all-transforming West but as a changing thing in itself, with its own capacity for movement and powerful inner sense of direction. To this extent, the new studies critically undermine the grip of the nineteenth century on our understanding of recent Chinese history. But insofar as they continue to be influenced by some form of the tradition–modernity contrast,[81] with its deep roots in nineteenth-century thought, they fall short of becoming fully emancipated from the world view of earlier generations.

To understand why this is so, it may be helpful in concluding this chapter to point up a number of problems that seem to be inherent in the tradition–modernity pairing, even in its most sophisticated formulations. One such problem is that the pairing's implied exclusivity forces upon us a rigidly bipolar view of reality. Even where, as in the case of the Rudolphs, tradition and modernity are seen as fluid, mutually interpenetrable states, with traditional societies containing modern potentialities and modern societies embodying traditional features, the assumption persists that all of the characteristics of a culture will arrange themselves someplace along a tradition–modernity continuum. There is no room for the possibility, occasionally alluded to by Schwartz in his writings, that there may be vitally important areas of human experience that, transcending time and space, are not readily identifiable as either "traditional" or "modern."[82]

The assumption of exclusivity is directly related to a second assumption, equally lethal, which J. H. Hexter describes as the "assumption of the conservation of historical energy, . . . the idea . . . that in a given society the energy expended on a single pair of polar elements is fixed, so that any flow of social energy in the direction of one such pole can only take place by way of subtraction from the flow of energy to the opposite pole." The corollary to this assumption, suggested by Hexter, is that, in any polar pair, an increase in the direction of one of the poles is *in itself* sufficient evidence of a decrease in the direction of the other pole. Hexter refutes the assumption of the conservation of historical energy by reference to the example of secular and religious activity in sixteenth-century Britain. The evidence unmistakably indicates an increase in both sorts of activity. For a long time, however, historians tacitly assumed that because secular activity had clearly increased, there had to be a decrease in religious activity. Only when it was realized that the religious and the secular, although polar to one another, *could,* both at once, rise to higher levels of intensity, did it become possible to recognize "that they both *did* so rise in the sixteenth century."[83]

Hexter's insight may be applied, with equal profit, to the tradition–modernity polarity.[84] As Dean Tipps has noted,

> Piecemeal "modernization" need not lead to "modernity." . . . Indeed, the introduction of modern medicine may only compound poverty by increasing population pressures, the transistor radio may be employed merely to reinforce traditional values, and a technologically sophisticated military may be placed in the service of the most reactionary of regimes. Thus, such selective modernization may only strengthen traditional institutions and values, and rapid social change in one sphere may serve only to inhibit change in others.[85]

A particularly apposite illustration from recent history is supplied by the religious leaders of post-Shah Iran who, according to a *New York Times* analysis, used "the technology of the electronic age literally to amplify their message of a return to centuries-old ways."[86]

A modified application of this very point is found in Friedman and Metzger, both of whom (though in quite different ways) argue that a net increase in revolutionary change may go hand in hand with an intensified commitment to older values. By challenging an assumption that has been virtually ubiquitous in Chinese historical studies—the assumption that, in seesaw fashion, China will automatically become less traditional as it becomes more modern—Metzger and Friedman open the door to a whole new world of possibilities in our understanding of the recent Chinese past.

A third problem with the tradition–modernity pairing is that it employs concepts that are neatly symmetrical to describe and explain realities that are fundamentally asymmetrical. "Modernity" may indeed denote a condition with enough uniform characteristics and cross-cultural regularities to enable people who inhabit modern societies to feel themselves, in some sense, part of the same universe. "Tradition," however, refers to no correspondingly uniform condition, in either a subjective or an objective sense. Subjectively, it is inconceivable that the inhabitants of cultures as different, say, as fourteenth-century France and tenth-century China would perceive themselves as living in the same *kind* of society. Objectively, the most we can say concerning the likeness of two such cultures is that neither is "modern." This, however, is a little like saying that fish and birds are alike in not being monkeys. Defining something in terms of what it is not—the word "non-Western" is another unfortunate example—may have a kind of low-grade descriptive utility. Analytically it is a dead end.

If "tradition" fails the test of conceptual congruity, in that it does not fit the reality it purports to describe,[87] "modernity" poses problems of a quite different sort. Two such problems are of paramount concern here. One is that "modernity" is a fundamentally closed concept, with a built-in picture of historical process that is tightly unilinear and highly teleological in nature. "The very words 'modern' and 'modernity,'" Joseph LaPalombara writes, "imply a social Darwinian model of political development. They suggest that change is inevitable, that it proceeds in clearly identifiable stages, that subsequent evolutionary stages are necessarily more complex than those which preceded them, and that later stages are better than their antecedents."[88] LaPalombara's strictures, although made with special reference to political development, are just as pertinent to historical change in general. Closed models of change force us, often without realizing it, to shape the data of the past to fit preformed conceptual frameworks. Only with open models of change, accompanied by open-ended questions, will historians be able to form a more empirically sensitive picture of the recent Chinese past.

A second problem with "modernity" stems from what Tipps calls "the fundamental ethnocentrism of modernization theory."[89] This is a special problem for Westerners because, as moderns ourselves, we are part of the very thing we are studying. Since we got there first, we think we have the inside track on the modern condition, and our natural tendency is to universalize from our own experience. In fact, however, our taste of the modern world has been highly distinctive, so much so that John Schrecker has seen fit to characterize the West as "the most provincial of all great contemporary civilizations." Schrecker's point is that the West alone "has had no outside view of itself" in modern times.[90] Never have Westerners had to take other peoples' views of us really seriously. Nor, like the representatives of all other great cultures, have we been compelled to take fundamental stock of our own culture, deliberately dismantle large portions of it, and put it back together again in order to survive. This circumstance has engendered what may be the ultimate paradox, namely that Westerners, who have done more than any other people to create the modern world, are in certain respects the least capable of comprehending it.[91]

This problem is particularly crippling for Western historians who, imprisoned in the parochial experience of their own modernity, seek to understand and explain processes of modernization in non-Western societies. Certainly there are degrees of sin here. And some historians will fall into traps that others will be clever enough to avoid. None of us, however, can escape entirely the cultural skins within which we live, which suggests that there may be merit in abandoning altogether the nomenclature of modernization theory—above all, the concepts "tradition" and "modernity"—and searching for alternative, less Western-centered modes of describing the large-scale processes that have overtaken the world during the past century.

CHAPTER THREE

Imperialism: Reality or Myth?

THE TERM *imperialism* has been used in two basic ways by American students of nineteenth- and twentieth-century Chinese history. Some of the more radical members of the profession, taking their cue from Mao Tse-tung's famous dictum that "the history of modern China is a history of imperialist aggression, of imperialist opposition to China's independence and to her development of capitalism,"[1] have approached imperialism in a broad, overarching way and seen it as the ultimate source of China's problems in the century from the Opium War to the Communist victory. Others, although taking sharp issue with this grand perspective (which I refer to in the ensuing pages as the imperialism approach), have been quite prepared to accept a more circumscribed role for imperialism, particularly in the political realm. On both sides of the issue, modernization theory—its origins, underlying assumptions, and intellectual functions—has been very much implicated in the discussion.

THE JUSTIFICATION OF EMPIRE: MODERNIZATION THEORY AS IDEOLOGY

In chapter 2, the "modernization" approach to recent Chinese history was treated essentially as an intellectual or analytical construct. Although formally developed and made explicit only after World War II, largely by American social scientists, this construct, I argued, had embedded in it assumptions about the West, China, and cultural change that extended back to the nineteenth century and even earlier. Because these assumptions, in subtle and often hidden ways, introduced severe distortions into our understanding of Chinese history, I concluded that modernization theory and its attendant nomenclature ought, on intellectual grounds alone, to be abandoned.

Toward the end of the 1960s, against the backdrop of America's growing military involvement in Vietnam and the intense feelings it aroused, the modernization approach to nineteenth- and twentieth-century China was challenged on an altogether different set of grounds. The opening salvo was fired by James Peck in the October 1969 issue of the *Bulletin of Concerned Asian Scholars*. In "The Roots of Rhetoric: The Professional Ideology of America's China Watchers," Peck argued that modernization theory was not just an intellectual construct, inadequate but harmless; rather, it was an ideological construct used by leading China specialists to justify America's political, military, and economic intervention in Asia in the postwar era.[2] Profoundly anticommunist, elitist, inclined toward reform over revolution as the best means of achieving societal change, supremely confident in the institutions, values, and ultimate goodness of America, and implicitly (if not explicitly) supportive of American interests around the globe, modernization theory ensured an unsympathetic, hostile, or at best psychologically patronizing view of the Chinese revolution, on the one hand, and complacent denial of the realities of American imperialism, on the other. It failed to explain China. But much more insidious, it explained away America, legitimizing American violence and brutality and masking the true nature and aims of American power in the postwar world.

According to Peck, the modernization approach of the

China experts not only disguised current American imperialist behavior, it also failed to take seriously the role imperialism had played in the last 150 years of Chinese history:

> Cultural conflict within an evolving world society—such is the China profession's perspective for understanding China's confrontation with the West. Thus "we discern two major factors that have shaped recent East Asian history—the forces of modernization originally introduced in large part from the West, and the native traditions." Since the external stimuli were so similar, the responses so different, the "more significant element in such situations of challenge-and-response was the way in which the local people reacted to the foreign stimuli."[3] Since, indeed, "in both China and Japan the external sources were virtually identical,"[4] we should focus on the particular internal qualities of the native traditions; therein rests the key to understanding why some responded effectively and some did not.
>
> Implicit in this concentration on internal factors is the obvious next question: which traditional values support or hinder the process of adaptation? And the obvious method: compare a successful society (Japan) with an unsuccessful one (China). So, the argument continues, China saw itself as the very "center of the world" with its self-sustaining society and its isolated self-sufficient culture. However, in the nineteenth century, confronted with the enormous wealth and power of the European countries, China's traditional civilization "let her down. The old ways were indeed inadequate to modern times."[5] . . . It was the very perfection, the "overall cohesion and structural stability of Chinese civilization that basically inhibited its rapid response to the Western menace."[6] To conclude from this inevitable cultural clash that one society victimized another would be to overlook the more profound nature of the conflict.

For the China specialist, Peck went on, the notion of imperialism was a fantasy, a myth, a psychological salve to wounded feelings, something the Chinese found emotionally satisfying because of their profound sense of victimization in the nineteenth and twentieth centuries and their understandable need to blame this sense of victimization on something more palpable than "modern history." Imperialism existed in Chinese people's heads. It wasn't real.

Peck, countering this perspective, offered a picture of imperialism as not only real but as the key explanatory variable in the past century and a half of Chinese history. He questioned "the China watcher's belief that internal factors were the primary reason for China's prolonged domination by Western powers," arguing instead (with support from Jack Belden) that before 1949 the Chinese "revolution never was completed for the simple reason that foreign imperialism was entirely too strong to permit the Chinese people to take control over their own destinies."[7] Rejecting the China specialist's contention that "China, unlike Japan, lacked the necessary cultural background and consequently bore the full brunt of Western imperialism," Peck proposed as being more nearly true the reverse: that "China bore the full impact of the Western powers and therefore could not respond," while "Japan's escape from imperial domination depended partly upon a unique configuration of external circumstances" rather than upon traditional Japanese culture's peculiar receptivity to Western-based innovation.

Finally, Peck pointed out that, although both the modernization and the imperialism perspectives "emphasize[d] the penetration of Western economic power into China," the former maintained that such penetration was beneficial, while the latter insisted that it was harmful. Edwin O. Reischauer could thus assert that the "economic tragedy" of the once colonial and semicolonial lands of Asia was not so "much that they formerly suffered from 'economic imperialism' as that they did not have enough of it in the form of solid investments by the West."[8] "Theories of imperialism," Peck countered, "insist that the exportation of capital and the control of foreign markets have been traditional instruments of foreign control and domination" and "that even trade by itself 'tends to have backwash effects and to strengthen the forces maintaining stagnation or repression.'"[9] The international economic system, in short, far from being conducive to the modernization of non-Western nations, provided a hostile environment in which such modernization was next to impossible.[10]

John K. Fairbank, the chief target of Peck's attack, published a reply in the April–July 1970 issue of the *Bulletin*. Fairbank commended Peck's article for striking "a welcome note of criticism" and acknowledged that "we are in a new climate of opinion where the greatest evil seems to come from over-extension, from 'American imperialism,' or at least from within the U.S.A. and thus from within ourselves." He was critical, however, of the black and white character of Peck's argument and questioned whether it actually got us "closer to the realities of our situation."

Fairbank raised several points in particular. He charged Peck with being insufficiently precise in his differentiation of "modernization" and "revolutionary Marxism," setting the two up as intellectual alternatives when they really weren't that at all. Modernization theory, Fairbank suggested, was essentially an academic thing, "a collection of bits and pieces, analysis-oriented," something used by people far removed from China to try to understand what was going on in that country. Revolutionary Marxism, in contrast, was "a more unified package, action-oriented," a doctrine employed by people in Asian countries for their own revolutionary purposes. Even as a basis for intellectual understanding, moreover, Fairbank questioned whether modernization and revolutionary Marxism were genuine alternatives. He saw them, instead, as differing like a part and a whole, "Marxism-Leninism as a theory" being "only one of the many theories of modernization, in the broad sense of explaining what has happened in modern times."

Fairbank found Peck's view of American China specialists as aiders and abettors of the official U.S. definition of reality in Asia incomprehensible:

> The "China-watchers" were not the United States government nor even the "ruling circles"; many if not most of them during the past twenty years have been critics rather than supporters of American policy. In order to get his black and white effect, it seems to me Mr. Peck has lumped together the ghost of John Foster Dulles and all the China specialists whose views that gentleman so ostentatiously con-

demned. They make strange bedfellows; if Mr. Peck persists in bedding them together, he can be sure they will continue to dream different dreams.

Turning next to the issue of imperialism, Fairbank noted the cyclical, *nei-wai* (inner-outer) oscillation in the treatment of nineteenth-century China by American historians. In the early twentieth century, as illustrated by H.B. Morse's *International Relations of the Chinese Empire*, excessive attention had been directed to external factors. Morse's book, in its day "the most comprehensive history of modern China," had essentially been "foreign-documented bluebook history," emphasizing "foreign wars and treaties, what was done in China and to China by foreigners." Then, in the 1930s, a reaction set in. A new generation of China specialists (led, Fairbank modestly neglects to mention, by himself) began to wonder about the Chinese part of the story, which "suggested the study of China's 'response' to the Western 'impact', a bit more on the *nei* side." More recently, this interest in internal factors had "gone much further—into studies of major traditional institutions, of indigenous rebellions, provincial developments, thought, and all the rest, not merely 'modernization.' "

Now, however, Fairbank detected a swing back to *wai*. Patriotic Chinese of all political persuasions were suffering "under a frustrating sense of grievance and victimization, evidently inspired in part by China's vanished glory as the central country," and the "imperialism" documented by Morse bulked large in their view of the past. For Americans, too, as we moved into the 1970s, "imperialism" had become "a wide open subject." We needed to understand our expansion in the nineteenth and twentieth centuries if we were going to have a chance of controlling it and surviving into the twenty-first century. "Imperialism," therefore, was "now a subject of vital concern in its own right as a part of our cancerous growth and expansion. Whether we [approached] it under the banner of 'modernization,' 'revolutionary Marxism' or merely 'international relations,' or all three, [was] a secondary question."[11]

Peck, in his rejoinder to Fairbank in the same issue, refused to give ground. Fairbank's response, he charged, had illustrated rather than refuted his (Peck's) original argument, revealing in the process why the ideology of various China specialists had become a "rhetoric of apology, a means of masking reality, and an obstacle to understanding and significant action."

Peck insisted on the legitimacy of lumping the liberal China specialists of the 1950s with the right-wing ideologues of that period, for although they did indeed quarrel among themselves, their basic premises about America and the world were identical:

> However bitter the conflict among [them], what emerges is an increasingly strong commitment to the anti-communist crusade, debates over tactics instead of assumptions, disputes which amounted to different ideological justifications for the American empire. The acceptance of the anti-communist perspective, its bi-polar and moralistic view of the world, the idealization of American power and the consequent justification of the role of chief nation builder and global cop, reduced the conflict to disagreement over the techniques for implementing a fundamentally rightist world view. . . . That is why even those liberal American China specialists can be put with Dulles (all dreaming) in the same bed.

To document his point, Peck devoted most of his reply to an analysis of three "outlooks" or "descriptive and evaluative perspectives" which liberals and conservatives shared: containment, "nation building," and "totalitarian" China:

> Each of these three widely shared perspectives fit snugly into [the] broad commitment to an anti-communist crusade. Each played its part in the prostitution of language. Each served to obfuscate the realities of Asia and help prevent a fundamentally critical analysis of America's role and power. For the China specialists spoke of America's international responsibilities and her global role (instead of the American empire), of modernization and nation building (instead of imperialism and neocolonialism), of non-violent change and stability (instead of counter-revolution and institutionalized violence), and of foreign aid and economic investment (instead of an international capitalist system).[12]

THE RADICAL CRITIQUE OF THE FIELD: AN ASSESSMENT

Peck's attack symbolized an important turning point in the development of the China field in America. During the 1950s and much of the 1960s, a broad consensus had indeed existed with regard to basic assumptions and questions. There had been skirmishes to be sure—one thinks of the controversy between Wittfogel and Schwartz over "Maoism" or that between Levenson and Arthur Hummel over the scholar's responsibility to the individual in history[13]—but the intellectual issues were of limited scope and the skirmishes never escalated into war. The editor of the *Journal of Asian Studies*, in a remark prefacing a symposium on "Chinese Studies and the Disciplines," which appeared in 1964, had to apologize to the readership that there was "more agreement among the authors than might ideally have been planned."[14] No one, it seems—and this reflected a pattern of resistance to critical self-analysis that, according to Hayden White, ran through the entire historical profession in America[15]—no one thought to ask of the field in general during this period: What are we doing? Where are we going?

As the 1960s wore on, discomfort with this consensus deepened. Self-criticism within the United States, especially among the young, became pervasive, and the horror of what Americans were doing in Southeast Asia in the name of freedom and honor began to trouble people deeply. Vietnam was an American tragedy, not just a tragedy for American Asian specialists. But many of the latter, because of their expertise, felt a special sense of responsibility to speak out. Some defended the war. Many, in time, became critics, though still within a moderate framework that failed to address basic assumptions. (This was the "wrong war to be fighting in the wrong place at the wrong time" school.) Still others, preponderantly graduate students and younger scholars, seeing the need for a more radical critique of the assumptions that had gotten us into Indo-China and were keeping us from getting out, formed an organization called the Committee of Concerned Asian Scholars and began publishing the *Bulletin of Concerned Asian Scholars* in 1968. It was the voice of this latter group that James Peck articulated.

Peck's article sent shock waves through the China field. It was written in a trenchant, hard-hitting style. It had a certain titillating aspect, in that the author, a youthful graduate student in sociology at the time, was taking on, in mass, the elders of the profession. Also, because of the way in which Peck's attack was structured, it inevitably resulted in a degree of nervous self-examination among his readership. Peck left the boundaries of the "China-watchers" cohort he was bringing under scrutiny vague and undefined, causing the unnamed (which was most of us) to wonder uneasily whether we had been consigned to the elect or the damned—or, perhaps mercifully, to some purgatory-like place in between.

Speaking for the damned, Fairbank made pointed reference at the time to "the usual American feelings of guilt" from which Peck's generation "unfortunately" suffered and suggested that, however appropriate Peck's sense of outrage, however useful even as "a starting point for new policy efforts," history did not operate on moral sentiments alone. "The fact that 'American imperialism' [had] very undesirable features [did] not mean that 'communism' or 'revolutionary Marxism' [did] not have very undesirable features too." Analysis and criticism of the one ought not to lead, inexorably, to idealization of the other. Fairbank concluded that Peck was "primarily concerned not with understanding Chinese realities but with combatting American imperialism." Peck himself, however, would surely have claimed that the two were inseparable, that the very same modernization theory that masked American imperialism also prevented Americans from acquiring a truer understanding of the Chinese revolution. In any case, Peck, however reluctantly, would have to agree with Fairbank that he was "not merely a watcher of China-watchers" now, but a China-watcher himself.[16] His views of Chinese history, too, would have to undergo scrutiny.

One of the more curious features of Peck's position is that it shares a number of fundamental premises with the "impact-response" and "modernization" approaches he assails. There are differences, to be sure, but the differences have to do more with evaluative labeling, with whether this or that aspect of the total picture was "good" or "bad," positive or negative, than with the picture itself.

To begin with, Chinese society, prior to the full impact of Western imperialism in the early nineteenth century, was in Peck's view both unchanging and apparently incapable of introducing fundamental change on its own. In a book Peck coedited with Victor Nee in 1975, he seemed to argue the opposite:

> Nothing is further from the truth than the portrayal of a peaceful, changeless, gracious China set ablaze by twentieth-century social and nationalist revolutions sparked by the Western impact; of China as a tranquil giant torn by foreign ideas from thousands of years of lethargy amidst a dazzling culture; of a stable, well-balanced society following a historical rhythm similar to a recurring seasonal cycle finally shattered by Western aggression. Underlying the grace and culture of the gentry and the rise and fall of dynasties was "one long chain of peasant revolts." . . . Bitter struggle and intense exploitation in China's long history were not the exception but the norm.

What Peck is really arguing here, of course, is that pre-nineteenth-century China was far from the nice, stable, happy place some Westerners imagined it to have been. He is not arguing that Chinese society underwent significant change. Quite to the contrary. "The Chinese peasants," he tells us a few pages later, "were never able to put China on a new historical path more favorable to their own interests. . . . [The] momentous uprisings throughout Chinese history led only to drastic but short-term action to divide the existing wealth rather than promoting a fundamental transformation of society."[17] "While peasant uprisings thus dealt blows to the prevailing feudal regime, the political and economic fabric of Chinese society remained basically unchanged."[18]

In short, despite Peck's rhetorical effort to dissociate himself from the cyclical view of Chinese history, the picture he presents us with is, for all its *Sturm und Drang*, quintessentially cyclical, a history drenched in blood in which nothing new ever happens. It is only with the intrusion of the nineteenth-century West, with its unprecedented wealth and power, that "fundamental transformation" becomes a genuine possibility in China:

> In the early nineteenth century, the waves of an expanding Western capitalism broke upon China's shores, giving rise to an epochal crisis in Chinese history. China's relative isolation from the rest of the world approached its end, widespread corruption in the government spread, administration deteriorated, peasant rebellions broke out, and the state public works projects began to break down. In addition, the unprecedented growth of population was a new and ominous sign of a crisis at the heart of traditional Chinese society. Even before the British victory in the First Opium War (1839-1842), a deepening internal crisis was interwoven with, and profoundly aggravated by, Western economic penetration. No longer was it a question of barbarian threats from the northern and northwestern frontiers which the Chinese could hope to assimilate. The new invaders came not only armed with superior weapons, but commanding a power unleashed by the Industrial Revolution in the West which was to undermine the foundations of China's self-sufficient agricultural economy and its traditional culture and values."[19]

The West thus created, as in Peck's view it alone *could* create, the preconditions for massive change in Chinese society. Having created these preconditions, however, it proceeded effectively to block any and all changes that were not in its interest. It did this partly by supporting those "conservative" and "backward" elements, such as the self-strengtheners, "who sought to preserve Chinese feudalism," partly by stimulating the emergence of new groups and social forces that, although "acutely sensitive to the heavy toll imperialism was exacting in China" and having "little stake in preserving the traditional Confucian state," unwittingly helped erect the infrastructure for even deeper imperialist penetration:

Both reformers and revolutionaries attacked the direct manifestations of Western imperialist and Japanese military presence, but the less obvious threads of imperialist power eluded them. Indeed, the reforms they advocated would only enmesh China more completely into the international capitalist economy. The growth of the "modern sector", improved communications, the modernization of China's customs service, and the growth of a Chinese banking system were all necessary for the increasingly sophisticated imperialist system which was evolving.[20]

As in the case of the self-strengtheners earlier, "those who sought to learn from the West were dominated by it. The dilemma remained: how could the country free itself from foreign domination and gain independence while using the reform methods and ideology of Western capitalism?" The answer, Peck tells us, was that it couldn't. When liberation finally came, it was led by a revolutionary movement that opposed imperialism frontally, had its roots in the Chinese countryside where imperialism was weakest,[21] and took place at a time (World War II and the immediate aftermath) when the forces of imperialism in China were either fighting it out among themselves or were in defeat and disarray.

Although Peck agrees with Levenson, Fairbank, and others in judging the impact of the West on China to have been a "disaster," he recognizes that China faced "an acute internal crisis in the nineteenth century" and does not, like Levenson, see all the problems of Chinese society as deriving from the West. Nor does he, in the spirit of Fairbank, Reischauer, and Craig, credit China's "transformation," when it finally does come, directly to the West; rather, he contends that it was the Chinese Communists who "almost alone . . . developed the theory and practice of revolution as a way of overcoming the traditional dynamics of chaos and violence or acquiescence and passivity."[22] The revolution itself, on the other hand, was, in Peck's view, first and foremost a product of the Western intrusion. Peck is quite explicit on this point, describing the revolution as "a protracted and continuous historical process which grew out of the Chinese response to the impact of Western expansionism in the mid-nineteenth century."[23] This clear echo of Mary Wright's "revolution from without," with its emphatic stress on the exogenous determinants of recent Chinese history, is further reflected in Peck's conviction that the *need* for China's "total transformation," if not the transformation itself, was immediately attributable to the West, which after 1840 placed "China's very culture and existence . . . in peril" and "brutally" showed "its ways . . . to be parochial."[24]

Although on one level Peck portrays a Janus-faced West, acting as both source of, and obstacle to, fundamental change in nineteenth- and twentieth-century China, on a deeper level he appears convinced that without the Western intrusion the revolution would never have taken place and Chinese society would have remained stuck where it had always been. This poses a problem for Peck's analysis. Since he appears to believe that, prior to the advent of the West, Chinese society, although shot through and through with suffering and exploitation, was incapable of self-generated change, he cannot very well argue, as have some, that the Chinese would have been better off without the West. But because he sees Western imperialism as a wholly negative and exploitative phenomenon, he also cannot maintain that China was better off with it.

A more focused statement of the same quandary is found in Peck's understanding of the relationship between China's "underdevelopment" and the world economic system. In his debate with Fairbank, Peck belabors the point that the "underdevelopment" of Chinese society was not sui generis, that it was a consequence of the world capitalist system into which China had been drawn by Western imperialism. Yet a few years later we find Peck arguing that, even prior to the nineteenth century, when Chinese society was (according to him) still relatively isolated from the world economic system—and therefore presumably not yet "underdeveloped"—it was nonetheless already in a state of seemingly permanent immiseration—incapable of "fundamental transformation," its "political and economic fabric . . . remain[ing] basically unchanged" for centuries.

It may seem that I have boxed Peck in too tightly. The reality is that Peck has done his own boxing. Peck acknowledges the internal crisis in nineteenth-century China and describes the population increase, in particular, as "unprecedented." Were he to delve more deeply into this crisis, he would find that fundamental changes were already under way in China at the time of the Opium War. Because these changes—urbanization of the east central coast region, monetization of the economy, growing popular literacy, expansion of the gentry class, commercialization of local managerial functions, to name some of the more important of them—had been building for several centuries, moreover, in order to gain a fuller understanding of them, he would have to give much more weight to internal factors and much less to the impact of Western expansionism (which, in his own estimation, became of critical importance only after 1840). This, however, is precisely what Peck, as we have seen, refuses to do.

The question is, Why? One reason for Peck's unwillingness—perhaps inability—to deal seriously with internal factors is his highly teleological vision of Chinese history. Like Levenson, Fairbank, and others, for whom the only change that really mattered in late imperial China was change leading toward "modernity," the only change that really counts for Peck is change that culminates in "the revolution." Since, however, Peck cannot conceive of the revolution except as a process emerging out of China's response to the West, the only change he is really interested in is change resulting directly or indirectly from the Western impact.

A second reason for Peck's downgrading of internal factors derives from his moral-psychological frame of reference. Profoundly unhappy with American conduct in Asia in the postwar era and outraged at the capacity of American scholars to see intelligence where he sees stupidity, humaneness where he sees brutality, Peck is driven to define Western expansionism as the key factor in the shaping of nineteenth- and twentieth-century Chinese history. To emphasize internal factors, in these circumstances, is tantamount to letting the West in general and America in particular off the hook, something Peck finds morally wrong and emotionally abhorrent. The trouble with this stance, from a historian's point of view, is that it is methodologically indefensible. As a hypothesis awaiting empirical proof, the notion of the paramountcy of Western imperialism in recent Chinese history is perfectly appropriate. As a given, which because it is given does not need to be proved, it is ahistorical nonsense.

A third reason for Peck's depreciation of endogenous determinants of change is that, with the important (but nonetheless ambiguous) exception of the emergence of embryonic capitalism,[25] such determinants have received little attention in the conventional Maoist historiography on which Peck's approach is closely based. Fairbank would see Peck's almost slavish adherence to Maoist historiography as illustrative of the perennial tendency of Americans to work out their guilt feelings by overidentifying with the victims—real or imagined—of American power. Whatever Peck's motives, his failure to depart in any significant respect from the Maoist approach to Chinese history—including, incidentally, the Maoist periodization model, which begins "modern history" (*chin-tai-shih*) with the Opium War and gives overwhelming stress thereafter to the Western impact[26]—renders him vulnerable to all of the criticisms that can be leveled against Maoist historiography: its extreme teleological character, its weak empirical foundation, its rampant use of vague and ill-defined labels (such as "feudalism"), and its ultimate acquiescence in a "stagnation-Western impact-transformation" paradigm of change that had its intellectual origins in the nineteenth-century West.[27]

IMPERIALISM IN NEW CLOTHES: THE WORLD ECONOMY THESIS

Although the intellectual challenge leveled by Peck was occasionally reiterated in the first half of the 1970s,[28] it was not until the publication in 1977 of *Japan, China, and the Modern*

World Economy by a sociologist named Frances Moulder that the imperialism approach received systematic book-length support. Moulder's study has attracted a good deal of scholarly attention, partly because of its iconoclastic thesis and partly because it represents the first serious effort to apply the theoretical perspective of Immanuel Wallerstein (the author's mentor) to East Asian history.[29] Moulder begins her book by asking why Japan was the only non-Western country to become a major industrial capitalist nation. Focusing on the comparison with China, she notes (as did Peck) that most scholars who have addressed this classic question have assumed that the Western impact experienced by Japan, China, and other East Asian countries in the nineteenth century was basically similar and that therefore the variations in the responses of these countries "must," to quote Reischauer and Fairbank, "be attributed mainly to the differences in [their] traditional societies."[30]

This emphasis on internal, sociocultural factors as the key variables in explaining the success or failure of a country's "development" is characterized by Moulder as the "traditional society" approach. Traditional society theories, with their essentially benevolent view of the world economy, further argue that incorporation into this economy is "development promoting" and that it is the insufficient openness of non-Western societies to such incorporation—an insufficient openness attributable to the internal makeup of these societies—that has been the principal reason for their underdevelopment. The alternative explanation of underdevelopment is characterized by Moulder as the "world economy" approach. World economy theories view "the influence of the industrial capitalist nations on the nonindustrial nations . . . as basically development blocking, not development promoting" and analyze underdevelopment "as a function of the subordinate or satellite position of the underdeveloped nations in a world economy that provides disproportionate benefits to the industrial nations."[31]

The purpose of Moulder's study is to show that, although

previous advocates of the world economy position (such as Paul Baran) have done an inadequate job of explaining the contrast between Japan's development and China's underdevelopment in the nineteenth century, the theory itself is basically correct. Japan's development was a consequence not of its unique sociocultural characteristics, as maintained by the traditional society theorists, but of its relative autonomy within the world economy, whereas China's underdevelopment was a result principally of its having been incorporated into the world system as a dependent satellite.

Moulder's study is divided into three parts. In the first part she argues "that traditional society theorists have exaggerated the differences between Ch'ing China and Tokugawa Japan on the one hand and the similarities between Tokugawa Japan and the societies of early modern Europe on the other." While not denying "certain similarities in *political* structure" between Japan and early modern Europe ("feudalism"), she insists that, taken as a whole, "the process of Japan's political-economic-social development . . . was more similar to that of China than that of Europe."[32]

My reactions to this part of Moulder's argument are complicated. I would agree, as suggested in the first chapter of this book, that there were indeed important similarities between China and Japan on the eve of the Western impact and that East Asianists, insufficiently attuned to a broader comparative perspective, have too often shown a tendency to overlook these similarities and exaggerate the contrasts. Moulder reminds her readership that both China and Japan were "fundamentally agrarian" and that peasants in both societies "produced largely the same things . . . by largely the same methods." She also maintains that both societies, prior to the nineteenth century, experienced similar patterns of social and economic transformation, in particular growing agricultural productivity, increasing population, improvements in transportation, the spread of "extensive" commercialization (which she distinguishes from "intensive" commercialization, which is marked by greater loss of regional self-sufficiency and greater domination of production by exchange relations), expansion (then relative curtailment) of foreign trade, and social changes accompanying commercialization.

Moulder also contends that there were basic similarities between Chinese and Japanese political processes, that they shared much more with each other than either did with the European "dynamic of development." Although Japan was feudal and China was imperial,

> neither showed signs of developing toward a centralized national state. In neither China nor Japan did governments have a comparably active mercantilist relationship to the national economy which would have strongly encouraged national industrialization and "intensive" commercialization. In neither country did accelerating military expenditures and a rapidly growing state apparatus, on a scale comparable to Europe's, give impetus to capital accumulation.

In terms of the political framework for development, Moulder concludes (quoting Baran) that on the eve of the Western intrusion, "conditions in Japan were as conducive, or rather as unfavorable, to economic development as anywhere in Asia." Had the West never appeared, she conjectures, the contradictions in Japanese feudalism "would most likely have resolved themselves through the creation of an imperial structure on the Chinese model." It is "highly unlikely," in her view, that in the absence of the Western impact, Japan would have moved, on its own, in the direction of industrial capitalism.[33]

The logic of Moulder's argument so far is fairly straightforward. According to traditional society theorists, the contrast between Chinese and Japanese development in the nineteenth century can only be explained on the basis of significant internal differences between the two societies. Therefore, if it can be shown that such internal differences were not present, that on the contrary China and Japan were moving in parallel or even convergent directions, a crucial building block in the traditional society analysis is demolished and serious doubt is cast on the interpretation's overall reliability. In scrutinizing Moulder's argument, the critical question that must be addressed is not whether her broad claims of parallelism or convergence are warranted—they may well be—but whether, in granting such claims, the possibility of significant, even decisive, internal differences between China and Japan is thereby negated.

I would argue that it is not, and I would rest my argument on several grounds. First, in contending that China and Japan were fundamentally similar societies in the mid-nineteenth century, Moulder has conveniently omitted from her analysis one area—that of values, beliefs, world views[34]—which traditional society theorists tend to regard as of major importance and in which they believe some of the most critical differences between China and Japan resided in the last century (an oft-cited example being the difference in attitude toward borrowing from abroad).

Second, even in the areas that Moulder does examine, she builds her case in a highly tendentious manner. This may be seen, for example, in her treatment of certain topics—social change in late imperial China, to cite one instance—on which there happens to be little hard information and much controversy. Repeatedly, in dealing with such topics, she extracts from an often highly interpretive secondary literature an analysis that supports her own thesis and then, without warning to the uninitiated reader, offers it up as "evidence."[35] On other occasions, most notably in her discussion of political patterns in Tokugawa Japan and Ch'ing China, Moulder is so intent upon showing that neither China nor Japan had the necessary ingredients for an indigenous birth of industrial capitalism—these ingredients, of course, being the ones that gave rise to industrial capitalism in early modern Europe—that she ends up defining the overall pattern of political-economic development in the two societies principally in terms of what they lacked: "Despite Japan's feudal form and China's imperial form, the dynamics of their development seem more similar than different, when compared to the development of the societies of Western Europe."[36] This analytical procedure, the careful reader will not have failed to note, rests on a variation of the zoological fallacy pointed out in the preceding chapter, whereby the bird (China) and the fish (Japan) are viewed as like in consequence of the fact that neither is a monkey (Western Europe).

A third reason why Moulder's argument is unconvincing is that it is pursued on a level of generality that is inappropriate to the problem at hand. It is possible to argue that certain broad similarities among societies in the East Asian cultural realm—not necessarily the precise similarities pointed out by Moulder—have been instrumental in facilitating economic development in all of these societies over the *long* term. But over the *short* term, variations in the "development experience" of such societies may depend much more on specific historical forces and conjunctions of events. Certainly it would not be hard to argue that, whatever general social, economic, political, and cultural features China and Japan may have shared, the concrete historical processes at work within the two countries in the middle of the nineteenth century were very different. The question then is: How decisive were these differences?

Before taking up this question, let us return to Moulder's argument. Having in the first part of her study disposed of the claim that, on the eve of the Western impact, the societies of China and Japan were fundamentally different, she proceeds in the second part to argue that the nature of the Western impact—in her terminology, the manner of incorporation into the world economy—differed radically in the two areas.

The key mechanism, for Moulder, is "incorporation." Her explanation of what she means by incorporation and how it works is, however, somewhat mystifying. Incorporation, as she defines it, is a political-economic phenomenon governed by four variables: the size and nature of trade between satellite and metropole; the extent and character of metropolitan investment in the satellite; the degree of political encroachment; and the degree of missionary penetration. At no point, unfortunately, does Moulder discuss the relative importance of these variables in determining the degree of incorporation, whether, as Shannon Brown asks, "twice as many missionaries [are] as important as twice as much investment" or "a dollar's worth of investment as important as a dollar's worth of trade."[37] Even more perplexing is her insistence that "the degree to which a society has been incorporated as a satellite (compared to others) is [to be] measured by the importance of that society (compared to others) for *metropolitan* economic and political interests, not vice versa." Were the reverse true, Moulder acknowledges, "it might be argued that China was less incorporated than Japan (or some other area) because the foreign trade or investment *per capita* was less." While she finds this line of reasoning "of interest," however, she is unpersuaded by it because "from the point of view of the *political* economics of development . . . the importance of a satellite to the metropole determines how hard the metropole will fight to take and to hold the satellite, which in turn determines the difficulties the people of the satellite nation will face in their efforts to liberate themselves and to develop the nation's economy."[38]

In football this is called an end run. End runs, however, are harder to get away with in historical scholarship. By defining incorporation in the way she does, Moulder neatly sidesteps the by now considerable body of literature by American economists and economic historians (to be dealt with further on in this chapter) which holds that the economic effects of Western imperialism in nineteenth- and twentieth-century China were negligible or—some argue—even beneficial. Moulder is well aware of this literature and uses the data from it liberally. At no point, however, does she directly confront the conclusions that the creators of the literature have derived from their data. Given her definition of incorporation, with its emphasis on the economic importance of satellite to metropole rather than the reverse, she does not have to.

What is principally wrong with Moulder's definition is that it rests on an oversimplified understanding of political behavior in general and of the relationship between political behavior and economic interests in particular. Two examples, one pertaining to foreign investment in China, the other to missionary activity, will serve to clarify the point.

In the early years of this century, the Chinese government, anxious to develop its northeastern frontier and to neutralize the penetration of Russia and Japan, offered the United States broad trade and investment concessions in Manchuria. The United States, like China, wanted to keep Manchuria from coming under the domination of one or more powers, and it was interested in business opportunities in the area. Yet, as Michael Hunt has shown, it either ignored or rebuffed a succession of Chinese overtures, partly because ignorance and ethnocentric blindness kept it from understanding what the Chinese were really up to, partly because the American stake in Manchuria was too small for it to care, and partly for a variety of other reasons.[39] What Hunt's analysis demonstrates, if nothing else, is that the situation in Manchuria was complex, far too complex to be encompassed by any simple interest calculus of political behavior. For one thing, the U.S. government in this case displayed considerable internal confusion over time as to what its own best interests were, and for another, if it had pursued more effectively and consistently the development-oriented approach advocated by Willard Straight, Charles Denby, Jr., Philander Knox, and others—and encouraged by the Chinese—a net increase in foreign (American) investment activity in China might well have resulted in a net decrease in foreign (Russian-Japanese) political domination—a subtlety for which Moulder's theory does not prepare us.

This same sort of obfuscation is seen in Moulder's treatment of the question of "missionary encroachment." "Nineteenth-century European governments," she tells us, "provided missionaries with the military protection that was essential to their activities only when the governments had important national political-economic aims that they hoped might be furthered through missionary influence." She further asserts, with respect to Japan specifically, that "in the absence of a build-up of economic interests, missionaries were not protected by the Western governments, as they were in China."[40] I will leave it to the reader to figure out how, if military protection was "essential" to the activities of missionaries, missionaries could have functioned at all in Japan (which they clearly did) without such protection, or how the leader of the largest Protestant mission in China (Hudson Taylor of the China Inland Mission) could have concluded in 1895 that in no circumstances was it appropriate for Protestant missionaries to appeal for redress to their governments.

Beyond this, there is again the problem in Moulder's analysis of oversimplification of governmental motivation. France undertook to furnish protection to Catholic missionaries in the late Ch'ing not because of French economic interests in China but because of power rivalries in Europe. Indeed, it was precisely France's lack of real interests in the Chinese empire that caused it to create unreal ones in order to counter the prestige and influence of Great Britain. The British, for their part, had a fairly significant commercial stake in nineteenth-century China. Yet anyone who has looked at the official correspondence for the period knows that, far from hoping that Her Majesty's government's political and economic interests "might be furthered through missionary influence," most British officials saw the missionaries as an impediment to the smooth development of Sino-British trade—people who, in Lord Clarendon's words (1869), had "to be protected against themselves." In these circumstances, when British protection was forthcoming, it was more often than not in spite, rather than because, of the official perception of Britain's interests.[41]

The bulk of the second part of Moulder's study consists of a fairly conventional recital of the external record of imperialism, first in China and then in Japan. Although the account is weakened by errors and oversimplifications,[42] it has the merit of accentuating the differences between the Western impacts on the two societies. Moulder emphasizes, in particular, that, in contrast to the Chinese case, Western political encroachment on Japan, in the form of the unequal treaty system, came *prior* to the development of significant Western economic interests in that country, and that it was some twenty to thirty years after the initial encroachment before such interests were established—an interlude she characterizes, following E.H. Norman, as Japan's "breathing space." Because of these and other differences, Moulder concludes, as we have already seen, that by the end of the nineteenth century China had become deeply incorporated into the world economy, while Japan retained a substantial degree of autonomy. A nagging problem with Moulder's analysis is its failure to specify how the effects of incorporation—or lack thereof—on either the satellite or the metropolitan country are to be identified and measured. This problem becomes critical in the final portion of the book.

In this final portion the central question Moulder addresses is: "Did Japan's 'breathing space' promote industrialization and did China's more intensive incorporation hamper it?" In pursuing this question, she places less stress than some world economy theorists on the purely economic concomitants of incorporation and much greater stress on what might be called the political infrastructure of industrialization. "Japan's industrialization," she maintains, "occurred *despite* a focus on production for export, despite the displacement of native products by imports, despite declining terms of trade, despite fluctuating export prices, despite the emergence of strata with a vested interest in the export-import trade, and despite the opposition of these strata to government tax policies." It occurred principally because of two political developments that had not taken place in China or Japan prior to the intrusion of Western capitalism "but had been an important aspect of the modernization of Western Europe." These were (1) the establishment of a centralized national state and (2) state encouragement of national industrialization. Both developments were made possible in Meiji Japan because of its relative autonomy vis-à-vis the world economic system; conversely, they failed to emerge in late Ch'ing China because of its strong incorporation into this system.[43]

This climactic stage in the evolution of Moulder's argument

is in many ways the weakest. No one would deny that a strong centralized state emerged in Japan during the latter half of the nineteenth century or that the Chinese state during this period became progressively weaker. Nor, despite disagreement over the precise nature of the Meiji state's role in Japanese industrialization, would anyone question the critical importance of this role overall. And surely most scholars would concur that, on the Chinese side, the state's efforts to encourage industrialization were on balance inadequate.

So far so good. The trouble comes when Moulder seeks to establish the causal factors leading up to these outcomes. Here her theoretical framework commits her so strongly to the primacy of external forces that instead of sifting through the evidence evenhandedly in order to see where it points, she appears to weight it in favor of a set of conclusions that have been preformulated in her mind. Moulder sees the Taiping uprising, for example, as having been a major factor in the weakening of the Chinese state in the middle of the last century. She is theoretically committed, however, to the view that the deterioration of the Ch'ing state was a consequence of China's intensive incorporation into the world economy. It is essential, therefore, that the Taipings be viewed principally in terms of incorporation. And indeed that is precisely what Moulder does. She writes,

> The Ch'ing government might have held on indefinitely without serious opposition had not the onset of relations with the West changed the situation in two ways that greatly increased the likelihood of large-scale revolt. First, the expansion of trade led to a dramatic increase in the hardships suffered by peasants throughout China and in South China in particular. Second, it increased the frequency and intensity of contacts among dissident groups—merchants, lower gentry, peasants, and artisans—thus facilitating the spread of revolt.[44]

There are two things wrong with this set of propositions. First, no one has ever demonstrated (or, as far as I know, even seriously argued) that prior to the middle of the last century peasant hardship *throughout* China suffered a *dramatic* increase *as a result* of the expansion of Sino-Western trade. Second, even though external factors undoubtedly played some part—possibly a very considerable one—in the origins of the Taiping uprising, most Taiping scholars would maintain that internal forces, which Moulder omits from her analysis entirely, were also—some would say much more—important.

An equally egregious manipulation of historical reality is encountered in Moulder's discussion of the "breathing space" issue in Japan's industrialization. Let us grant, with Moulder, that the Meiji Restoration took place largely as a consequence of the onset of relations with the West. (This is at least an arguable proposition.) The question is why, between 1870 and 1890, the Meiji rulers proceeded to fashion a strong, centralized national state and to bring the state's increasing power to bear on the promotion of Japan's industrialization. Moulder's answer to this question is that the Western powers, for various reasons, were relatively uninterested in Japan for trade and investment purposes until the turn of the century and therefore did not impose upon that country the sorts of political constraints that in China resulted in underdevelopment. Given this "breathing space," Japan's leadership seized the "opportunity"—an opportunity denied China—to promote state centralization and start the country on the path toward industrialization.

What is wrong with this thesis? One thing wrong with it is that Moulder fails to point out the serious implications for the "external factor" approach of the fact that the Meiji Restoration was victorious while the Taipings went down to defeat. Since both movements, in her judgment, had "centralizing or rationalizing" tendencies and "aimed . . . at strengthening state control over society," the presumption must be that, had the Taipings won, they would have propelled China in the direction of political centralization, making the country less vulnerable to incorporation into the world economy and creating, as in Meiji Japan, an environment conducive to industrialization. Since such a result, in terms of Moulder's argument, would be inimical to the interests of the Western powers, one would expect the latter to take a strong hand in assisting the Ch'ing in its suppression campaign. This is not, however, what happened, according to the author, who argues, on the contrary, that "Western support does not seem to have played a decisive part in the success or failure" of either the Taiping or the Meiji movements.[45] If such is the case, and I think Moulder is absolutely right in this instance, are we not left with the conclusion that internal factors were of critical importance in the determination of both outcomes?

A second problem with Moulder's thesis is that it assumes, without proof, that it was Japan's freedom from substantial Western economic involvement between 1870 and 1890—the "breathing space"—that enabled it to build a strong centralized state, when it could as easily be maintained that the opposite was more nearly the case (that the breathing space was facilitated by the centralization process) or that it was some combination of the two or that there really was no breathing space at all and that Japan's state-building efforts succeeded *in spite of* the negative effects of economic relations with the West (a thesis, incidentally, for which the author herself supplies evidence). Let us grant, however, for the sake of argument, that there really was a breathing space and that it really was this circumstance that furnished the Meiji leadership with the opportunity to create a centralized state. This still leaves us with a third set of problems, namely, why Japan's rulers seized the opportunity to begin with, and why, once it was seized, they were so effective in implementing their goals. These, curiously, are questions that Moulder never poses. She seems to assume that any government, faced with foreign political encroachment, will want to transform itself as rapidly as possible into a powerful centralized state and that, in the absence of strong external constraints, it will know exactly how to go about this task.

Moulder's failure to confront these questions is, of course, not really curious at all. Were she to confront them, she would have to acknowledge the very real contribution that internal *as well as* external forces made to the political and economic history of Meiji Japan (to say nothing of Ch'ing China which, it has been argued by some, also experienced a "breathing space" in the period prior to 1895). She would also have to abandon the Europocentric bias that permeates her thesis and causes her to assume that industrialization, when it occurs in a non-Western society, must follow essentially the pattern that it followed in Western Europe. Although it may not be immediately apparent, there is an all-important connection between Moulder's Europocentrism and her facile disregard of internal historical forces in China and Japan. For it is precisely the belief that Chinese and Japanese, if given half a chance, will act like Europeans that makes it superfluous to scrutinize painstakingly the real sources of their behavior.

Moulder's one-sided presentation of the evidence, on the other hand, cannot be attributed entirely to her Europocentric bias. It is also, I fear, a consequence of her having failed to work out a satisfactory relationship between her political orientation and her scholarly commitment to illuminating what she calls "the sociological theory of economic change."[46] Moulder argues, from a neo-Marxist ideological perspective, that governments behave according to their political and economic interests and that imperialism—the global pursuit of such interests by Western capitalist countries—has been the prime cause of the problems experienced by non-Western societies over the past century and a half. Certainly there is nothing inherently wrong with either of these propositions. The crucial question, in scholarship, that must be asked of an author's political convictions is whether they serve to stimulate or to foreclose serious inquiry. It is here, I believe, that Moulder fails her readership. Although she claims to be in quest of the truth, the key propositions in her study operate more as givens than as hypotheses in need of testing. Evidence that does not support her conclusions is disregarded instead of being carefully weighed. In the end, we are left with one more contribution to the "empirical vacuum" in which so much of the controversy over the economic effects of imperialism on China and Japan has taken place.[47]

THE ELEPHANT AND THE FLEA: IMPERIALISM MANQUÉ

Let there be no question about it. Everyone—or, at any rate, almost everyone—today regards imperialism as bad,[48] and most would agree with James Peck that it was not just a figment of the Chinese imagination but had real, measurable effects. That is not the issue. The issue is: What were these effects? On one hand, we have people like Peck and Frances Moulder, who view imperialism as the principal moving force in the century of Chinese history from the Opium War through World War II and who maintain, specifically, that imperialism distorted and restructured the Chinese economy, forcing it into a condition of underdevelopment from which it was able to escape only after a Communist-led revolution threw the imperialists out and "decisively broke the ties that chained China to the imperialist system."[49] On the other hand, there are a by now sizable number of individuals, mostly economists and economic historians, whose researches have brought them to very nearly the opposite conclusion. These people do not argue that imperialism had no consequences whatever. Many of them, in fact, judge it to have been of vital importance in the political and intellectual history of nineteenth- and twentieth-century China, in particular as a stimulus to the rise of nationalism. In the economic sphere, however, they believe the effects of imperialism—good or bad—to have been, on balance, modest. Like the proverbial flea in the elephant's ear, foreign economic encroachment could act as an irritant, as a source of localized disruption, even (within limits) as a positive stimulus. But the Chinese economy as a whole was too gargantuan, too self-sufficient, and too poor to be substantially affected.

The picture of the crippling economic effects of imperialism that these scholars challenge was first put forward in the

1930s by Western-trained Chinese social scientists. Within the Chinese world it has had wide support ever since, not only among scholars but also among political spokesmen of all persuasions (Chiang Kai-shek, for example, as well as Mao Tse-tung). As recapitulated by Chi-ming Hou, one of the critics of the picture, its central ingredients are as follows:

> First, it is argued that foreign economic intrusion—that is, foreign trade and investment in China—upset the economy by ruining the handicraft industries and disrupting agriculture. Second, foreign trade and investment are alleged to have drained the economy of its wealth because of the secularly unfavorable balance of trade and the large amount of income that was made or remitted to their home countries by Western enterprises. Third, it is maintained that foreign enterprises in China were so effective in their competitive power or enjoyed so many advantages secured by their respective governments that the Chinese-owned modern enterprises were utterly and hopelessly oppressed and had little, if any, chance to grow.

In challenging this overall picture, different authors have focused on different parts of the whole. Hou himself, in a book published in 1965, concentrates on the impact of foreign investment. He argues that, mainly because of the size of the population, foreign investment per capita was extremely low in China (less than U.S. $8, as late as 1936), that it was mainly concentrated in the treaty port sector, and that it took the form for the most part of direct investment in fields associated with foreign trade (the low level of foreign investment in primary production—agriculture and mining—being due to the restrictive nature of Chinese mining regulations and persistently strong barriers to the infusion of foreign capital into the rural economy). Hou further maintains that competition from foreign capital did not have a destructive effect on Chinese-owned enterprises or on the traditional sector and also did not result in lopsided export development. On the contrary, he concludes, through linkage and other effects, "foreign capital was largely responsible for the development of whatever economic modernization took place in China before 1937."[50]

Although Hou is to be commended for reopening the question of the economic effects of imperialism and for formulating a radically alternative hypothesis concerning these effects, his study has been criticized from a number of quarters on methodological grounds. Hou's main contention, in Cheryl Payer's view, is a tautology and therefore meaningless, because "no definition is ever given of 'modernization' which could analytically distinguish it from the effects of foreign capital and thus make the contention a testable hypothesis."[51] Although Payer, by her own admission, writes from the standpoint of "the opposition," Hou has also been severely judged by scholars who agree with his more important conclusions. Robert F. Dernberger, for example, charges him with having set out to disprove the "negative effect" hypothesis by citing contrary examples—a procedure that, Dernberger rightly asserts, may work in mathematics and the natural sciences but is inadmissible in the social sciences.[52]

Central to the "negative effect" hypothesis is the assumption that the traditional sector of the Chinese economy underwent a sharp decline during the late Ch'ing and republican periods and that this decline was due in great measure to the foreign intrusion. One way of countering the hypothesis, therefore, is to show that the decline did not take place at all or that, insofar as it did take place, it was a result of factors other than imperialism. Hou pursues the former of these two lines of argument, but his book is not centrally concerned with the rural sector. In a book that is, Ramon Myers' *The Chinese Peasant Economy* (1970), both positions are argued.

Focusing on the north China region, Myers contends that changing patterns of land utilization, more intensive cultivation, rising farm prices, slight improvements in farm technology (mainly new seed strains), and increased opportunities for nonagricultural employment in the urban sector made possible a rise in total farm income for the 1890–1949 period that was roughly commensurate with population increase (about 1 percent yearly). Except during periods of natural or manmade calamity (such as World War II and the Civil War), therefore, peasant living standards did not decline over this time; in fact, they may even have shown a slight improvement due to the expanding commerce and industry of the treaty port–market town economy. Myers does not argue that peasants in north China prospered. He is insistent, however, that "there is no evidence to suggest that large sections of the countryside became so impoverished that their living standards in the mid-1930s were lower than in the 1890s." The fundamental problem faced by the rural economy during this period, he further maintains, was not socioeconomic; land distribution, although already very unequal in the late nineteenth century, did not become more so, and Myers finds "scarcely any evidence that exploitation of one group by another was . . . severe." Rather, the problem lay in the absence of any system for generating rapid technological progress in agriculture—a failure the responsibility for which Myers lays squarely on the shoulders of the Chinese government and the educated classes, neither of which took the development of the agrarian economy seriously.

Myers is aware of the enormous size and diversity of Chinese agriculture and counsels caution in applying the conclusions reached from his study of north China to other regions of the country. He notes, in particular, that in the northwest masses of peasants were perpetually on the verge of starvation owing to famine, while in the central provinces commerce was more highly developed and rural conditions were generally more prosperous and stable. Myers is hopeful, nonetheless, that his study will stimulate others to do work on different regions so that in time "a general theory of the Chinese peasant economy can be advanced."[53]

Myers' own conclusions, however, have by no means inspired universal acceptance. For one thing, Myers, even more than Chi-ming Hou, is guilty of the fallacy of argument by counterexample. The hypothesis of agricultural decline that he sets out to test—Myers calls it the "distributionist" hypothesis—is framed for the Chinese economy as a whole. Yet, the north China region with which he tests it had, according to

John Lossing Buck, the highest rate of owner-cultivators, the second lowest rate of taxation, and the highest percentage of farms hiring laborers of any region in China. "If there was any part of China which escaped the 'agrarian crisis,' " Thomas Wiens writes, "it was this region where, between 1911 and 1933, the tenancy rate remained stable at 13 percent, while it was rising from 28 to 32 percent for China as a whole."

Wiens' rigorous assessment of Myers' book raises a number of other potentially damaging questions concerning both the author's evidence and his interpretation of it. Although Myers has scoured an intimidating quantity of material, most of his generalizations rest on two sources of data: Japanese (Mantetsu) surveys of four Hopei and Shantung villages during the war and the Buck survey data, also for Hopei and Shantung. The Japanese materials were collected from potentially hostile informants under conditions that can only be described as tense and awkward. Even granting complete accuracy, however, Wiens challenges the representativeness of Myers' data, demonstrating that the sample selection procedures used in both the Buck and the Mantetsu surveys were biased. (The Buck data oversampled the more prosperous owner-cultivator group and undersampled tenants. Both sources of data suffer from geographical bias in that they sampled counties or villages that lay along or in close proximity to major transportation routes.)

From his analysis of Myers' data, Wiens concludes that the author "has no material basis at all for generalization on the questions at issue . . .; at most he can discuss the trends in his sample data as *sui generis*." Even here, moreover, he finds that Myers repeatedly misreads his own evidence, drawing from it conclusions that suit his preoccupations but are not in fact warranted.[54]

While Hou focused on foreign investment and Myers on agriculture, Rhoads Murphey, in his assault on the "negative effect" position, concentrates on foreign trade and the port cities in which this trade centered. Murphey's book, *The Outsiders,* appeared in the same year (1977) as Frances Moulder's and, like Moulder's study, treats China in a comparative context. The principal country he compares China with is, however, India, rather than Japan, and he arrives at conclusions that are diametrically opposed to Moulder's.

The big question, at the heart of Murphey's book, is why Western imperialism had such contrasting effects in China and India. Although granting "basic differences in the Western impact from one area to another," the "grand colonial design," Murphey contends,

> was essentially uniform in the Western mind, . . . Missionaries, traders, and consuls or colonial administrators played similar roles in India and China as elsewhere in Asia. The [treaty] ports themselves were . . . strikingly similar, not merely in physical layout . . . but in their ideological world. The empire builders, taipans, adventurers, and even to a degree many of the missionaries, were from the same stamp in each port. . . . They jostled each other, but they were jointly trying to do the same kinds of things in each country, and to impress uniformly on the Asian landscape their vision of the grand colonial design.

The outcomes of their efforts were, however, far from uniform. The historical and societal settings of countries like India and China were fundamentally different, and this internal variation was powerful enough to produce very different end results.

In India, for a variety of reasons, Western colonialism, instead of being resisted, found broad acceptance, at least until well into the nineteenth century. Politically disunited, commercially weak, and governed by an alien dynasty of conquest (the Mughals) that had little indigenous support, "India was in a condition to accept not merely colonial rule but fundamental change along the lines offered by the British. Individual Indians were . . . willing to become collaborators as fellow entrepreneurs and fellow administrators. . . . To most Indians who had any degree of political consciousness . . . the Western-British model, if not British colonial rule, was genuinely attractive." In this hospitable climate, what began in the colonial port cities spread in time "to create and shape virtually all change which took place in the country and to create virtually de novo the people, groups, institutions, and ideas which ruled India at independence. The treaty port Indian became, without need for apology, the dominant modern Indian."[55]

Things could not have been more different in China, where the same overarching Western colonial design met with steady and persistent frustration. To be sure, there were treaty ports galore, and, as in India, the Chinese ports produced their share of native collaborators. But "the Shanghai model did not spread—except to other treaty ports" and "the treaty port Chinese, . . . who seemed to be following the Indian path, [did] not achieve a similar conquest." Repeatedly Murphey refers to the Chinese treaty ports as enclave economies and enclave worlds ideologically and institutionally. Even while noting the criticisms leveled against Ramon Myers' study, Murphey accepts—indeed extends—Myers' conclusions, maintaining that "for China as a whole it is exaggerating to picture even the 1920s, 1930s, and 1940s as a period of unrelieved, universal, and limitless mass misery." But none of this is, in the end, of much account for Murphey's thesis, for in his view no matter how much deterioration took place in the rural economy, "the foreigners and their aggressively ambitious activities were only marginal factors" in causing it. The psychological and intellectual impact of the treaty ports was profound, Murphey argues, but "their influence was slight in material terms." Not only on a per capita basis but in absolute terms as well, China's foreign trade was insignificant. With one-fifth of the world's population, its foreign trade "never exceeded 1.5 percent of the total value of world trade, and exceeded 1 percent only briefly."[56]

Much of Murphey's account is devoted to explaining why the Chinese were so effective in resisting the economic impact of the West. Partly, it was a matter of sheer physical bulk. A strong proponent of the elephant-flea theory, Murphey frequently reminds the reader that China, "well over twice the size of India, . . . was simply too vast to be moved, let alone transformed by marginal seacoast contact with a relative handful of foreigners, however vigorous or effective they were." Size, moreover, lent itself not only to inertia but also to inaccessibility, a point the author underscores by comparing China with Japan, where over 90 percent of the population lived (and still lives) within fifty miles of the coast and within the same distance of Japan's half-dozen leading cities, all of them seaports.[57]

At least as important as the size of China was its nature—politically, psychologically, and as a functioning economic system. Murphey stresses a number of themes here. One is China's retention of its territorial sovereignty, which he judges (rightly in my view) to have been of critical importance in enabling it to contain the spread throughout Chinese society of the treaty port model. As part of his argument, Murphey notes that it was in those areas and only in those areas where Chinese sovereignty either was lost entirely (Manchuria) or remained at best nominal (the treaty port sector itself) that China's economy underwent genuine transformation in response to the foreign impact.

Another reason in Murphey's view why China was so effective at fending off Western influence was the enormous strength of its self-image: "The Chinese self-image more than anything else was what blunted the Western effort, what kept it from achieving the degree of success, in its own terms, which it won in India." Where, in other cultures, confrontation with the West had produced an erosion of national-cultural identity, the Chinese sense of identity, Murphey argues (following Lucian Pye), was if anything sharpened in the process. "What identity crisis there was . . . was limited to a few, and almost wholly in the non-Chinese world of the treaty ports."[58]

A third factor emphasized by Murphey was the strength and effectiveness of the traditional Chinese economy, above all its commercial structure, right through the nineteenth century and into the twentieth. The Chinese economy was highly productive and drew on centuries of experience in organization and management.

> It was not, as the foreigners perennially complained, the resistance of officials, the foot dragging of the gentry, the "backwardness" or xenophobia of the Chinese consumer, the inadequacy of railways, the continuation of the *likin* (internal transit tax), the transit pass system, or the lack of support from their home governments which aborted their dreams of trade profits. They were attempting to invade an economy and a set of producers and entrepreneurs who were able to beat them at their own game, especially on home grounds, enough so at least to remain in charge.[59]

The Outsiders starts out as an almost archetypical illustration of what Frances Moulder calls the "traditional society" approach. The uniformities of imperialism are accentuated and the different outcomes of the imperialist eras in India and China are explained above all in terms of internal contextual factors. As the book proceeds, however, the ground of Murphey's argument shifts noticeably. More and more emphasis is placed on the distinction between full colonialism, as experienced in India and much of the rest of Asia, and semi-colonialism, as experienced in China. The uniformities of imperialism begin to recede into the background and a more complex picture of the imperialist experience emerges. In itself, this is praiseworthy. Yet, unfortunately, the complexities are not worked out with sufficient analytical clarity, and in the end one is left with an uneasy sense of uncertainty—and confusion—regarding the comparative importance of internal and external causal agents.

This confusion is best illustrated in Murphey's handling of the issue of territorial sovereignty. Murphey does not really get to this issue until the second half of the book. When he does, however, we are told that it was "critically important," that indeed "for effective impact on any established Asian system, complete colonial control or territorial sovereignty was necessary."[60] I quite agree with Murphey on this point, and I am convinced, as I think he is, that we can begin to deal intelligently with the question of imperialism only after we have clearly recognized that China was a semicolony, not a colony. Where Murphey's analysis falters is not with respect to the *consequences* of China's retention of significant territorial sovereignty, but with respect to the *causes*.

There are at least two possibilities here (or some combination thereof): (1) that the Western powers wanted to establish full colonial control over all or part of China but were unable to because of internal factors; and (2) that the powers were not motivated or were unable to establish complete control, irrespective of the internal Chinese context. Murphey seems to acknowledge both of these possibilities when he states with what appears to be deliberate circularity: "China could resist a colonial takeover in part because its indigenous system was able to continue functioning effectively in its own way, and it was enabled to do so because China was never politically or militarily taken over by the West."[61] He also pays lip service at one point to the part played in the retention of Chinese sovereignty by such external circumstances as intra-Western rivalries and the dismaying prospect of full colonial responsibility for the Chinese empire.[62] The overwhelming thrust of Murphey's analysis, however, is to emphasize the first of the two above-stated possibilities. He assumes—as, indeed, he must, if the notion of a uniform grand colonial design is to have any meaning—that the foreigners wanted full colonial control over China. And he argues very explicitly that China's ability to prevent this from happening, where other Asian countries had failed, was due first and foremost to endogenous factors: "a single-minded determination to do so by any available means . . ., an adroit diplomacy, a deeply based confidence that sovereignty was worth preserving, plus the support of an ongoing system of production and organization which owed nothing to foreigners and was capable of continuing without them at an acceptable level of success."[63] (Conversely, Murphey argues that the impressive degree of transformation achieved by the Japanese in less than forty years in Manchuria was, in no small measure, due to the fact that Manchuria was thinly populated up to about 1900 and had none of the "built-in drags against change" that characterized China in general.)[64]

What is wrong with this analysis, chiefly, is its one-sidedness: its heavy emphasis on the distinctiveness of the Chinese setting and its failure, conversely, to delve seriously into the foreign end of things. If we accept the assumption that the foreigners *wanted* to convert China into a full colony, the factors on the Chinese side preventing such an outcome naturally assume paramount importance, and Murphey's analysis is hard to fault. But if we do not accept this assumption—if, indeed, the assumption turns out to be unsubstantiated and very possibly incorrect—then the elaborate edifice erected by Murphey collapses of its own weight. One does not, after all, explain a baseball team's victory in terms of its inherent strength when the other side has thrown the game.

When we look at the foreign side more closely, what do we in fact find? Is there solid evidence that the foreign powers at any point contemplated assumption of full colonial responsibility in China? To be sure, there were individual foreigners who would have welcomed such an outcome, and there was one country, Japan, that eventually did assume colonial control over portions of China. But no other foreign power (with the possible exception of Russia) seems to have been so motivated. There is ample evidence, certainly, that Great Britain was not, despite its leading position in Sino-Western trade. A close scrutiny of the motives of the Western powers would undoubtedly reveal that there were differences from power to power, as well as shifts over time. It might also show that the magnitude of the task, in terms of China's size and its strengths, did indeed play some role in discouraging the powers from seriously contemplating a colonial takeover. But the magnitude of the task was relative not only to the size and circumstances of China but also to the circumstances of the powers themselves (such as the coexistence of rival powers on the scene and, in the case of Great Britain specifically, the fact that it already had a major colony in India). That Murphey goes into none of these complexities with care constitutes a major weakness in his analysis.

Another problem with this analysis is its heavy reliance on the impact–response model of change. As long as Murphey sticks close to his main theme—the failure of the Chinese economy to "modernize" in response to the treaty port challenge—he is reasonably safe. The treaty ports and Sino-foreign trade clearly belong to what I characterized in chapter 1 as the outermost zone of Chinese history, where the impact–response approach is most applicable. Murphey's problems here have to do less with his conceptual framework than with his failure to identify clearly and accurately the *nature* of the Western impact, in particular of Western goals. Where the impact–response approach gets Murphey into real trouble, on the other hand, is in his portrayal of the Chinese revolution. Although characterizing the revolution as "indigenous" and emphasizing its roots in what he refers to as the "real China," he sees it, in the final analysis, as a response, however negative and negating, to the Western challenge, the "treaty port goad."[65] The Chinese revolution was this. But it was also much more. As long as we continue to portray it as a response to the West, our understanding of it will remain limited and severely distorted.

Although the studies of Hou, Myers, and Murphey may each be faulted in one way or another, their broad conclusion that the economic effects of imperialism were small and perhaps marginally favorable, rather than strongly negative, is widely supported by other scholars. Albert Feuerwerker has argued the point in many of his writings, most impressively perhaps in his work on rural handicraft industry. Feuerwerker acknowledges a sharp decline in the handspinning of cotton yarn in the last decades of the Ch'ing due to competition with machine-spun yarn (more than half of which was imported). More generally, he does not deny "either that significant structural changes in the handicraft industrial sector took place in these . . . decades or that the strain and dislocation occasioned by these developments adversely affected substantial parts of the population." He, nonetheless, maintains that the handicraft industry as a whole was not seriously undermined in the late Ch'ing and that even in the republican era total demand for handicrafts did not decline. "Anyone," Feuerwerker insists, "who would claim that the Hunan or Szechwan peasant in the 1930s dressed in Naigaiwata cottons, smoked BAT cigarettes, and used Meiji sugar has a big case to prove."[66]

On a more theoretical level, Thomas Rawski, an economist, points out that the relationship between handicraft industry and foreign manufactured imports ought not, in any case, to be viewed in isolation from events in the rest of the economy, in particular the agricultural sphere. "A rapid decline in handicraft output and employment, such as occurred in U.S. history," Rawski observes, "may reflect a prosperous farm sector, while rising craft activity can indicate agrarian distress"[67]—the latter, other economists have noted, being precisely what happened in China in the nineteenth century.[68] More broadly, Rawski argues that, on the basis of China's "vast space," its limited transport system, and other factors,

> without detailed evidence to the contrary, our safest course is to begin by assuming that the strategic factors in China's prewar economic evolution came from within, and that whether the net impact of international contacts was beneficial or harmful, the presence of privileged foreign communities, low tariffs, uncontrolled foreign investment, indemnity payments and other trappings of imperialism made only a marginal impact on China's prewar economy.[69]

Shannon Brown takes a basically similar position with respect to the nineteenth century. While acknowledging the expansion of Sino-foreign contacts after 1860, Brown maintains that the economic effects of these contacts were hindered by two kinds of impediments, economic and political. The former, which would have existed even if the Chinese government had adopted a policy supportive of laissez faire and free trade, included the size and structure of Chinese demand (the great majority of Chinese being too poor to buy Western goods and the minority of wealthy Chinese being, for the most part, too conservative in taste to want to buy them), the high cost of internal transportation, China's large population and geographical expanse, the inapplicability of much of Western technology, and the effective competition offered by Chinese businessmen. On the political side, Brown emphasizes, among other factors, the dampening effects of the Chinese fiscal system (which hindered domestic as well as foreign commerce), exclusion of foreigners from participation in certain trade areas (such as salt) because of the powerful resistance of vested native interests, official restriction of Western business to the treaty ports, and above all the attitude of the central government, which before 1900 did almost nothing to promote economic change and much to discourage it. Brown concludes that, whatever may be said of the intellectual, psychological, and political impact of the West in the nineteenth century, its economic impact, certainly for the 1860s (on which he concentrates), and probably until at least 1895, was "virtually insignificant."[70]

Parts of Brown's analysis echo themes earlier advanced by Robert Dernberger in his theoretically rigorous, tautly argued treatment of the problem, covering the entire period from 1840 to 1949. Dernberger's aim is to determine whether the economic activity of the foreigner during this century made a positive contribution, direct and/or indirect, to China's economic development. His conclusion is that it did, most significantly in terms of a gross transfer of productive capital and technology that, without a foreign sector, would not have been possible. At the same time, Dernberger argues, the direct foreign contribution was strictly limited by the narrow geographical constraints within which foreigners were compelled to operate and by a structure of foreign investment that restricted favorable backward and forward linkages between the foreign and domestic sectors of the economy. These limitations Dernberger attributes largely to the policy of a succession of Chinese governments that, on the one hand, deliberately sought to limit foreign contact with the domestic economy and, on the other hand, failed to provide a legal, financial, and economic environment supportive of the emerging Chinese modern sector. Though individual Chinese entrepreneurs "were able to escape the inhibiting limits of their tradition and reacted favorably to the forces of modernization, the government did not."[71] The one area where economic change was substantial was colonial Manchuria, where a non-Chinese government held sway and foreigners had free rein.

Although by no means insensitive to the costs in terms of human suffering and national humiliation, Dernberger appears to some extent to fit James Peck's category of China specialists who feel that, from the standpoint of economic development narrowly construed, China's problem in the nineteenth and twentieth centuries was not that it had too much imperialism but that it did not have enough. Even at the existing level of imperialist impact, on the other hand, Dernberger is persuaded that the Chinese government could have done more than it did, that it was hamstrung less by imperialism than by its own built-in traditional preferences and habits.

The trouble with this line of argument, in my view, is that it is too single-dimensional. As Murphey (explicitly) and Brown (implicitly) both emphasize, the Chinese government, at least in the nineteenth century, took many actions that, although counter to the spread of a Western capitalist model of economic change, can be interpreted as having been very much in China's vital interests in other respects. The same political obduracy, in other words, that Dernberger sees as a failing, Murphey, in particular, sees as a source of strength.

A related shortcoming of Dernberger's account, especially considering the long time span it covers, is its ahistorical, static nature. As just suggested, the motives, actions, and interests of the imperial government in the late Ch'ing cannot be assumed to have been identical with those of the Kuomintang government in the 1930s, even though the consequences for economic change of government action or inaction in the two cases may have been, in the very broadest sense, comparable.

A third problem with Dernberger's analysis is its stated assumption, following Elvin, that Chinese agriculture (and by extension the economy as a whole), by the end of the nineteenth century, was caught in a "high-level equilibrium trap" (meaning that increasing output to provide for an increasing population was no longer possible without significant changes in technology or available land) and that this trap could be broken only by an exogenous shock. If one accepts the idea of a trap and also (as Dernberger apparently does) the notion that the capitalist mode of economic change was on balance good, one would be hard put *not* to argue that the foreign contribution to China's economic development was positive (even if marginal). I have already expressed, in chapter 2, my general reservations with the trap concept. Others have questioned its applicability to China on specifically economic grounds.[72] The broader problem with Dernberger's analysis is that it is heavily parochial in its assumptions as to what constitutes a "positive" contribution to China's economic development and is built around a question (like that of Levenson discussed in chapter 2) that, by its very nature, narrowly constrains the range of possible answers. Where Dernberger is to be strongly commended is in his forthright acknowledgment that economists are still far from agreeing on the facts of China's economic situation in the century from 1840 to 1949 and that the high-level equilibrium trap represents his understanding of those facts.[73]

This last statement, in a sense, takes us to the very heart of the problem. Agreement on the facts, however, as every scholar knows, is a sticky business, involving, on the one hand, finding out what the facts are (the empirical part of the process) and, on the other hand, determining which ones are important and how they interrelate (the conceptual part). So far, in the debate among American scholars over the economic impact of imperialism, the side that minimizes this impact would appear to have the upper hand. It has not been able to bring the controversy to a conclusion, however, and the reasons why it has not point to problems concerning the nature and productiveness of the debate itself. I would like, in the concluding section of this chapter, to explore some of these problems.

THE PROBLEM WITH THE PROBLEM OF IMPERIALISM

Before doing so, however, it is well to reiterate that the focal point of controversy is the *economic* impact of foreign imperialism, not its impact in other areas. In the political realm, above all, there is a fairly broad consensus at this juncture on the importance, one way or another, of the imperialist presence. Numerous scholars have taken the position, developed in greatest depth by Rhoads Murphey, that imperialism, particularly in its treaty port incarnation, was a major stimulus to the flowering of Chinese nationalism.[74] Joseph Esherick, arguing that imperialism was an important cause of the Changsha riot of 1910, has stressed the close association in the popular mind between Western-inspired reform and Western imperialism, both of which were viewed by the Hunanese masses of the day as inimical to their interests. Mary Wright and Edward Rhoads show how fear of foreign intervention affected the calculations of Chinese revolutionaries in 1911, dissuading them from prolongation of the civil conflict and encouraging compromise with Yuan Shih-k'ai (1859–1916). And, for much the same reason, Edward Friedman and Ernest Young maintain, Yuan himself chose compromise over confrontation in his response to the Japanese-issued Twenty-One Demands of 1915.[75]

In most of these examples, the political impact of the foreign presence was indirect. It was the psychological and intellectual impact that was immediate. The foreign powers may or may not have been prepared in 1911 to intervene militarily to restore order to a Chinese polity verging on chaos. The treaty ports may or may not have been beachheads for the undermining of the Chinese economy. What was important was that numbers of Chinese believed these things to be so and responded accordingly.

The foreign impact on the position and power of the Chinese government, on the other hand, was often far more direct, and there is general agreement, on all sides of the imperialism controversy, that since this impact was to a greater or lesser extent subversive of China's national sovereignty, it hampered the government's ability to provide the leadership role everyone agrees was essential for healthy economic growth. This is, of course, the very essence of Frances Moulder's argument. Rhoads Murphey also, although in so many respects at odds with Moulder, observes that in a larger sense the chief effect of the foreign presence on the Chinese economy was "a weakening of the state, which contributed to the state's inability to provide the kind of leadership which played such a crucial role in Japan's economic success after 1870." Even Dernberger, although emphasizing the drag effect on Chinese governmental policy of traditional habits and practices, readily concedes that *some* of the factors that limited the capacity of the government to take positive economic action "were imposed by the West."[76]

Where, then, does this leave us? It suggests, I believe, that on both sides of the debate there is an important item of unfinished business. There appears to be general agreement that a proper political infrastructure is absolutely crucial if successful economic change is to occur, and everyone also seems to agree that foreign imperialism played some part in preventing such an infrastructure from coming into place. Beyond this, however, the consensus ends, and there is not likely to be a consensus, or anything even approaching one, until the negative effects of foreign encroachment on the Chinese government's capacity to supply effective leadership in the economic sphere at different points in time are carefully and systematically weighed against other factors—domestic political turmoil, the class interests of China's rulers, "traditional" values and behavior, and so on—that also hampered this capacity.

A second problem with the debate over the economic consequences of imperialism is that both sides seem to feel constrained to adopt the entire Chinese economy as the only—or at least the only truly significant—unit of analysis. This is partly due to the fact that the original framers of the problem, Marxist-Leninists in the early decades of this century, had an analytical orientation that happened to be national in scope. It is partly because Chinese nationalists themselves have focused on the nation as the natural object of their concern. And it is partly because economists in general seem to have a pronounced tendency to favor the national unit as the most appropriate unit of analysis.

Whether it is in fact the most appropriate unit in this instance is another matter. The averaging out of data for a large-scale unit may conceal extremely significant variation within that unit. Two societies, to take a purely imaginary example, might have the same average age but very different internal age structures in terms of sexual and geographic distribution. For most analytic purposes, it is the internal variation, rather than the society-wide average, that would be of interest to a demographer. Similarly, in the case of the economic impact of imperialism, the vast scale of the Chinese economy virtually assures that certain basic phases of foreign economic activity, such as trade and investment, will appear to be of negligible consequence in terms of the economy as a whole. But if China were subdivided into regions and very specific questions asked regarding the impact of exogenous factors on each region and, within a given region, on core and peripheral areas, as regional systems theory proposes, one might come up with a far more complex—and more textured—picture than either side in the imperialism controversy now provides. The effects of shifting world market conditions on the tea growers of nineteenth-century Fukien or the antimony producers of post–World War I Hunan would assume greater importance. The peasant households from cotton-spinning areas whose precarious livelihoods were "profoundly shaken by the decline in handicraft spinning" would not somehow get lost in the shuffle.[77] The flea, defined in terms other than its size relative to the elephant, would appear less small.

A third problem with the imperialism debate—really a cluster of problems—centers on the concept of imperialism itself. One basic difficulty with this concept is that most standard definitions of it, for the period up through World War II, refer to a situation in which one society establishes full colonial control over another. Application of the concept to the Chinese case is therefore confusing. Questions get asked, based on expectations derived from "normal" imperialism, that are not quite relevant, while other questions that really are relevant never get asked at all. Murphey's book stands as an important exception to this pattern in that it compares China with an example of full colonial domination and underscores the difference that China's retention of territorial sovereignty made.[78] Murphey does not, however, go nearly far enough in my view. The phenomenon of semicolonialism is addressed—up to a point. But two other peculiarities of the colonial experience in China, its multiple and its "layered" or "spliced" character, are barely touched on.

By "multiple colonialism" I refer, of course, to the circumstance that China in the nineteenth and twentieth centuries was faced with encroachment and partial domination not by one but by a plurality of foreign nations. This may have redounded to China's advantage, to the extent that competition and rivalry among several powers served as a brake on the capacity or will of any one power to establish full colonial authority and also enabled the Chinese government, in certain situations, to play one country off against another (as it sought to do in Manchuria in the final years of the Ch'ing). On the other hand, it has also been argued, by none other than the father of the Chinese revolution, Sun Yat-sen, that there were distinct disadvantages to such an arrangement. Because colonial domination was parceled out among several powers, no one power manifested the sort of responsible concern for the welfare of its charge that was sometimes encountered in single-ruler colonies such as India. The Chinese people therefore suffered not less, but more, than other colonial populations, reaping all of the disadvantages of colonialism and none of its benefits.[79]

The third peculiarity of the colonial framework in China was that the partial colonialism of the Western powers (and later Japan) was until 1912 spliced onto the full colonialism of the Manchus, creating a curiously layered pattern of colonial authority. We do not customarily think of Ch'ing China as a Manchu colony, and in certain respects—above all, the subordination of Manchu to Chinese culture and the absence of metropolitan exploitation of the satellite's economy—it was significantly different from most Western colonies. In other respects, however, it bore a decided resemblance to the Western colonial pattern. The Ch'ing was established by military conquest. Even more important, its successful rule over Chinese society was heavily dependent upon native collaboration, in return for which, as in India and other more "typical" colonial situations, the collaborators were given substantial political power.

These three features of the colonial experience in China—its partial, multiple, and layered character—add up to a highly idiosyncratic pattern, a pattern that both sides in the imperialism debate have been remiss in describing and analyzing closely. That this is so is not surprising. For, as already suggested, the debate has been cast in terms of questions derived from classical theories of imperialism, and these theories were originally advanced to explain situations that differed markedly from the Chinese case. All the same, the failure to scrutinize with care the distinctive colonial environment that prevailed in China has been a major limitation on the productiveness of the entire imperialism controversy—almost as great a limitation as the failure of the proponents of the "negative effect" position to take China's internal sociocultural setting with any degree of seriousness.

A further difficulty with the imperialism concept is its vagueness and imprecision. This does not hamper it in the least as an idea against which people can react emotionally.

But it makes it of questionable value for serious analytic purposes, unless it can be broken down and its component parts carefully defined. This is difficult to do, but not impossible. Sherman Cochran, in his superbly crafted study of Sino-foreign rivalry in the cigarette industry, employs five distinct definitions of imperialist exploitation in his assessment of the performance of the British-American Tobacco Company in China. For each definition he carefully appraises BAT's record and determines whether and, if so, to what extent the company can be characterized as imperialist.[80] Pursuing such a strategy, Cochran ends up not with a simple label but with a complex balance sheet. The more general significance of his study is that it shows how one can make an important contribution to the imperialism debate without becoming yet another polarized participant in it.

A final difficulty with the imperialism concept is that, apart from its looseness, it is also, even more than "modernization," highly charged politically. This is clearest in the arguments of Peck and Moulder, which seem at times propelled more by the need to indict America or the West than by the commitment to understand China. But it is by no means absent from the more empirically grounded analyses developed on the other side. Everyone who argues that imperialism's effects on the Chinese economy were negligible knows that, in so doing, he or she is taking a position that the entire community of historians in China, at least in its public stance, finds anathema. Some may revel in this knowledge secretly; others may experience sadness or even guilt. But no one can remain politically unencumbered.

The encumbrance, moreover, is not just political; it is also cultural. And, in its cultural dimension as well, it is present on both sides. For in a number of important respects the assumptions that guide Peck, Moulder, and other espousers of the imperialism approach are scarcely different from those that inform the work of their adversaries, most of whom have been influenced by modernization theory. The overriding concern, on both sides, is economic development. Economic development is seen by both as a good. Moreover, on both sides it is assumed that without the impact of the industrialized West—the all-important exogenous shock—China would not have been able to industrialize on its own. This assumption is explicitly stated by Levenson, Elvin, and Dernberger. It is implicit in the writings of Moulder, Peck, Fairbank, Murphey, and others. Where the two sides in the controversy differ sharply is on the issue of why China *failed* to develop or modernize—a profoundly Western-centric question in itself—not on the desirability of such development or modernization.

When all of these problems concerning the concept and the consequences of imperialism are taken into account, it may well be questioned whether the term has not outlived its scholarly usefulness. Be this as it may, since there is no sign that it is about to go away, the immediate practical problem is to reformulate the agenda of issues concerning imperialism that need resolution. Clearly, the question posed in the title of this chapter has heuristic value only. We can't say whether imperialism was reality or myth until we have some reasonably clear notion in our minds as to what it was. My own view, as argued in the preceding pages, is that imperialism, seen in metahistorical terms as the master key to an entire century of Chinese history, was indeed a myth. Seen as one force among several, operating in a wide range of concrete historical situations, on the other hand, imperialism was, I believe, not only real but of critical explanatory importance. The challenge for historians is to define with precision—much greater precision than has generally been exercised in the past—the specific situations with regard to which imperialism was relevant and then to show *how* it was relevant. When this challenge has been met, we should end up with an understanding of the impact of imperialism on nineteenth- and twentieth-century China that is more complicated—and far more historically interesting—than anything presently available.

CHAPTER FOUR

Toward a China-Centered History of China

ONE OF the first principles of equity, learned by everyone in earliest childhood, is that if there is one piece of cake that two people must share, the person who does the cutting should not do the choosing. This principle rests on the assumption that people are self-interested and that, if the cutter is also the chooser, he or she will not be so careful about—indeed, may deliberately avoid—cutting pieces of equal size.

In his novel, *A Bend in the River,* V. S. Naipaul describes the colonial experience in the following terms:

> The Europeans wanted gold and slaves, like everybody else; but at the same time they wanted statues put up to themselves as people who had done good things for the slaves. Being an intelligent and energetic people, and at the peak of their powers, they could express both sides of their civilization; and they got both the slaves and the statues.[1]

What both of these cases have in common is a recognition that, where power is unevenly distributed, where cutter can also be chooser, a degree of imbalance or inequity is likely to result. Someone is going to get more. This is also the point

Edward W. Said makes, on an epistomological level, in his recent critique of the assumptions underlying Western study of Middle Eastern history and culture. There is no simple one-to-one correspondence, Said tells us, between knowledge and truth, between reality and the ways in which reality is represented. For "all representations, because they *are* representations, are embedded first in the language and then in the culture, institutions, and political ambience of the representer."[2] All representations of reality must, in short, also be misrepresentations, a form of intellectual dominion exercised by the knower over the known.

The particular example of intellectual dominion with which Said is concerned is the field of Orientalism, a body of knowledge created in the West by people who style themselves Orientalists and focused on an object invented by Westerners that they call the Orient. One need hardly agree with all of Said's strictures about Orientalism to accept the more general insight that all intellectual inquiry, all knowing, partakes of a kind of "imperialism" and that the dangers of misrepresentation are greatest, the imperialism especially virulent, when the inquirer—or more precisely the cultural, social, or political world of which he or she is a member—has also had some part, historically, in shaping the object of inquiry. The inquirer, in this situation, chooses as well as cuts. He gets both the slaves and the statues—and even exercises some superintendence over the latter's design.

THE INTELLECTUAL IMPERIALISM OF AMERICAN HISTORIANS

It is the argument of the present book that a dualism of much this sort has marked American involvement with Chinese history in the nineteenth and twentieth centuries. As actors on the Chinese stage, Americans took direct part, along with other Westerners, in the making of Chinese history. But we have also taken a leading part, as historians, in the creation of conceptual paradigms for understanding it. American power vis-à-vis China has thus been expressed on two levels—first, on a physical or material level, and second, on a level of intellectual superintendence or comprehension. The second sort of power would exist under any circumstances, as a natural consequence of the process by which all historians inject something of themselves into the historical reality they seek to represent. It is rendered all the more potent, however, by the added existence of the first sort of power.

Viewed from this perspective, it is no surprise to discover that all three of the paradigms examined in this book share a high degree of Western-centeredness—a Western-centeredness that robs China of its autonomy and makes of it, in the end, an intellectual possession of the West. Each paradigm accomplishes this in a different way. The impact–response paradigm portrays Chinese reality primarily in terms of the responses of Chinese (positive or negative) to the Western challenge. In so doing, it offers a more interior view of Chinese history than was supplied by the "bluebook" reconstructions of an earlier generation of American historians. But it is an interior perspective that is sharply skewed in the direction of the Western impact. As a consequence, it sometimes misreads Chinese thought and action as responses to the West when they really are not and sometimes overlooks important developments altogether because they are not related, or are only tangentially related, to the Western presence. In the upshot, certain aspects of Chinese history are distorted, while other aspects are simply omitted from view and, in the process, trivialized.

The modernization or tradition–modernity paradigm is essentially an amplification of the impact–response paradigm. It contributes to the latter a much more sophisticated theoretical scaffolding. But it is suffused with the same basic assumptions about China and the West. Where the impact–response model depicts China as passive and the West as active, the modernization approach, particularly in its 1950s and 1960s guise, portrays China as a "traditional" society, stuck in time, capable of being stirred from its eternal repose only by the life-giving force of a dynamic and "modern" West. The West thus plays Beauty to China's Beast, transforming by its kiss the torpor of centuries, releasing with its magical power the potential for "development" that must otherwise remain forever locked up. The implications of this paradigm for a reasonably balanced appreciation of recent Chinese history are of course devastating. Apart from the West's being cast uncritically and self-servingly in the role of savior, significant historical change is defined parochially as that process or combination of processes which the West itself passed through on the way to modernity. China is thus presented with a no-win situation. The possibility of modernizing change taking place without the West becomes unthinkable; equally unthinkable is the possibility that change other than modernizing change can be historically important.

Advocates of the imperialism paradigm as the best means of explaining nineteenth- and twentieth-century Chinese history—and I refer here not to scholars who merely take imperialism more or less seriously but to those scholars, such as Frances Moulder and James Peck, who judge it to be *the* key variable—regard themselves as being in the opposite camp from those who espouse the impact–response and modernization paradigms. And in some respects they are. In other respects, however, they share important ground with their putative adversaries. Like both of the other two approaches, the imperialism approach portrays modernization qua industrialization as a positive good. Like them, moreover, it sees Chinese society as being without the historical preconditions needed to produce an industrial revolution on its own and therefore dependent, directly or indirectly, on the intrusion of the West to supply these preconditions. True, the proponents of the imperialism paradigm also believe that such economic modernization must be accompanied by a genuine social revolution—a crucial assumption not shared, or at best half-heartedly or belatedly shared, by upholders of the other two approaches. All three, however, either implicitly (the impact–response and modernization paradigms) or explicitly (the imperialism paradigm), insist that the only important change China is capable of experiencing in the nineteenth and twentieth centuries is change that is a consequence of or response to the Western impact. A truly interior, China-centered view of recent Chinese history thus becomes impossible.

If the major American approaches to post-1800 Chinese history err both in misrepresenting the role of the West and in misreading the realities of China (the two forms of error being historically, if not logically, linked), where does this leave us? Is it possible for Americans to approach the history of this period without ethnocentric distortion or prejudgment of any sort and to acquire an understanding that is fully in keeping with Chinese realities? Or is this only an idle dream? So stated, it is indeed an idle dream. Historians are incapable of writing history that is totally free of distortion and prejudgment, and it would be pure mischievousness to suggest that American historians of China can somehow be different. There is, however, a question of degree. It is not naive to believe that the cruder, more crippling forms of ethnocentrism can be overcome and that we can inform our understanding of recent Chinese history with a more interior, less Western-centered perspective, one that, at the very least, locates the starting point of this history in China rather than in the West.

CENTERING CHINESE HISTORY IN CHINA

In fact, as already noted in chapter 2, a more interior approach to late imperial and postimperial China has been steadily gaining ground in the United States since about 1970 (if not earlier). As yet, however, no one has really taken the trouble to describe this approach—to articulate its salient characteristics, show how it differs from earlier approaches, and spell out its consequences for our understanding of Chinese history.[3] It is to such a description that I should like to devote this final chapter, asking the reader to bear in mind that what we are dealing with is really much more a set of tendencies than a single, well-defined approach (though I shall continue to refer to it as an approach for the sake of convenience) and that *my* understanding of these tendencies and of their import may differ in some respects from that of other scholars.

The main identifying feature of the new approach is that it begins with Chinese problems set in a Chinese context. These problems may be influenced, even generated, by the West. Or they may have no Western connection at all. But either way they are *Chinese* problems, in the double sense that they are experienced in China by Chinese and that the measure of their historical importance is a Chinese, rather than a Western, measure.[4] The conventional paradigms of the past, all of which begin history in the West and incorporate a Western measure of significance, are thus explicitly or implicitly repudiated. The narrative of the most recent centuries of Chinese history is not commenced in Europe with Prince Henry the Navigator and the first stirrings of Western expansionism; it begins in China. As more and more scholars search for a Chinese story line, moreover, they find, magically, that there really is one, and that this story line, far from grinding to a halt in 1800 or 1840 and being preempted or displaced by the West, continues to be of central, paramount importance right through the nineteenth century and on into the twentieth.

This restructuring of our picture of recent Chinese history can be seen in a number of areas. For example, reformism in nineteenth-century China is now viewed by many scholars as an outgrowth of indigenous reformist traditions. Few would argue that the West was unimportant or that it did not in time have a significant shaping effect on Chinese reform thought and activity. But there has been a strong reaction against the customary representation of reform as Western-oriented and Western-inspired and an equally strong sense of the need to redefine the entire phenomenon of reform in Chinese perspective.[5]

When the early nineteenth century is not "viewed backwards, over the historical shoulder of the events of the 1840s and 1850s—the Opium Wars, the Taiping Rebellion," but is instead "understood from a perspective that looks ahead, out of the context of developments of the late eighteenth century," as urged by Susan Mann Jones and Philip Kuhn, a picture emerges of reform-minded Chinese responding to a wide range of political and social problems, partly associated with dynastic decline (which is seen by many as beginning around 1775–1780) and partly resulting from unprecedented changes of a secular sort, such as the increasing commercialization of Chinese society.[6] Initially, the problems scrutinized—for example, the effects of population growth, as discussed by Hung Liang-chi (1746–1809) in 1793—are entirely domestic in nature. But even as, very gradually, the issue of maritime defense against the Western threat begins to intrude on the Chinese mental landscape, the intrusion remains sharply circumscribed. Kung Tzu-chen (1792–1841), writing in the early decades of the nineteenth century, is aware of a foreign menace and comments upon it, but his overarching preoccupation is with the moral deterioration of Chinese political and social life. The problem of the West is more central for Kung's friend, Wei Yuan (1794–1856). But Wei establishes his reformist credentials in an indigenous context first, long before encountering the West, and although he comes to regard the commercial and military presence of the foreigners on the coast as an unprecedented situation in Chinese history, his reactions to this presence form part of a broader contemporary reassessment of the bearing of maritime Asia on the security of China's coastal frontier. The principal aim of Wei's influential treatise on the maritime countries (*Hai-kuo t'u-chih,* 1844), as recently reinterpreted by Jane Kate Leonard, is not to introduce new information about the geography and conditions of the West but to describe Western expansion into maritime Asia—a Chinese concern of long standing—and to probe the dynamics of this expansion.[7]

Examples can also be cited from the latter half of the nineteenth century. Wang T'ao, the quintessential Western expert and proponent of Western-oriented reform in the 1870s and 1880s, cut his teeth as a social and political critic and reform advocate in the early 1860s in response not to the West but to the Taiping uprising. Wo-jen (d. 1871), well known to students of "China's response to the West" as the archconservative who opposed the establishment of a school for the teaching of Western subjects in the 1860s (the T'ung-wen-kuan), was better known to his Chinese contemporaries as an educational reformer who wanted the local academies revitalized in order to achieve political renovation.[8] The first organized efforts to reform the status of women, at the turn of the century, although commonly portrayed as a simple emulation of the Western example, were preceded, Paul S. Ropp tells us, "by over two centuries of progressively more articulate criticism of the oppression of women . . . by both orthodox Confucian scholars and unorthodox writers of poetry and fiction."[9] Even Liang Ch'i-ch'ao, for all his importance in the late Ch'ing as a popularizer of Western ideas, operated out of an intellectual tradition, dominated by statecraft and New Text thinking, that had been gathering force in China since well before the Opium War.

It is thus no accident that Hao Chang, in his study of Liang, takes as his point of departure not the foreign challenge but the native intellectual setting and portrays Liang as responding not just to the West but also to a vast and complex Chinese intellectual world with its own inner variety and competing currents of thought.[10] American scholars have only recently begun to penetrate this intellectual world. But as the foregoing examples all in one way or another suggest, our understanding of Chinese reformism in the nineteenth century has been transformed in the process.

Another dimension of this altered picture of reform has been supplied by John Schrecker and James Polachek, both of whom interpret the reform movement of the 1890s as a consequence, at least in part, of political and social problems encountered among China's educated elite. Schrecker argues that there was an important internal bond between the *ch'ing-i* movement that began in the 1870s and the reform movement of 1898, that indeed the two movements "formed an unbroken opposition movement within the government and elite" during the last two decades of the nineteenth century. This is radically different from the conventional picture, which, as we saw in chapter 1, portrays the *ch'ing-i* as a conservative, xenophobic force and the 1898 reformers as a "progressive" faction, open to strong Western influences. Revising this conventional picture, Schrecker finds that, when the two groups are viewed in political rather than intellectual terms, there are striking parallels between them. Both were dominated by young, highly educated, political outsiders who stressed the importance of morality in government and were bitterly critical of the dynastic policy of appeasement. Frustrated over their lack of access to power, both groups denounced the sale of office and called for the opening up of channels of communication to the throne (*yen-lu*) and for disregarding the rules of seniority in the promotion of capable men. Finally, Schrecker notes, there was a very considerable overlapping between the two groups in personnel terms, symbolized most dramatically in the figure of K'ang Yu-wei, who behaved in characteristically *ch'ing-i* fashion and had close ties with members of the *ch'ing-i* movement but who was also the most prominent of the 1898 reformers.

Schrecker locates the source of the steady rise in political opposition after 1870 in the social history of the period. Because large numbers of younger men had advanced quickly during the Taiping Rebellion and the T'ung-chih Restoration, they were still in power in the 1870s and 1880s, and so blocked the promotion of lower-level bureaucrats. Moreover, the chances of gaining even low office via the regular (or examination) route had diminished sharply because the increase in examination quotas in the post-Taiping era had enlarged the pool of those seeking jobs, while the great rise in the sale of office had reduced the number of positions available.[11]

While Schrecker sees the frustration resulting from this situation as fueling political opposition, Polachek finds in the same frustration a possible source of the intellectual radicalism of reformers like K'ang Yu-wei and T'an Ssu-t'ung (1865–1898). The content of this radicalism does not interest Polachek particularly. What intrigues him is the sense of social stress it conveys. The pseudoscientific metaphysical soundings, the wild attacks on the family system and its ethics, the wholesale reinterpretation of the classics—all suggest a fairly high level of discontent both with the standard curriculum and with the social infrastructure of elite education. In research that is still in the preliminary stages, Polachek hypothesizes that there was a direct relationship between the elite alienation reflected in this new intellectual orientation and the late-century decline of family and community assets that had been built up in the course of the struggle against the Taiping and other insurgencies of the 1850s and 1860s. This decline in assets engendered a career crisis for lower and middle gentry in certain areas of Kwangtung and Hunan—Polachek's own research is centered on Nan-hai hsien, Kwangtung, the home county of K'ang Yu-wei—and encouraged them to carve out new career opportunities. The quest for new careers, in turn, led many of them to become leaders of the reform movement in their respective provinces.[12]

The very different picture of nineteenth-century reformism that results when it is approached from within—either in terms of China's indigenous intellectual setting or in terms of the festering political and social problems to which reform was in part a response—has a parallel in the new understanding of the 1911 revolution that has emerged since the late 1960s. Initially, American scholarship on 1911 was concentrated almost entirely upon Sun Yat-sen and the revolutionary organization he headed, the T'ung-meng-hui.[13] Hawaii-educated and American-influenced, Sun was a familiar figure. By placing him at the center of the 1911 revolution and relating its development largely in terms of his career, we effectively domesticated the revolution, making it into an event Americans could comprehend and be comfortable with.

Then, in 1961, Chün-tu Hsüeh published a book on one of Sun's fellow revolutionists, Huang Hsing (1874–1916), which suggested that Sun was not the only leader of 1911, that there were other leaders who were of comparable importance.[14] These other leaders had not been given their due, however, in part because of the natural pro-Sun bias of American historians and in part because of the influence on American scholarship of Kuomintang historiography, which was also (although for very different reasons) strongly Sun-centered.

A third—and more decisive—stage in the evolution of American understanding of 1911 came with the appearance in 1968 of a volume of essays edited by Mary Wright.[15] Wright herself, in an important introductory chapter, argued that one of the distinctive characteristics of the 1911 revolution was its *lack* of strong, effective leadership. Most of the other essays reflected this point in one way or another, laying less stress on the leadership of the revolution and more on the social, political, economic, and intellectual context out of which the revolution was spawned. With this shift in the focus of American scholarship from revolutionaries to the revolution,[16] a far more internal, more China-centered perspective on 1911 began to take shape.

One particularly interesting byproduct of this new perspective has been the debate over the relationship of the gentry class to the revolution. Wright argued forcefully that the gentry were a progressive force in 1911, new men in a new world, determined to create a strengthened China through constitutional reform. Chūzō Ichiko, a Japanese contributor to the Wright volume, voiced the contrary view that the gentry were a conservative element, interested in Westernization and reform, if at all, only insofar as they contributed to their preservation as a class. Joseph Esherick, in a stimulating analysis of the revolution in Hunan and Hupei that goes beyond either Ichiko or Wright (though tilting toward the former), portrays the gentry class in more stratified terms, breaking it down into a rural segment that was conservative and opposed to reform and an urban component that was progressive and favored reform. The latter supported the revolution. Its support, however, was "contingent upon its own acquisition of political power." Moreover, once the revolution had taken place, the urban reformist elite's greatest preoccupation was with stability. The revolution, therefore, like the reforms that helped bring it about, was "both politically progressive and socially regressive."[17]

The relationship of the gentry to the revolution can also be seen in the context of a broader historical process that had its inception long before 1911. At the time of the Ming–Ch'ing transition the class character of the gentry had still been defined principally in terms of landholding. However, as the size of the gentry swelled (mainly as a consequence of population expansion) and certain regions of China became heavily commercialized, new sources of income began to replace landed wealth as the chief economic basis of gentry status. These new sources of income consisted in a range of quasi-official, managerial roles that the gentry came increasingly to play at the local level from the seventeenth century on: mediation of legal disputes, supervision of local schools and academies, proxy remittance of peasant taxes to yamen clerks, management of municipal services, the recruiting and training of militia, and so on.[18] This shift in the economic basis of gentry status reached a high point during and after the insurrections of the mid-nineteenth century, when gentry managers were called on to assume a wide assortment of new military and civil functions, enabling them to become more entrenched than ever in local government. In the waning years of the dynasty the situation became even more complex, as increasing numbers of gentry—Bastid-Bruguière calls them "business gentry" (*shen-shang*)[19]—entered trade or invested in new forms of enterprise at the local level. The reliance of the gentry on administrative-managerial roles or business, or both, for their economic survival, became so great that when the central government, as part of its post-Boxer reform program, tried in the first decade of the twentieth century to increase dramatically the scope of its own administrative and economic activity, the gentry—and many merchants as well—felt their lifeline threatened.

The 1911 revolution looks very different when viewed in this light. The role of Sun Yat-sen and his fellow revolutionaries, so much emphasized by earlier historians, recedes into the shadows. Indeed, the revolution seems less a revolt of Western-influenced radicals against a conservative Manchu political establishment than a product of conflict and tension between a *reforming* Manchu dynasty and local elites, in some respects quite *conservative,* who saw the dynasty's reform program, with its strong centralizing tendencies, as a menace to their own economic and political well-being.

Certainly there were important Western influences at work. In fact, one of the surface issues that triggered the revolution was the conflict between the central government and the provinces over who was to assume responsibility for building China's railroads. The real issue, however, was not railroads but the dynasty's challenge to a whole complex of prerogatives—financial, commercial, political, managerial—that local elites had increasingly come to regard as theirs. The revolution, from this perspective, emerges not as a triumph (however qualified) of the forces of "modernity" over the forces of "tradition" but as the culmination of a long-drawn-out contest for power within Chinese society.

Clearly, this is only one of many ways in which the revolution of 1911 may be viewed. But even in the schematic and oversimplified form presented here, it suggests a rather different picture of the twilight years of the imperial era than that articulated by past generations of American historians. The West is still significantly involved in this picture. But its involvement is understood in very much more complicated terms, as we begin to see it interacting not with an inert, passive China but with a China that has long been undergoing important changes on its own, a China riven with tensions and conflicts of the most basic sort, a China that, seen in its own frame of reference, is not at all bizarre and exotic but is peopled by real human beings, preoccupied, as in any society, with the messy business of surviving in a harsh, unforgiving, and often incomprehensible world.

A second identifying feature of the China-centered approach is that it attempts to cope with this incomprehensibility by breaking the Chinese world down into smaller, more manageable spatial units. In this sense it is not *China*-centered at all, but region-centered or province-centered or locality-centered. The key assumption on which this strategy rests is that, because China encompasses a wide range of regional and local variation, the content and extent of this variation must be delineated if we are to gain a more differentiated, more contoured understanding of the whole—an understanding of the whole that does more than blandly reflect the least common denominator among its several parts.

This strategy of spatial differentiation may be pursued on various levels of specificity and in accordance with an array of different variables, depending upon the nature of the problem under consideration. In my study of late Ch'ing reformers, I found it useful for classification purposes to divide China into two broad cultural zones, which I loosely characterized as littoral (or coastal) and hinterland (or interior).[20] I was particularly interested in the former, because the reformers I was studying had all lived and worked in the littoral zone and had been profoundly shaped by the experience.

The basic underlying contrast between the littoral and hinterland cultures went back, of course, many centuries. However, it reached a new stage in the early sixteenth century, as inhabitants of China's southeastern littoral became more and more deeply involved in a new maritime civilization of global embrace. With the establishment, after the Opium War, of Hong Kong as a British colony and Shanghai, Canton, Ningpo, Foochow, and Amoy as treaty ports, the differences between littoral and hinterland widened still further and the culture of the rapidly growing emporia on the coast acquired an increasingly distinctive stamp that persisted until at least the middle of the twentieth century.

The distinctiveness of the littoral culture lay not only in the contrast to the culture of the Chinese heartland but also in the very considerable resemblances that emerged among the various components of the littoral culture itself. This was manifested in physical terms in the heavy flow of goods and people back and forth among the coastal ports. More important than the matter of movement per se, however, was the degree to which these cities formed interchangeable parts of a homogeneous, self-contained environment. In the final analysis, it was the common cultural, institutional, and economic character of the littoral that made movement within it natural.

Some of the characteristics that gave the culture of the littoral internal consistency and at the same time differentiated it from the rest of China may be briefly enumerated. First, the littoral was physically and culturally under direct (though highly selective) Western influence. (This should be immediately qualified by noting (1) that, in strictly numerical terms, the populations of all littoral cities were overwhelmingly Chinese, and (2) that, by the end of the nineteenth century, nonlittoral cities, in particular treaty ports along the Yangtze and its main tributaries, had also come under significant Western cultural influence, though never on the scale of the larger coastal cities.) Second, the economy of the littoral was geared to commerce, including inter–treaty-port (intralittoral) commerce, littoral–hinterland commerce, and commerce between the littoral and the non-Chinese world. Third, although there were small numbers of Chinese and foreign officials and large numbers of Chinese industrial and nonindustrial working people living in the port cities, littoral society was strongly colored by the bourgeois values of its Chinese and Western merchant elites. Fourth, the littoral was administratively and legally mixed, with elements of Western sovereignty and practice alongside elements of Chinese sovereignty and practice. Fifth, the orientation of the littoral, in sharp contrast to the hinterland, was global and outward-looking, focused as much on the world as on China.

The littoral–hinterland distinction is useful for addressing historical problems in which the role of external (especially Western) influence is of paramount importance. It can be seriously misleading, however, if, as a result of its heavy emphasis upon the cleavage between the foreign-influenced part of China and the non-foreign-influenced part, it is understood to imply a homogeneous, undifferentiated hinterland culture.

One of the great merits of G. William Skinner's regional systems approach, from this perspective, is that it draws attention to critical variation *within* the vast Chinese "hinterland."

Skinner introduces the regional approach in conjunction with an effort to determine the extent of urbanization in nineteenth-century China.[21] Early in his research on Chinese cities, he observed that in late imperial times they formed not a single integrated national system but several regional systems, each only tenuously linked to its neighbors. He further discovered that these regional urban systems coincided very closely with physiographic units, defined in terms of drainage basins. All told there were nine such units—Skinner calls them macroregions—in nineteenth-century China: Manchuria (which is excluded from the author's analysis because of its negligible urbanization prior to the twentieth century), North China, Northwest China, Upper Yangtze, Middle Yangtze, Lower Yangtze, Southeast Coast, Lingnan, and Yun-Kwei.

The two main variables in Skinner's analysis are *geography,* taken in the broadest sense to include physical features, resource endowment, and distance, and *technology,* particularly transport technology. Where transport technology was unmechanized, as was the case in China prior to the introduction of the steamship in the nineteenth century, the high costs of moving people and goods long distances—the cost of transporting grain 200 miles on the back of a pack animal, for example, was as high as the cost of producing the grain in the first place—served as an effective limit on the overall dimensions of regional systems and also as a depressant on virtually all forms of interregional intercourse. In this situation, physiographic barriers to movement (such as high mountains), by raising transport costs, formed natural regional boundaries, while physiographic facilitators of movement (such as navigable waterways), by lowering transport costs, formed natural core areas within regions. Population and resources tended to concentrate in these core areas and to thin out progressively as one moved away from the core to the peripheries of a region.

Major cities, of course, were located in regional core areas or along major transport routes leading to them.

Skinner's approach has very substantial strengths. Not the least of these is that it supplies us with a new conceptual vocabulary that enables us to look at old problems in new ways and to see connectedness where previously we had been blind to it. More specifically, regional systems analysis is spatially dynamic, in the sense that it deals with cities not as discrete, isolated units but in terms of their interactions with their hinterlands and with other cities of higher and lower orders of magnitude within their respective regions. It is also temporally dynamic in that it sees all regional systems as going through cycles of development and retardation, to some extent coincident with the cyclical flourishing and decline of dynasties, but to some extent following their own distinctive rhythms. The greatest strength of Skinner's approach, in my view, is that it highlights spatial and temporal variation, both *among* regions and also between core and peripheral areas *within* regions. Different regions are differently endowed, in terms of their internal geographic features and natural resources. They are also differentially affected by discrete natural and historical occurrences. Skinner reminds us that the major catastrophes—droughts, floods, rebellions—that have punctuated Chinese history have nearly always been regional, not national, in scope. (Disastrous droughts affected Northwest and North China more severely than other regions. The primary impact of the Taipings, on the other hand, was felt in the Lower Yangtze region and the Kan basin in the Middle Yangtze region.) Also, imperial decisions typically affected the development cycles not of the entire empire but of specific regions. (The monopoly of overseas trade granted Canton in 1757 accelerated development in the Lingnan region but depressed the economy of the Southeast Coast for nearly a century.)

The impact of Skinner's analysis on American students of Chinese history has already—and deservedly—been far-reaching. The approach is, however, not without its potential shortcomings. One of these, which Skinner himself has pointed out, is that systems analysis is best at describing regularities—the functional interactions of the component parts of a system—and worst at capturing causal relations.[22] This is especially marked—at least for a historian—in the temporal sphere, where cyclical change tends to be emphasized at the expense of secular change, and one is left with the impression (unfortunate in my judgment) that cycles were the characteristic form of change in late imperial China, secular change becoming important only in the twentieth century with the introduction of mechanized technology.[23] A second potential shortcoming of Skinner's approach is its pronounced substructural bias, its almost exclusive emphasis upon geographical and economic determinants. Where the problems being addressed center on economic development and retardation, urban growth and decline, and demographic expansion and contraction, this geoeconomic determinism may be quite appropriate. There are times, however, when Skinner appears to make more broadly inclusive explanatory claims for systems analysis, extending it to embrace political and perhaps even intellectual and cultural transactions, as well as social and economic ones. Here, it seems to me, the ice becomes thinner and one skates with increasing peril—just how much peril, time and further empirical testing alone will tell.

One of the points repeatedly made by Skinner is that, in doing research on a problem, scholars should identify the appropriate human interaction system for that problem. If, for example, the problem is an economic one, we ought not to take a political-administrative unit such as a province or a county as our relevant spatial system. While few would question the wisdom of this counsel in theory, most historians, for reasons of both habit and convenience, find it hard to resist dividing China up into provinces and counties. The Chinese subjects we study tend to think in such terms, and the materials we work with (such as gazetteers) are often organized in accordance with administrative subdivisions. Appropriately or inappropriately, province-level studies in particular have mushroomed in recent years.

These studies have dealt with themes as diverse as social disorder in mid-nineteenth-century Kwangtung, German imperialism in Shantung during the last years of the Ch'ing, and rural revolution in Hunan in the period from 1911 to 1927.[24] The greatest clustering of provincial studies, however, has been around the 1911 revolution and the ensuing warlord period. While some studies, such as Donald Sutton's of militarism in Yunnan, span both the pre- and post-1911 periods,[25] most have concentrated on the one or the other. For 1911 and the years immediately preceding it, there are published accounts focusing on Kwangtung, Hunan and Hupei, and Chekiang, as well as several unpublished dissertations.[26] Provincial studies of warlordism are even more numerous, although, as Diana Lary observes, the provinces studied—Shansi, Yunnan, Szechwan, Kwangsi, Kwangtung, and Manchuria (really a three-province region)—all happen to be on the periphery of China, where provincial (and, in the case of Manchuria, regional) boundaries are geographically distinct. Lary warns against assuming, on the basis of these studies, that warlordism was invariably, or even typically, a *provincial* phenomenon. Sometimes the range of a warlord's power was, as in Manchuria, multiprovincial; often it was subprovincial.[27]

Province-centered studies have begun to give us a more diverse China, and with greater diversity has come increased questioning of received historiographical wisdom. Although it has long been held, for example, that the differences between reformers and revolutionaries in the late Ch'ing were insurmountable—K. S. Liew speaks of the "permanent and unbridgeable gulf" separating the two camps[28]—the more localized, in-depth studies of Rankin (Chekiang and Shanghai), Rhoads (Kwangtung), and Esherick (Hunan and Hupei) all maintain that (to quote Rhoads) "the reform movements and the revolutionary movement were so intertwined that they sometimes seemed to be indistinguishable from each other."[29] Another instance of this revisionist thrust is supplied by Keith Schoppa, whose research on Chekiang in the early decades of the twentieth century leads him to question the validity of the conventional periodization, which refers to the years from 1916 (or earlier) to 1928 as the age of warlordism in China. "Chekiang's history during this period," Schoppa writes, "was not (at least until late 1924) one marked by the 'traditional' evils of warlordism."[30]

The built-in revisionist tendency of spatially delimited research is also seen in the smattering of prefecture- and county-level studies that have so far appeared. I have already noted this in Polachek's analysis of the relationship between declining community assets in Nan-hai county, Kwangtung, and the radical reformism of K'ang Yu-wei and his associates. James Cole's research on what he calls the "Shaohsing connection"—the capacity of Shaohsing prefecture in Chekiang to produce throughout the Ch'ing a disproportionate share of low-level government functionaries and to reap disproportionate economic rewards in consequence—provides another example. Cole's work demonstrates, among many other things, that the advantage to an official of hiring into his yamen *mu-yu* (private secretaries with special expertise) from Shaohsing did not rest, as was once believed, on the superior ability of Shaohsing *mu-yu* but rather on the organizational advantage they brought with them. For there were Shaohsing *mu-yu* in all yamens, from the governors-general down to the counties, and because they spoke the same dialect and communicated readily among themselves, officials in lower-level yamens were forced to rely on them in order to gain access to yamens at higher levels.[31]

Another county-level study, Hilary Beattie's exploration of local elites in T'ung-ch'eng county, Anhwei, in the Ming and Ch'ing dynasties, challenges a number of the standard generalizations made about elites in late imperial China. Two such generalizations, supported by the seminal studies of Chung-li Chang and Ping-ti Ho,[32] are that passage of the examinations was an essential step in the acquisition of gentry status and that there was a high level of upward and downward elite mobility in the Ming and Ch'ing. In T'ung-ch'eng, according to Beattie, neither of these patterns held true. The great preponderance of people of elite standing in the county were drawn from six lineages, all of which had become firmly established by the late Ming and continued to dominate local society through the Ch'ing years. The composition of this elite, moreover, was quite different from what Ho and Chang would lead us to anticipate. Only a few of its members, at any point in time, were degree holders. The main sources of elite status, throughout the period, were landholding and lineage organization.[33]

Some spatially delimited studies raise the question of representativeness or typicality. Others do not. If one is interested, as Polachek is, in the local sources of K'ang Yu-wei's radicalism, K'ang's county, Nan-hai, is the only one that needs to be examined (though, presumably, if one could show that other counties with declining community assets did *not* produce reformers with radical ideas, parts of Polachek's argument would be weakened). Similarly, although Shaohsing was not the only prefecture to produce a disproportionate number of subofficials in the Ch'ing, it is not absolutely necessary to study Soochow and Hangchow, two other prefectures that produced more than their share, in order to find out how the Shaohsing "vertical administrative clique" came into being and operated. In Beattie's case, however, the problem framework consists of a set of generalizations that have been made about elites *throughout* China. Finding a single county (out of some 1,500) that fails to support these generalizations, therefore, does not in itself disprove the generalizations. All it shows is that the generalizations are not universally valid. The great benefit of studies like Beattie's is that they point the way toward the eventual creation of more complex, differentiated—and hence less general—statements about the Chinese elite. Before we can make such statements, however, we need parallel studies of additional counties, representing a spectrum of spatial characteristics.[34]

This same issue of representativeness has been of critical importance in research on another and very different topic: the growth of the Chinese Communist movement in the 1930s and 1940s. The problem framework in this case was set by Chalmers Johnson in his seminal work, *Peasant Nationalism and Communist Power,* published in 1962.[35] In seeking to account for the dramatic extension of Communist strength during the Sino-Japanese War, Johnson argued that the Communists' implementation of social and economic reform measures to alleviate rural misery was far less crucial than their identification with (and exploitation of) the political force of nationalism, which the Japanese invasion—and in particular the brutality of Japanese "mopping up" campaigns in the countryside—had aroused among the Chinese peasantry.

The "Johnson thesis," which was framed for the Communist movement as a whole, came under sharp criticism, first from Donald Gillin (1964) and later from Mark Selden (1971), both of whom, on the basis of spatially delimited research (Gillin on Shansi, Selden on the Shen-Kan-Ning [Shensi-Kansu-Ninghsia] base area), were led to conclude that social and economic reforms were of vital importance in generating peasant support for the CCP. While Selden was on safe ground as long as he stayed with Shen-Kan-Ning, which was unique among base areas in domiciling the headquarters of Mao and the central CCP apparatus and in never having experienced direct Japanese attack, he extended his conclusions concerning the primacy of socioeconomic reform to other base areas as well, thus overreaching his data and generalizing, like Johnson (but unlike Gillin), for the entire Communist experience.

To Johnson's emphasis on peasant nationalism and Selden's on socioeconomic reform, Tetsuya Kataoka (1974), building in part on the earlier insights of Roy Hofheinz, added a third broad answer to the question of how the CCP came to power. In an important essay published in 1969, Hofheinz had insisted that "perhaps the most important . . . of all the possible explanations of Chinese Communist success [was] the behavior of the Chinese Communists themselves" and that "any general theory of the rise of Chinese communism that [omitted] the importance of organizational presence and vitality [would] remain only a partial explanation." According to Kataoka, it was precisely the organizational strength of the CCP that enabled it (once the threat of Kuomintang encirclement had been deflected by the War of Resistance and the second united front) to bend the Chinese peasantry to its will. The peasantry, in Kataoka's view, although a source of great potential power, was basically apolitical, atomistic, and localist in orientation. For "thousands upon thousands of separate, isolated . . . cellular units" to be welded into a unified, coherent force, "a thoroughly modern organization"—the CCP—had to be "imposed from above." Once this "frame of steel" was securely in position, village China, ultimately malleable, could be brought to support a range of alternative policies and goals.[36]

Although all of these theses embody some measure of truth, because they prematurely supply us with general characterizations of the Communist experience as a whole, each has proved vulnerable in the face of the more spatially focused scholarship of recent years. The strength of this scholarship, as represented by the work of Yung-fa Ch'en, Kathleen Hartford, David Paulson, and Elizabeth Perry,[37] derives from a number of factors. First, as stressed by Lyman Van Slyke in his perceptive overview of new American research on the base areas, it is extensively based on CCP inner-party documents and classified Kuomintang intelligence reportage, both of which present a more candid picture of ground-level reality than that found in open sources designed for public consumption.[38] Second, the new research is region-specific, more intent upon illuminating the complex processes by which the Communists gradually won popular support in a given base area than upon formulating generalizations applicable to base areas throughout China. Third, the new scholarship exhibits a high degree of sensitivity to spatial differentiation and temporal change *within* each base area and incorporates a wide spectrum of variables in its analysis. Paulson, for example, in his work on Shantung, shows how Communist appeals for mass support were affected by shifts in the Japanese military situation, the gradual accumulation of military and organizational experience by local party cadres, fluctuating levels of tension within the united front, the changing strength of Kuomintang guerrilla forces, the gradual acclimatization of the population to the CCP, and a host of other factors, most of which varied both from place to place within the region embraced by the base area and from point to point in time.[39]

The new research on base areas has not only undermined China-wide generalizations pertaining to the rise of the Communist movement. It has also shifted attention away from the question to which these generalizations were initially presented as answers. This question, as Van Slyke points out, by focusing on the reasons for Communist success, *assumed* Communist success and pushed into the background prior questions concerning what actually happened. The new scholarship, more oriented toward such prior questions, has challenged older assumptions and begun to lay the groundwork for "fuller, more sophisticated, and more nuanced generalizations" regarding the Communist experience in wartime China.[40]

A third feature of the China-centered approach—implicit in the new research on Communist base areas—is that it sees Chinese society as being arranged hierarchically in a number of different levels. To the spatial or "horizontal" differentiation just discussed is thus added a "vertical" axis of differentiation. Where American research on China prior to the 1970s tended, with few exceptions,[41] to focus on the view from the top—the policies and actions of the central government and of powerful provincial rulers (governors-general and governors under the empire, warlords under the republic), events or developments of national moment (the Opium War, May Fourth, the Communist movement), intellectual and cultural figures of more than local or regional prominence (Liang Ch'i-ch'ao, Lu Hsun), and so forth—the new approach concentrates more on the lower reaches of Chinese society. The distinction, it cannot be too strongly stressed, is not one between elites and nonelites. There were elites—that is, social stratification—at every level of the hierarchy, right down to the very lowest. As Skinner puts it:

> Those who provided *de facto* leadership within the [basic-level] marketing community *qua* political system and those who gave it collective representation at its interface with larger polities were gentrymen—landed, leisured, and literate—the very antithesis of any reasonable definition of the peasantry. It was artisans, merchants, and other full-time economic specialists, not peasants, who sustained the heartbeat of periodic marketing that kept the community alive. It was priests backed by gentry temple managers, not peasants, who gave religious meaning to the peasants' local world.[42]

Even the bottom-most stratum of Chinese rural society, in short, was anything but an undifferentiated mass of peasants.

This stratification at the lowest level of Chinese society is clearly reflected in recent excursions into popular history. In these accounts a much broadened conception of "elite" emerges, one that includes merchants, religious specialists, lower gentry, militarists, and even local bullies and bandits—people, in other words, of all social types who played leadership roles on the local scene—in addition to elites more narrowly and exclusively defined, whose visibility extended to the upper reaches of society. Also, as lower-level social reality has been freed from the self-serving perspectives of upper-level elites, our perception of this reality has been substantially altered. We can see things now that before we were unable to see.

Take, for example, Evelyn Sakakida Rawski's account of education and popular literacy in the Ch'ing. For a long time it was assumed that the vast majority of Chinese in the late imperial period were illiterate, that this high level of illiteracy was a direct consequence of the nonphonetic nature of the Chinese writing system, that the time and expense needed to become literate were more than most Chinese—especially rural Chinese—could afford, and that the manifold difficulties attending the acquisition of literacy in China constituted one of the main impediments to Chinese modernization during the past century.

John Fairbank, in his widely read book, *The United States and China,* gave the problem its classic expression:

> The Chinese writing system was not a convenient device lying ready at hand for every schoolboy to pick up and use as he prepared to meet life's problems. It was itself one of life's problems. If little Lao-san could not find the time for long-continued study of it, he was forever barred from social advancement. Thus the Chinese written language, rather than an open door through which China's peasantry could find truth and light, was a heavy barrier pressing against any upward advance and requiring real effort to overcome—a hindrance, not a help, to learning.[43]

Rawski turns this entire set of assumptions on its head, fundamentally transforming in the process our understanding of the issues involved. Using a variety of analytical strategies and many different kinds of data, she concludes that elementary education in the Ch'ing period was extremely cheap and therefore available to almost any male Chinese (even those from poor rural areas) who wanted it badly enough; that it was possible to acquire functional literacy relatively quickly; that by the late nineteenth century (if not earlier) 30 to 45 percent of China's men and from 2 to 10 percent of its women "knew how to read and write," making for "an average of almost one literate person per family"; that the male literacy rate at this time was roughly comparable to those of contemporary Japan and mid-seventeenth-century England; and that the late Ch'ing literacy level, far from impeding, served as an invaluable asset in China's efforts to modernize.

The key feature in Rawski's restructuring of our picture of popular literacy in the Ch'ing is her redefinition of what constitutes literacy. Highly educated Chinese in the late imperial period, not unlike American literati today, tended to define literacy as the capacity to read books—and very difficult books at that. This is, however, a narrow, self-indulgent definition that ignores the reason writing systems first came into being thousands of years ago—more for the purpose of keeping books than for writing them—and conveniently overlooks the comparative economic advantages conferred in late imperial China by even a minimal knowledge of letters. To be a merchant or a shopkeeper in nineteenth-century China did not require a reading knowledge of the classics. But some ability to read, however limited and specialized, was both helpful and apparently very common. Indeed, it is precisely in what Rawski calls "the everyday usefulness of literacy" that the key is to be found, in her view, "to understanding the motivations underlying popular literacy, not just in the early twentieth century, but in the eighteenth and nineteenth centuries as well. The economic demand for literacy . . . was high, not only in the cities but in the Chinese countryside."[44]

Rawski's analysis is not unassailable. Her estimates of the quantitative extent of the literate sector may be on the high side. Her contention that basic education was cheap has to be set against the income levels of the rural poor, which in Ch'ing China were extraordinarily low. And her argument that even minimal functional literacy, which she defines as mastery of a few hundred characters, made a potentially significant difference in an individual's social and economic power is too impressionistic to be fully convincing.[45] The author's overall thesis, nevertheless, puts the problem of literacy and popular education in the Ch'ing in a wholly new light, and future research in this area will have to take up where she has left off.

What Rawski does for literacy and popular education, Daniel Overmyer and Susan Naquin have done for popular religion and rebellion in the late imperial era. Exploiting new kinds of source materials—sectarian scriptures or "precious scrolls" (*pao-chüan*) in Overmyer's case, rebel confessions in Naquin's—and operating explicitly from a "bottom–up" rather than a "top–down" perspective, both authors strive to establish an interior view of thought and behavior at the lowest levels of Chinese society, a view of reality as actually experienced by convinced participants rather than as defined by remote—and often hostile—outsiders.[46]

Overmyer is chiefly interested in the sectarian tradition of Chinese Buddhism, or what he refers to in the title of his study as "folk Buddhism." This tradition, he contends, has been subjected to grave distortion, initially, by Confucian scholar-officials inclined to see popular sects as socially disruptive groupings that used religion as a cover for political subversion and, more recently, by those modern scholars who have insisted upon portraying religion as a mere superstructural manifestation of deeper, underlying social and economic forces. Either way, the possibility of true religious commitment on the part of sect members is, if not denied, greatly minimized.

Overmyer is convinced that this picture is wrong, that "for some people religious belief has . . . a shaping power in its own right," and that if we are to deal adequately with Chinese Buddhist sects we must recognize "the central role of their religious vision." Although readily admitting that sectarians did, from time to time, engage in political activity, and that the boundaries between sects and rebellious groups, on the one hand, and sects and secret societies, on the other, could become quite blurred, especially in times of social breakdown like the nineteenth century, the author insists upon the basic separateness of the sects in terms of their underlying intentions. Sects might be forced to behave like secret societies because of government surveillance, but the elaborate secret codes and obscure practices of the secret societies were at bottom antithetical to the long sectarian tradition of simplified doctrine and vernacular ritual. And however much rebel movements might seek divine assistance in the carrying out of social and political reforms, it was not the same as "sectarian movements engaged in eschatological warfare," with the "specific commitment to a saving deity and [to the implementation of] its paradise on earth." Religion played a part in both types of movements. But the basic intention of the former was to solve local socioeconomic problems, while that of the latter was to bring about a new spiritual order for all mankind.[47]

The best known of the Chinese sectarian traditions was the White Lotus, which was active in various guises from the twelfth century, although it did not apparently form a distinctive religious tradition until the mid-sixteenth century. In its peculiar amalgamation of piety with politics and rebellion—it was this sect, it is widely thought, that served as the religious inspiration for the Boxer uprising of 1900—the White Lotus was "the classic example of Chinese folk Buddhist sects."[48] Overmyer focuses on its religious dimension, giving much interesting information on beliefs and myths, leadership, scriptures, and ritual. Naquin's first book, although also supplying an intimate picture of White Lotus religion, stresses the rebellious side of the tradition, as exemplified in an uprising of White Lotus sects calling themselves the Eight Trigrams in the fall of 1813.

This uprising, which took place on the north China plain and attracted more than 100,000 supporters, was a prime example of Overmyer's "eschatological warfare." Rebellion, for the participants, was not an alternative to religion; the two were "different phases of the same salvational process." This point is driven home by Naquin again and again:

> Followers of [the White Lotus] religion, normally concerned with private devotions, also anticipated a period of great cataclysms when they would cast aside their ordinary lives and, following the deity sent to lead them, join together and rise up to usher in a new and perfect world in which all people found salvation through their faith and their faith alone.

It was precisely this that happened in 1813. Although, after five good harvests, parts of northern Honan had experienced drought in 1811, followed by two years of worsening agricultural conditions, the drought was clearly not the cause of the uprising. Of all the counties on the north China plain where the rebels were eventually active, only two were beset by economic difficulties in 1811. The drought, if anything, was taken by the organizers of the rebellion as confirmation of the beginning of the period of kalpa calamities, just as a great comet, which also appeared in 1811, was interpreted by them as a sign of heaven's favor. The inspiration for the Eight Trigrams uprising was, from first to last, religious in nature. Convinced by prophetic statements in their sacred literature, "members of certain previously uncoordinated and nonviolent religious sects . . . anticipated the imminent destruction of existing society and its replacement by a better world and joined together to bring about this change."[49]

The great merit of Naquin's book is that it invites us into a world to which we rarely are granted access. With sumptuous attention to detail and taut narrative power, the author guides us through this world and, to a remarkable extent, breathes life into its inhabitants. Thus, we not only learn about the idiosyncratic occupations of White Lotus sect members (many of whom earned their livings as healers and martial arts instructors), the loose chains of teachers and pupils that comprised the building blocks of the sects in normal times, and the step-by-step process by which an assembly of faithful was transformed "from a religious sect into its alter ego, a vehicle for millenarian rebellion."[50] We also find out where the rebels-to-be procured their weapons (including how many knives they could commission from a blacksmith without arousing suspicion), how much they had to pay for the white cloth they needed for identifying sashes and pennants, what the sources of their money were, where the insurgents charged with the task of storming the imperial palace in Peking hid their weapons (in peddlers' baskets of sweet potatoes, dates, and persimmons), and what they fortified themselves with as they sat about in teashops and wineshops in the vicinity of the palace walls, nervously waiting to do their part in the launching of the millennium.

Although Overmyer and Naquin dwell on different dimensions of the Chinese sectarian tradition, both scholars take the religious beliefs of their subjects with utmost seriousness and see these beliefs as playing a primary role in people's lives. Other scholars, in recent years, though not necessarily dismissing such "subjective" forms of motivation outright, have been more intent upon probing the social and economic roots of popular behavior, sometimes, though by no means invariably, within an implicitly Marxist or Marxist-influenced framework. Esherick's analyses of the socioeconomic causes of the Boxer movement and of popular antireform violence in Hunan and Hupei on the eve of the 1911 revolution have already been noted (see chapter 1). The sharp increase in census- or tax-related protests in the first decade of the twentieth century has been explored in studies by Roxann Prazniak (Lai-yang, Shantung, 1910) and Edward Rhoads (Lien-chou, Kwangtung, 1910).[51] June Mei has analyzed the social and economic background of emigration from southern Kwangtung in the latter half of the nineteenth century.[52] And on a more structural level there have been numerous efforts by historians to reexamine and reformulate inherited generalizations concerning the class makeup of the Chinese countryside during the republican era, focusing in particular on the nature, extent, and historical impact of landlordism and tenantry.[53]

Although the range of different interests and approaches reflected in these studies is very wide, all of them satisfy the minimum criterion of popular history, in that they are centrally concerned with the intellectual, social, economic, and/or institutional environment within which ordinary Chinese functioned. Not all lower-level history, however, has this popular dimension. Philip Kuhn's study of the growing militarization of Chinese society in the nineteenth century deals at length with village-level and multivillage-level organization for defense. Kuhn's main preoccupation, however, is not with rank-and-file militiamen but with the leadership role played in the militarization process by elites (normally, though not invariably, degree-holding gentry) and the enhanced power that accrued to local elites in particular as a result of their exercise of this leadership.

Kuhn's work, which appeared in 1970, marks an important breakthrough in American historiography on China. While to a degree *Rebellion and Its Enemies in Late Imperial China* is still encumbered by the tradition–modernity mindset so pervasive in the 1950s and 1960s, it moves beyond this pattern of thought in decisive ways, embodying in its analytical framework all of the new tendencies I have been delineating. The book has, as its title suggests, a Chinese point of departure: The key problem it addresses is the breakdown of the Chinese social order beginning in the late eighteenth century and the ways in which Chinese elites responded to this breakdown. Its subject matter is spatially circumscribed, focusing on south and central China. It emphasizes different levels of military organization, thus treating Chinese society in hierarchical, vertically differentiated fashion. Also, it embodies a fourth facet of the new approach that, although in itself hardly "China-centered," has exerted a marked influence on practitioners of China-centered historiography. I refer to the high receptivity the latter have shown to the techniques and strategies of other disciplines, in particular the social sciences, and their serious commitment to incorporating these techniques and strategies into historical analysis.

The desirability of applying social science analysis to the study of Chinese history has long been recognized. For years, however, the insights applied were linked, explicitly or implicitly, to modernization theory, with its heavy burden of Western-centric assumptions, and this resulted, as we have seen, in an understanding of China that was seriously flawed. Then, in the 1960s, two developments took place that significantly altered the context for cross-fertilization between the social sciences and the data of Chinese history. One was the awakening, on the part of the American historical profession generally, to the importance of social history—an awakening that, once it occurred, uncovered a wide spectrum of previously unrealized possibilities for fruitful collaboration between history and the social sciences.[54] The second development was the emergence, however limited and halting, of a more critical awareness among Western and more particularly American social scientists of the degree to which social science theory was parochially grounded and in need of radical restructuring.

In the China field, it was the anthropologists, accustomed by training to the investigation of non-Western societies and more sensitive than most social scientists to the perils of ethnocentric bias, who led the way.[55] This is evident in Kuhn's analysis, some of the most important building blocks of which clearly reflect the influence of two anthropologists specializing in China, Skinner and the late Maurice Freedman of England. Freedman's influence is seen in Kuhn's discussion of the role of lineage in local militarization and in his preference for a conception of elite status based on functional as well as formal (degree-holding) criteria.[56] Skinner's impact, much more marked, is discernible in the author's analysis of the relevance of the marketing community to militia organization, the distinction he draws between natural and administrative (or official) modes of societal organization, and more generally in the key concept of progressively higher levels of military organization, each level defined by its capacity to perform certain functions. (The size, for example, of the highest local-level military organizations, the "extended-multiplex confederations," which rose spontaneously throughout south and central China in the 1850s, was generally limited, according to Kuhn, by "intractable realities of communications and economics." If too large, the gentry leadership of a confederation would be unable to maintain contact with its constituent parts; if too small, it would be incapable of mustering large enough amounts of money and manpower.)[57]

The influence of anthropology, in particular ecological anthropology, is also vitally important in Elizabeth Perry's provocative study, *Rebels and Revolutionaries in North China, 1845-1945* (1980). Perry's book, even more explicitly than Kuhn's, incorporates all of the features of the China-centered approach. Interested in the question of the origins of the Chinese revolution and, more specifically, how this revolution related to earlier patterns of peasant rebellion in China, she begins by asking why *some* Chinese peasants rebelled and why peasant rebellion occurred persistently and frequently only in certain geographic areas. The nature of her questions, of course, literally compels Perry to pursue a spatially delimited approach—the book is focused on the Huai-pei region in North China—and to concentrate her attention on the lowest levels of Chinese society. In building her theory of rebellion "from the bottom up" (as she words it), Perry starts with the premise that in unusually harsh natural environments like Huai-pei, where resources were in perennially short supply, collective violence constituted a rational strategy for survival. She breaks such violence down into two subcategories: predatory and protective. The former strategy (exemplified in nineteenth-century Huai-pei by the Nien) involved illegal expansion of the resources of some members of the community at the expense of others. The latter (represented by the Red Spear Society, which was active in Huai-pei during the republican period) involved the effort of propertied elements to safeguard their possessions against predatory threat. The author views both of these strategies as adaptive responses to an environment dominated by scarcity. Moreover, historically considered, both were highly parochial in nature and inhospitable to radical structural change.

Thus, when the Communists moved into Huai-pei in the late 1920s, hoping to transform the Red Spears into a truly revolutionary force, they encountered staunch resistance. Later, during the war against Japan, when the interests and priorities of the CCP and the Red Spears were less in conflict, relations between the two groups improved. The long-term goals of the CCP were, however, basically different from those of either the Red Spears or their predecessors, the Nien. The Communists, moving beyond the parochialism characteristic of both earlier groups, were committed to a fundamentally new strategy, which sought to transform peasant protest "from its vicious predatory-protective cycle into a positive articulation of new social arrangements." In the end, Perry is forced to conclude (contrary to the supposition with which she started out) that the discontinuities between "traditional" rebellion and "modern" revolution were basic and, at least for Huai-pei, "any simple positive relationship between a history of rural insurrection and the success of modern revolution" must be firmly ruled out.[58]

While Kuhn and Perry, because of the particular nature of

their research interests, draw heavily on ideas from the field of anthropology, students of the phenomenon of warlordism in the twentieth century have been more inclined to turn to political science for their theoretical stimulus. Given the subject matter, this has seemed a natural marriage, raising hopes that the chaotic and densely impenetrable character of warlord politics might be illuminated and our understanding placed on a new footing. The hopes, unfortunately, have been only partially fulfilled. Certainly our knowledge of the warlord era, in a factual sense, has been greatly advanced. But new interpretive insight, flowing directly from the application of social science theory, has lagged behind. Recent efforts in this direction have been criticized in a number of quarters for being strained and artificial. Too often, it is argued, the theory seems to have been "tacked on" to the data, rather than being genuinely integrated with it, and readers have been left with the uncomfortable sense of being witness to a marriage that has been inadequately consummated.

Andrew Nathan's analysis of warlord politics in Peking in terms of factionalism is a case in point. Nathan, a political scientist with strong historical proclivities, performs his separate duties as historian and as political scientist with consummate skill. He develops a complex model of factional behavior, and his historical account of the abortive revival of constitutionalism in the post–Yuan Shih-k'ai era is well documented and lucidly presented. But as Diana Lary points out, "the relationship between the empirical half and the theoretical half [of Nathan's book] is not as clear as the two halves are individually. The Fengtian Clique in practice looks closer to the ramshackle, makeshift, and heterogeneous outfit described by [Gavan] McCormack [in his study of Chang Tso-lin] . . . than it does to Nathan's immaculate model [of factional behavior]."[59]

Hsi-sheng Ch'i, another political scientist, and Odoric Wou, a historian, encounter much the same criticism. Both scholars are praised for the empirical portions of their studies: Ch'i for his perceptive chapters on the recruitment, training, and weaponry of warlord armies and the economics of warlordism; Wou for his detailed description of the life and career of Wu P'ei-fu.[60] But Ch'i's effort, in the final part of his book, to relate international systems analysis to warlordism, and Wou's postulation of a parallelism between warlord cliques and Chinese lineage organization, using a fictive kinship construct and the Krech–Crutchfield–Ballachey star-shaped model of leader–follower relationships, have stretched the patience of well-intentioned reviewers.[61] In contrast to Kuhn and Perry, who weave the insights they have gleaned from anthropology tightly into the fabric of their historical analyses, enabling us thereby to see the phenomena of militarization and rebellion in Chinese society in truly new ways, Nathan, Ch'i, and Wou have written accounts of Chinese militarism in the twentieth century that, failing to achieve a comparable level of integration, are of value to the historian in spite, rather than because, of their introduction of social science constructs.

I have touched on these somewhat less successful examples of the marriage of social science analysis to Chinese historical data not in order to damn the enterprise as such but to suggest how very difficult it is to do well. Finding the right theory—right both in terms of its applicability and in terms of its sensitivity to Western-centric bias—and integrating it effectively with the data is only one hurdle that has to be surmounted. Another is what may be called the stylistic barrier: the challenge of incorporating social science concepts into historical narrative without succumbing to the almost total disregard of art to which formulators of the former seem disposed. A third hurdle, perhaps the most humbling of all, is the demand that the mastery of theories, methodologies, and strategies from a wide range of disparate disciplines (often extending beyond the social sciences to mathematics and even, in some instances, the applied natural sciences) places on the human brain—a brain that, if it happens to be lodged in the head of an American historian of China, has already put in years of time and effort doing battle with one, if not two, of the world's most daunting languages.

"Very few scholars," Marc Bloch tells us, "can boast that they are equally well equipped to read critically a medieval charter, to explain correctly the etymology of place-names, to date unerringly the ruins of dwellings of the prehistoric, Celtic, or Gallo-Roman periods, and to analyze the plant life proper to a pasture, a field, or a moor. Without all these, however, how could one pretend to describe the history of land use?" Almost any important human problem, Bloch felt, posed a comparable challenge. The deeper one delved into the problem, the greater the variety of different kinds of evidence one encountered; and the more heterogeneous the evidence, the greater the strain on the individual historian's capacity to master the diverse skills required to interpret it. The only remedy, in Bloch's view, was "to substitute, in place of the multiple skills of a single man, the pooling of techniques, practiced by different scholars, but all tending to throw light upon a specific subject." This form of cooperative historical endeavor was still only a distant goal in 1944, when Bloch died. Nevertheless, its successful realization would, he predicted, "unquestionably govern the future of our science."[62]

Recent undertakings in the China field in the United States suggest that Bloch's future may finally be at hand for students of the Chinese past. A landmark event was the publication in the 1970s of three thick volumes on Chinese urban history, a collaborative effort by representatives of numerous disciplines—history, sociology, geography, political science, anthropology, and religion, among others—to study the Chinese city in the late imperial, republican, and contemporary periods.[63]

Even more ambitious, in terms of disciplinary input, was a workshop on food and famine in Chinese history, held at Harvard University in the summer of 1980. Participants in the workshop were presented with two- and three-day intensive "minicourses" offered by specialists in fields as far-flung as regional systems, geography, water engineering, agricultural economics, nutrition, and demography. When it was all over, they had learned something about the use of cost–benefit and multi-objective analysis in water management decision making; how to construct a food balance sheet for China; how land tenure systems, commercialization, taxation, and other institutional arrangements affect levels of food output and food distribution and consumption; the value of satellite photography (LANDSAT) for study of contemporary Chinese agriculture and water control (a technique Bloch, who pioneered in the use of aerial surveys to map medieval French land arrangements, would have eagerly embraced); how mathematical models can be employed to plot the time it takes for a population, in aggregate terms, to bounce back after a mortality crisis; and a host of other potentially invaluable techniques and approaches.

Significantly, Lillian Li, the organizer of the food and famine workshop, in reporting on its results, made direct reference to the *Annales* school, of which Marc Bloch was a principal founder, and expressed the hope that subsequent work on Chinese history would emulate the example set by this school in European history. The particular facet of *Annaliste* historiography to which Li referred was its emphasis on interdisciplinary collaboration—an emphasis for which, in her view, the study of famine offered "enormous potential."[64]

THE CHINA-CENTERED APPROACH: IMPLICATIONS AND CONSEQUENCES

The approach to Chinese history described in the preceding section possesses four distinct characteristics: (1) It begins Chinese history in China rather than in the West and adopts, as far as humanly possible, internal (Chinese) rather than external (Western) criteria for determining what is historically significant in the Chinese past; (2) it disaggregates China "horizontally" into regions, provinces, prefectures, counties, and cities, thus making regional and local history possible; (3) it also disaggregates Chinese society "vertically" into a number of discrete levels, facilitating the writing of lower-level history, both popular and nonpopular; and finally (4) it welcomes with enthusiasm the theories, methodologies, and techniques developed in disciplines other than history (mostly, but not exclusively, the social sciences) and strives to integrate these into historical analysis.

This approach is not entirely new; nor does it represent a single, coherent "approach." It embodies, nonetheless, a set of tendencies that became increasingly marked among American historians—predominantly younger and more recently trained practitioners of the craft—from about 1970, in response partly to changes that had occurred in the American historical profession generally in the 1960s and partly to the anti-imperialist and self-critical orientations of the antiwar movement of the late 1960s and early 1970s. The impact of the antiwar movement was complex and seemingly contradictory. In the case of some scholars—Edward Friedman, Ernest Young, and Joseph Esherick may be cited as examples—it was immediate and direct, resulting in heightened interest in imperialism as an explanatory variable in late Ch'ing and republican history. In the case of other scholars, however, the impact was less direct and harder to demonstrate with conclusiveness, though in the end it may have been equally profound. These scholars—represented most clearly, perhaps, by people like Polachek and Kuhn—have evinced little apparent interest in imperialism (or, for that matter, the West in general) as a material factor in recent Chinese history. But by moving away from the Western-centric paradigms of the 1950s and 1960s and adopting a more interior, more Chinese sense of historical problem, they have dealt a critical blow to the intellectual imperialism inherent in earlier American historiography.

Although the differences between these two groupings are pronounced and should not be slighted—members of the first grouping, aside from their greater emphasis upon the impact of foreign imperialism on the Chinese environment, are more likely to accent the political activities of "the masses" and to be principally interested, in their research, in the processes of revolutionary change beginning in the late nineteenth century—the ground both share is considerable. Esherick's conception of a differentiated or stratified elite shows the influence of Kuhn's earlier work.[65] Polachek and Esherick both attach paramount importance to the motivational role of political and economic interests and share a radical aversion to the proposition that ideas and values significantly influence human behavior. More generally, members of both groupings have a strong interest in social change and in the social context and consequences of change in the political, economic, and other spheres. On both sides, moreover, there is a deep commitment to the notion that the study of Chinese history should, in some meaningful sense, be rooted in China. Thus, while Young emphasizes the problems posed for China in the early republican era by the "towering presence" of foreign imperialism, the central theme of his study of the Yuan Shih-k'ai presidency is how these problems became enmeshed in the centuries-old Chinese controversy over the comparative advantages of centralized (*chün-hsien*) versus decentralized (*feng-chien*) authority.[66]

When a major new orientation emerges in any field of study, it is bound to have a profound effect on the shaping of that field's subject matter. The present instance is no exception. In contrast to much of the historical scholarship of the 1950s and 1960s, when practically every book published opened up a new subject area but where existing paradigms, although modified over time, were not altered fundamentally, the scholarship of the 1970s and early 1980s, by questioning seriously the intellectual structures of the preceding decades, paved the way for a much more pronounced revisionist thrust. There was still plenty of room, in a young field, for path-breaking research into previously unworked topics. But more and more, as documented in the body of this chapter, the accent came to be placed on the pioneering of new analyses and new research strategies, rather than brand-new problems. Generalizations of long standing, based on the entire geographic expanse of China or on the upper stratum of Chinese society, were sharply challenged when the focus of research became more spatially delimited or shifted to the lower social strata. Old familiar problems began to be reworked, sometimes several times over, and around increasing numbers of them—the genuineness of the T'ung-chih Restoration, the role of the gentry in 1911, the nature and antecedents of the May Fourth movement, the character of the social base of Kuomintang rule during the Nanking decade,[67] the sources of the Chinese Communist Party's success in the 1940s—a genuine historiography, marked by deep cleavages and lively controversy within the field, emerged.

Another important concomitant of the China-centered approach has been a gradual shift away from *culture* and toward *history* as the dominant mode of structuring problems of the recent Chinese past. During the 1950s and 1960s, when the impact–response and tradition–modernity paradigms held sway in American scholarship, enormous explanatory power was invested in the *nature* of China's "traditional" society or culture—and, of course, either explicitly or by implication, in the ways in which this society-culture differed from that of the West or Japan. Studies of clash between China and the West—Fairbank's *Trade and Diplomacy on the China Coast,* my own *China and Christianity*—although devoting much space to political, economic, social, institutional, and other factors, tended to view cultural difference and misunderstanding (as expressed, above all, in the realm of attitudes and values) as the ultimate ground of conflict.[68] Similarly, influential treatments of such themes as China's failure to industrialize in the late Ch'ing (Feuerwerker), the ineffectiveness of China's response to the West as compared with Japan's (Fairbank, Reischauer, and Craig), the fruitless efforts of the Confucian state to modernize (Wright), and the inability of Chinese society to develop on its own into "a society with a scientific temper" (Levenson) all attached fundamental explanatory importance to the special nature of Chinese society and culture.

This emphasis upon the social or cultural factor was a natural by-product of intellectual paradigms that were built around the notion of sociocultural contrast and that sought to explain China principally in terms of its social and cultural differences from the West. It is not surprising, therefore, that when these paradigms began to be sharply challenged, beginning in the late 1960s, the sociocultural mode of explanation also was vigorously contested. The challenge assumed its most explicit formulation in the hands of people like James Peck and Frances Moulder, both of whom, it will be recalled, were profoundly hostile to sociocultural explanations. Peck and Moulder, however, in their one-sided—and almost wholly unempirical—stress on imperialism, attached little explanatory value to factors internal to Chinese history. In the end, the challenge to the sociocultural mode of explanation was leveled far more effectively by practicing historians,[69] who, regardless of how they felt about imperialism in nineteenth- and twentieth-century China, were committed to operating with real data within a China-centered framework.

The reason why the China-centered approach lends itself to a structuring of the Chinese past more in historical than in cultural terms is that its locus of comparison is not the differences between one culture and another (China and the West) but the differences between earlier and later points in time within a single culture (China). The former kind of comparison, by drawing attention to the more stable, ongoing attributes or properties of a culture—a culture's intrinsic nature—encourages a relatively static sense of the past. The latter, by stressing variation over time within one culture, fosters a more dynamic, more change-oriented sense of the past, one in which culture, as an explanatory factor, recedes into the background, and history—or a heightened sensitivity to historical process—moves to the fore.

A fine example of this more history-oriented structuring of the Chinese past is found in the conference volume, *Conflict and Control in Late Imperial China* (1975), edited by Frederic Wakeman and Carolyn Grant. The contributors to the volume, focusing for the most part on social and lower-level political history, convey a picture of Chinese society from the late Ming to the early republican period that is full of movement and change. In place of the familiar story of a China in its dotage, staid and bone-weary, just waiting for a dynamic West to intervene and inject new life, what we get is a China not beholden to others for the gift of history but quite capable of generating it on its own.

The *Conflict and Control* volume also points to another

consequence of the China-centered approach, which is that it calls into serious question the standard periodization of late imperial history. For many decades, 1840—or, more precisely, the Opium War of 1839–1842—was viewed by a preponderance of both Chinese and Western historians as the most important temporal boundary in China's recent past. Chinese historians, Marxist and non-Marxist, settled upon this date out of a patriotic concern with the issue of foreign imperialism; 1840 became, for them, the beginning of modern history. Western historians, of course, also were interested in dating the advent of modern Chinese history, and, convinced that modernity could only be Western-carried, they too fastened upon 1840 as the great divide.

As of 1980, historians in the People's Republic of China, although differing among themselves over when "modern" (*chin-tai*) history ended and gave way to "contemporary" (*hsien-tai*) history (some saying 1919, others 1949), were still virtually unanimous in the opinion that 1840 was when it all began.[70] American historians, however, as they either repudiated the tradition–modernity paradigm altogether or gravitated toward the view that, prior to the arrival of the West, China was already, in Evelyn Rawski's words, "an advanced society, with many modern characteristics,"[71] came increasingly to challenge the overarching significance of the Opium War. This was particularly so among practitioners of the new tendencies described in this chapter.

For those inclined to abandon completely the periodization of Chinese history into traditional and modern phases, the question of when modern China began became a nonquestion; but even for the rest, for whom it remained a question, the terms of the answer were changed. No longer was it necessary to suffer, with Immanuel Hsü, over which Western impact—the Opium War or the earlier arrival of European traders and missionaries in the late Ming—was most instrumental in giving birth to "modern China."[72] The very assumption of an ironclad causal linkage between the intrusion of "forces exogenous to Chinese society" (Kuhn) and the advent of China's modern history was declared null and void.

The same kinds of questions that caused one old time boundary to seem less meaningful, moreover, also challenged other old boundaries. As 1840 receded increasingly into the shadows, so too did conventional Chinese dynastic periodization. In his introduction to *Conflict and Control in Late Imperial China,* Wakeman writes,

> Gradually, social historians began to realize that the entire period from the 1550s to the 1930s constituted a coherent whole. Instead of seeing the Ch'ing as a replication of the past, or 1644 and 1911 as critical terminals, scholars detected processes which stretched across the last four centuries of Chinese history into the republican period. The urbanization of the lower Yangtze region, the commutation of labor services into money payments, the development of certain kinds of regional trade, the growth of mass literacy and the increase in the size of the gentry, the commercialization of local managerial activities—all these phenomena of the late Ming set in motion administrative and political changes that continued to develop over the course of the Ch'ing and in some ways culminated in the social history of the early twentieth century.[73]

A similar note is struck by Ramon Myers who, also from the perspective of social and economic history, argues that "Ming and Ch'ing China experienced changes as profound and far-reaching as those of the Sung" and urges scholars to consider these two dynasties as "a single epoch in Chinese history."[74] While Wakeman and Myers both see fundamental transformations commencing in the late sixteenth or early seventeenth centuries, Joseph Fletcher, arguing from a somewhat different perspective, suggests that the great watershed in late imperial history came in the eighteenth century:

> The change that has received the most scholarly attention is the solid establishment of Europe's presence. But two other changes [that occurred in the eighteenth century] may prove to have been of greater significance in the long run. One of these was a doubling of the territorial size of the Chinese empire. The other was a doubling of the Han Chinese population. . . . The indigenous social and economic processes of a demographically and territorially expanded China, no less than pressures from outside, have underlain the modern transformation of Chinese society that is still under way.[75]

From Ming to Ch'ing (1979), a multi-author book edited by Jonathan Spence and John Wills, argues persuasively that both of these perspectives—the one emphasizing long-term secular trends spanning Ming and Ch'ing, the other laying stress on peculiarly Manchu–Ch'ing contributions to late imperial history—are valid. Spence and Wills are impressed by the "internal coherence" of the period from late Ming (the 1590s) to high Ch'ing (ca. 1730), as illustrated in "an individuality and intensity of Confucian moral-seeking . . . that ran from the Tung-lin heroes through such great early Ch'ing scholars as Wang Fu-chih; or a continuity of half-controlled official exploitation of commerce that carried over from the eunuch mines commissioners of the 1590s to the 'Emperor's Merchant' at Canton after 1700."[76] But they are equally struck by the differences between Ch'ing and Ming, differences relating to the events of the conquest and to the specific characteristics of the Manchu ruling elite.

Among the latter they point in particular to the conspicuous alienness of the Manchus (in matters of custom, language, dress, diet, and so forth) and the ethnic anti-Manchuism it aroused; the far-reaching changes the Manchus introduced in the military organization of the empire (the banner system) and in the structure of the "extrabureaucratic elite" (which served vitally important functions as a control mechanism); and, above all, the Manchu orientation toward Inner Asia. Insofar as this last characteristic revived an interior, overland focus that had marked the foreign policy of earlier Chinese dynasties, it was not entirely new. The combination of Manchu political and military skills in the handling of Inner Asia with Chinese administrative experience and economic power, however, established "a new level of control over China's inland frontier zones" and ushered in "a very basic change in the geopolitics of East Asia."[77]

Spence and Wills underscore the "immense consequences" that the continued orientation of Ch'ing foreign policy toward the inland frontier and away from the coast had for Chinese history in the nineteenth century. Other writers have attached comparable weight to the strong centralizing tendencies exhibited under Manchu rule. Tsing Yuan emphasizes the repressive side of the centralization phenomenon, seeing in the cringing submissiveness the Manchus demanded of their Chinese subjects, the harshness of the throne's response to urban riots, and the literary inquisition of the eighteenth century, "the overpowering hand of the Ch'ing state."[78] Other scholars have probed the institutional aspect of Manchu centralization. The Yung-cheng Emperor's effort to enhance the throne's direct control over state affairs through creation of the Grand Council has been described as "a milestone in the development of Ch'ing autocracy."[79] Equally important in this regard was the inauguration of the palace memorial system in the K'ang-hsi reign to strengthen, through closer imperial management of communications, the court's supremacy over the bureaucracy.[80]

The impact of this centralizing penchant of the Manchu monarchy on the late imperial—and perhaps even postimperial—Chinese state is not yet well understood. But we may guess it to have been considerable.[81] Like the other internal determinants noted in this chapter,[82] it offers a sharp challenge to any periodization of recent Chinese history that misstates or overstates the role of external agents.

One form of "false periodization," David Hackett Fischer tells us,

> appears when a historian takes a time scheme which may be valid and functional in problem A and transfers it to problem B, where it is invalid and dysfunctional. American history is still periodized in the textbooks by presidential administrations, which are perfectly proper for a history of the presidency but not for the development of American society, which possesses its own set of inaugurations and retirements.[83]

The same is of course true of the Opium War in Chinese history. It is not that it was of no consequence. But its consequences were bounded. They had to do with diplomatic history, the history of China's foreign trade, even the social, economic, and local political history of Kwangtung and other coastal areas, but not with the evolution of Chinese society as a whole. Chinese society, like American, has had its own set of inaugurations and retirements, to many of which the Opium War did not speak in ways that were significant.

The abandonment of 1840 as a *general* time marker (by all but the most old-fashioned and the most radical of American historians) has symbolic implications that extend far beyond the Opium War itself. The symbolism, however, is subject to variant readings. American historians may interpret their gravitation away from 1840 and the accompanying search for a more interior perspective on recent Chinese history as a sign of maturation, of the coming of age of American historiography, an indication that at last we have transcended the intellectual imperialism of the old paradigms and are treating Chinese history on its own ground, in its own terms. From the vantage point of Chinese historians, however, the American move toward a more bounded assessment of the role of the West may seem a little like our lecturing underdeveloped countries on the ill effects of DDT. As long as the experience of the Western intrusion remains fresh and resentment against it alive and warm, it will be difficult for Chinese to accept a scaled-down appraisal of imperialism's role in the last century and a half of their history, and they may well view American efforts in this direction as ultimately self-serving, a new and more subtle form of foreign intellectual aggrandizement.

Irony of ironies: outsiders moving toward an inside perspective; insiders insisting on the crucial importance of outside factors. The irony is more apparent, however, than real. True, the China-centered approach adopted by increasing numbers of American historians has the potential to degenerate into a new form of parochialism that, by underestimating the part taken by the West in nineteenth- and twentieth-century China, simply turns the old parochialism, with its overestimation of the West's role, inside out and takes us no closer to the truth about the Chinese past. There is nothing in the new orientation, however, that necessitates such an outcome.

The idea that the China-centered approach tries to encompass is that there is an internal structure or direction to Chinese history in the nineteenth and twentieth centuries that proceeds from the eighteenth and earlier centuries. Forces of enormous shaping significance are at work: unprecedented population pressure and territorial expansion, commercialization of the rural economy, increasing domestic political frustration at all social levels, and so on. What we have is not a "traditional" order going no place, marked by "inertia," definable largely if not exclusively in terms of its incapacity to cope with the West, but rather a genuine historical situation, bristling with tensions and problems that countless Chinese are trying to deal with in countless ways. Enter the West. The West creates new problems—and this is the aspect that until recently has mesmerized American historians (Fairbank and Levenson being prime examples). But it also creates a new *context,* a new *framework* for the perception and understanding of old problems, and finally, it offers for the solution of problems both old and new a radically different stock of ideas and technologies. Throughout, however, although the context is increasingly influenced by the West, the internal history remains Chinese.

My use of the term *China-centered* is not intended to describe an approach to this history that ignores external determinants and treats China in isolation from the rest of the world; nor, certainly, do I mean to revive the old concept of "Sinocentrism," with its connotations of a world centering on China. Rather, *China-centered* is intended to delineate an approach to recent Chinese history that strives to understand what is happening in that history in terms that are as free as possible of imported criteria of significance.

Where, as in many of the concrete examples cited in the pages of this chapter, the focal point of inquiry centers on the lower levels of Chinese society or on geographically circumscribed parts of China or on the nineteenth century (when the West had only recently arrived on the scene and had not penetrated Chinese life very deeply), the overall picture that emerges is indeed one in which external factors play a sharply reduced role. This is a valuable corrective to the picture we used to have of this phase of Chinese history, and it is what justifies the search for alternative periodizations—periodizations that do not imply that the history of China after 1840 was exclusively or overwhelmingly governed by external forces. Where, on the other hand, the focal point of inquiry is the upper levels of society (which would include cultural and intellectual elites of national stature, as well as central government functions such as diplomacy) or more extensive geographic areas (particularly along the coast or embracing major urban centers) or the twentieth century, the chances are that exogenous determinants of change will loom much larger. Although to date the China-centered approach has been applied much less frequently to these latter areas of inquiry than to the former, it is perfectly capable of being extended to them. When this happens, moreover, the result is likely to be a further correction of the old picture. For, being less bound than earlier American approaches to Western determinants of what is historically important, the China-centered approach is in a position to treat even exogenous sources of change from a more interior perspective.[84]

Be this as it may, it will be countered, as long as the practitioners of China-centered historiography are Americans, no matter how hard we try to get "inside" Chinese history, we will still end up insinuating into this history vocabulary and concepts that are American. Outsiders can never really develop an inside perspective. The very notion of Americans pursuing a China-centered approach to Chinese history is a contradiction in terms.

This is true—up to a point. But it is also false in that it lays too much stress on a particular kind of outsideness and in so doing betrays a fundamental misconception concerning the nature of the limitations under which historians *in general* operate in their efforts to retrieve the truth about the past. The fact is, all historians—not only Americans approaching Chinese history from without but also Chinese historians approaching it from within—are, in some sense, outsiders. All of us are to an extent prisoners of our environments, trapped in one or another set of parochial concerns. And the truth we retrieve is inevitably qualified by the intellectual and emotional preoccupations each of us, through our vocabulary and concepts, brings to bear on the study of the past.

To qualify the truth is not, however, to nullify it. In the last analysis, all historical truth is qualified, in that it consists not in the whole truth about the past but in a limited set of factual statements, adequately supported by evidence, that constitute the answers to a particular question or set of questions that the historian has in mind. Historians with different concerns and preoccupations will naturally pose different questions. This is not a problem. The problem arises when historians are insufficiently aware of the assumptions buried inside their questions, with the consequence that "truth" is imposed upon the data of history instead of being derived from it and we end up with a picture of the past—of the kinds of historical change that are important—that is defined too much by the historian's own innermost reality and too little by the reality of the people he or she is writing about. This is truly *outside* history. It can be written by Chinese as well as Americans. And it can never be avoided by any historian altogether. But all of us, to the extent that we are conscious of the problem and take it seriously, can find ways to moderate its impact. In this sense, China-centered history written by Americans is not a contradiction in terms but an entirely appropriate—perhaps the only appropriate—goal for American historians to aspire to in our study of the Chinese past.

Notes

INTRODUCTION

1. Ping-ti Ho, *Studies on the Population of China, 1368–1953* (Cambridge: Harvard University Press, 1959); Ping-ti Ho, *The Ladder of Success in Imperial China: Aspects of Social Mobility, 1368–1911* (New York: Columbia University Press, 1962); Chung-li Chang, *The Chinese Gentry: Studies on Their Role in Nineteenth-Century Chinese Society* (Seattle: University of Washington Press, 1955); Chung-li Chang, *The Income of the Chinese Gentry* (Seattle: University of Washington Press, 1962); Kung-chuan Hsiao, *Rural China: Imperial Control in the Nineteenth Century* (Seattle: University of Washington Press, 1960); Franz Michael, "Military Organization and Power Structure of China During the Taiping Rebellion," *Pacific Historical Review* (1949), 18(4):469–483; Franz Michael in collaboration with Chung-li Chang, *The Taiping Rebellion: History and Documents*, vol. 1, *History* (Seattle: University of Washington Press, 1966).

2. Some readers will be reminded of Thomas S. Kuhn's discussion of the role that paradigms play in "normal science." A paradigm, Kuhn tells us, supplies a "preformed and relatively inflexible box." In the operations of "normal science," phenomena of nature "that will not fit the box are often not seen at all." *The Structure of Scientific Revolutions*, 2d ed. (Chicago: University of Chicago Press, 1970), p. 24.

3. See Philip D. Curtin, "African History," in Michael Kammen, ed., *The Past Before Us: Contemporary Historical Writing in the United States* (Ithaca, N.Y.: Cornell University Press, 1980), pp. 113–130, esp. 119–130; Nikki Keddie, "The History of the Muslim Middle East," in *ibid.*, pp. 131–156, esp. 141, 148, 151, 154–155. See also Charles Gibson, "Latin America and the Americas," in *ibid.*, pp. 187–202, esp. 194–195.

1. THE PROBLEM WITH "CHINA'S RESPONSE TO THE WEST"

1. Teng and Fairbank, *China's Response to the West: A Documentary Survey, 1839–1923* (Cambridge: Harvard University Press, 1954), p. 1.

2. Clyde and Beers, *The Far East: A History of the Western Impact and the Eastern Response (1830–1965),* 4th rev. ed. (Englewood Cliffs, N.J.: Prentice-Hall, 1966), p. 6.

3. See Fairbank, Reischauer, and Craig, *East Asia: The Modern Transformation* (Boston: Houghton Mifflin, 1965), esp. pp. 81–82, 404–407.

4. A paperback edition with a new preface was issued by Harvard University Press in 1979. But although the preface acknowledges criticisms of the impact–response framework (some of them voiced by the editors themselves in the original edition), the text itself is unaltered. See n. 6, this chapter.

5. In the most recent edition of the Clyde–Beers text (6th ed., 1975), the introductory discussion of impact and response remains essentially unmodified except for the fact that "impact" and "response" are pluralized, as is the book's new title, *The Far East: A History of Western Impacts and Eastern Responses, 1830–1975*. In Franz H. Michael and George E. Taylor, *The Far East in the Modern World,* 3d ed. (Hinsdale, Ill.: Dryden Press, 1975), the second part of the text, dealing with China, Japan, and Southeast Asia in the nineteenth century, is entitled "The Response to the West." The latest edition of the Fairbank–Reischauer–Craig text is a one-volume condensation entitled *East Asia: Tradition and Transformation* (Boston: Houghton Mifflin, 1978). The portions dealing with nineteenth-century China follow the same basic pattern as in the original text.

6. Although Teng and Fairbank, to their credit, alluded in their introduction to *China's Response to the West* to some of the basic flaws of the impact–response framework, subsequent historians (including Fairbank himself) tended to take over the framework without paying much heed to these qualifications. "The terms 'stimulus' (or 'impact') and 'response,' " Teng and Fairbank wrote in 1954, "are not very precise. We are in danger of assuming that there was a previous 'Western impact' merely because there was a later activity which we call a 'Chinese response.' This 'Chinese response' or activity is the thing we want to study, but it obviously was part of Chinese conduct as a whole. In other words, the Western impact was only one of many factors in the Chinese scene. The response to it can only be unscrambled with difficulty from Chinese history in general. Until we can work out a more precise analytic framework, the title of this study will remain more metaphorical than scientific" (p. 5).

7. Schwartz, *In Search of Wealth and Power: Yen Fu and the West* (Cambridge: Harvard University Press, 1964), pp. 1–2.

8. To cite another illustration, the term *ch'ün-hsueh,* first used by Yen Fu to translate "sociology," was widely misunderstood among late Ch'ing intellectuals, who took it to refer to the need to develop a "sense of community." See Wang Erh-min, *Chung-kuo chin-tai ssu-hsiang shih lun* (Essays on the history of modern Chinese thought) (Taipei: Hua-shih ch'u-pan-she, 1977), p. 43. That distortions in cross-cultural transmission of ideas are not confined to cultures as distinct as China and the West is suggested in a recent article by Bruno Bettelheim, who maintains that some of the most basic concepts of Freudian psychoanalytic theory have been completely misunderstood by the American psychoanalytic profession as a result partly of faulty translation and partly of American cultural orientations that differ from German. See Bettelheim, "Reflections: Freud and the Soul," *New Yorker,* March 1, 1982, pp. 52–93.

9. All the text accounts earlier referred to emphasize the endogenous origins of the Taiping movement, and none attempts to interpret the movement in direct, concrete

terms as a response to the West. But at the same time they all place the Taiping phenomenon within a loose, overarching, impact–response perspective. Fairbank is the most specific in this regard, seeing the Taipings as the first in a succession of failed Chinese responses to foreign encroachment in the nineteenth century ("after ten years' development [they] proved themselves old-fashioned rivals for power and showed little capacity for remaking the traditional order"). See Fairbank, Reischauer, and Craig, *East Asia: The Modern Transformation,* p. 404. John Whitney Hall, a leading Japan historian, in a recent review of postwar American scholarship on Asia, is also quite explicit in characterizing the Taipings as a response to the Western challenge. See Hall, "East, Southeast, and South Asia," in Michael Kammen, ed., *The Past Before Us: Contemporary Historical Writing in the United States* (Ithaca, N.Y.: Cornell University Press, 1980), p. 177.

10. See especially Franz Michael in collaboration with Chung-li Chang, *The Taiping Rebellion: History and Documents,* vol. 1, *History* (Seattle: University of Washington Press, 1966), pp. 3–4 and passim; Philip A. Kuhn, "The Taiping Rebellion," in John K. Fairbank, ed., *The Cambridge History of China,* vol. 10, *Late Ch'ing, 1800–1911, Part 1* (Cambridge: Cambridge University Press, 1978), p. 279; and Joseph R. Levenson, *Confucian China and Its Modern Fate,* vol. 2, *The Problem of Monarchical Decay* (Berkeley: University of California Press, 1964), pp. 87, 91, 101–103.

11. Michael and Chang, *The Taiping Rebellion,* vol. 1, p. 84; see also *ibid.,* pp. 190, 198–199.

12. See, e.g., Ida Pruitt, *Old Madam Yin: A Memoir of Peking Life* (Stanford, Calif.: Stanford University Press, 1979), p. 58.

13. Mary C. Wright, *The Last Stand of Chinese Conservatism: The T'ung-chih Restoration, 1862–1874,* rev. ed. (New York: Atheneum, 1965), pp. viii–ix.

14. This theme is brought out repeatedly in Paul A. Cohen and John E. Schrecker, eds., *Reform in Nineteenth-Century China* (Cambridge: East Asian Research Center, Harvard University, 1976). It is further addressed in chapter 4.

15. Wright, *The Last Stand of Chinese Conservatism,* ch. 8. For a more recent treatment of the T'ung-chih Restoration, which supports Wright's analysis in some respects and modifies it in others, see Kwang-Ching Liu, "The Ch'ing Restoration," in Fairbank, *The Cambridge History of China,* 10:409–490, 606–608.

16. This is a major point in James Polachek's piece, "Gentry Hegemony: Soochow in the T'ung-chih Restoration," in Frederic Wakeman, Jr., and Carolyn Grant, eds., *Conflict and Control in Late Imperial China* (Berkeley: University of California Press, 1975), pp. 211–256.

17. Cited in Teng and Fairbank, *China's Response to the West,* p. 48.

18. Wright, *The Last Stand of Chinese Conservatism,* pp. 8, 9.

19. Some have questioned whether a genuine restoration even took place. See Polachek, "Gentry Hegemony," passim; Franz Michael's introductory essay, "Regionalism in Nineteenth-Century China," in Stanley Spector, *Li Hung-chang and the Huai Army: A Study in Nineteenth-Century Chinese Regionalism* (Seattle: University of Washington Press, 1964), p. xlii; and Jonathan Ocko, *Bureaucratic Reform in Provincial China: Ting Jih-ch'ang in Restoration Kiangsu, 1867–1870* (Cambridge: Council on East Asian Studies, Harvard University, 1983).

20. Wright, *The Last Stand of Chinese Conservatism,* p. 9.

21. See Philip A. Kuhn, *Rebellion and Its Enemies in Late Imperial China: Militarization and Social Structure, 1796–1864* (Cambridge: Harvard University Press,

1970); and Polachek, "Gentry Hegemony." Mary Rankin makes a similar point for the Kuang-hsu period in " 'Public Opinion' and Political Power: *Qingyi* in Late Nineteenth-Century China," *Journal of Asian Studies* (May 1982), 41(3):459–460.

22. Summaries of Feng's reform ideas on local administration may be found in Liu, "The Ch'ing Restoration," pp. 487–488, and Philip A. Kuhn, "Local Self-Government Under the Republic: Problems of Control, Autonomy, and Mobilization," in Wakeman and Grant, *Conflict and Control in Late Imperial China,* pp. 265–268.

23. Kuhn, "Local Self-Government Under the Republic," p. 265. Wang T'ao held views quite similar to Feng's. The likelihood of direct Western influence on Wang's political reform thought is, however, much greater. See Paul A. Cohen, *Between Tradition and Modernity: Wang T'ao and Reform in Late Ch'ing China* (Cambridge: Harvard University Press, 1974), pp. 210–226.

24. Liu, "The Ch'ing Restoration," p. 488.

25. Levenson, *Confucian China and Its Modern Fate,* 2:89.

26. This is certainly the burden of Levenson's analysis (see especially *ibid.,* p. 113); it has also, at least in some contexts, received support from Fairbank (see *East Asia: The Modern Transformation,* p. 330).

27. The case against this assumption is made by Albert Feuerwerker in his *State and Society in Eighteenth-Century China: The Ch'ing Empire in Its Glory* (Ann Arbor: Center for Chinese Studies, University of Michigan, 1976), pp. 69–71.

28. Wright, *The Last Stand of Chinese Conservatism,* p. 7.

29. See especially Teng and Fairbank, *China's Response to the West,* and Joseph Levenson, *Confucian China and Its Modern Fate,* vol. 1, *The Problem of Intellectual Continuity* (Berkeley: University of California Press, 1958).

30. Levenson, *Confucian China and Its Modern Fate,* 1:59–78. Levenson's analysis has been sharply challenged by Wang Erh-min and Lü Shih-ch'iang, among others. The revisionist position is summarized in Thomas L. Kennedy, "Self-Strengthening: An Analysis Based on Some Recent Writings," *Ch'ing-shih wen-t'i* (November 1974), 3(1):3–35. For a critical examination of the assumptions informing Levenson's approach, see chapter 2.

31. Ch'üan Han-sheng, "Ch'ing-mo te 'Hsi-hsueh yuan ch'u Chung-kuo' shuo" (The late Ch'ing theory that "Western learning originated in China"), in Li Ting-i et al., eds., *Chung-kuo chin-tai-shih lun-ts'ung* (Collected essays on modern Chinese history), 1st ser. (Taipei: Cheng-chung shu-chü, 1956), 5:216–258. See also Wang Erh-min, *Chung-kuo chin-tai ssu-hsiang shih lun,* pp. 50–51.

32. See Schwartz, *In Search of Wealth and Power.*

33. Cohen, *Between Tradition and Modernity,* pp. 152–153.

34. On K'ang's thought and the New Text revival of the nineteenth century, see Kung-chuan Hsiao, *A Modern China and a New World: K'ang Yu-wei, Reformer and Utopian, 1858–1927* (Seattle: University of Washington Press, 1975); Frederic Wakeman, Jr., *History and Will: Philosophical Perspectives of Mao Tse-tung's Thought* (Berkeley: University of California Press, 1973), pp. 101–136.

35. Self-strengthening efforts during the T'ung-chih period are detailed in Tingyee Kuo and Kwang-Ching Liu, "Self-Strengthening: The Pursuit of Western Technology," in Fairbank, *The Cambridge History of China,* 10:491–542.

36. Although it has been customary to portray Tz'u-hsi as an archconservative and Kuang-hsu as a supporter of radical reform, this picture has been sharply revised by recent research, which sees both Kuang-hsu and Tz'u-hsi as proponents of *moderate*

reform and explains the coup d'état more as a function of court politics (above all Tz'u-hsi's fears concerning her nephew's impetuosity and political ineptitude) than of ideology. See Sue Fawn Chung, "The Image of the Empress Dowager Tz'u-hsi," in Cohen and Schrecker, *Reform in Nineteenth-Century China,* pp. 101–110; Luke Kwong's forthcoming book, *A Mosaic of the Hundred Days: Personalities, Politics, and Ideas of 1898* (Cambridge: Council on East Asian Studies, Harvard University).

37. Kwong in *A Mosaic of the Hundred Days* radically downgrades K'ang's influence over Kuang-hsu and his contribution to the reform decrees of the Hundred Days; he sees K'ang's importance in the period as being primarily political and argues that he probably made more enemies of, than converts to, reform.

38. Kwong argues that the emperor played an essentially passive role in the reform process. Instead of formulating a well-designed, grand imperial strategy of reform, he in effect yielded the initiative to the bureaucracy, accumulating and sifting the reform proposals sent up by others in the form of memorials and issuing decrees in response. *Ibid.*

39. This point is suggested in James Polachek, "Reform at the Local and Provincial Level," in Cohen and Schrecker, *Reform in Nineteenth-Century China,* pp. 211–212.

40. The complex mix of indigenous and Western influences on local reform efforts in Chekiang in the latter decades of the nineteenth century is indicated in Mary Backus Rankin, "Local Reform Currents in Chekiang Before 1900," in Cohen and Schrecker, *Reform in Nineteenth-Century China,* pp. 221–230.

41. W. G. Beasley, ed., *Select Documents on Japanese Foreign Policy, 1853–1868* (London: Oxford University Press, 1955), introduction.

42. Spector, *Li Hung-chang and the Huai Army,* p. 153.

43. Marilyn Blatt Young makes much the same point in connection with Li's railroad-building plans for south Manchuria in the 1890s. See Young, *The Rhetoric of Empire: American China Policy, 1895–1901* (Cambridge: Harvard University Press, 1968), pp. 37–38. In the controversy over Li's goals as a self-strengthener, on the other hand, some scholars have placed more emphasis on his patriotic motives. See Kwang-Ching Liu, "The Confucian as Patriot and Pragmatist: Li Hung-chang's Formative Years, 1823–1866," *Harvard Journal of Asiatic Studies* (1970), 30:5–45; Liu, "The Ch'ing Restoration," p. 427; and Kuo and Liu, "Self-Strengthening," pp. 610–611.

44. Teng and Fairbank, *China's Response to the West,* p. 116; David Pong, "Confucian Patriotism and the Destruction of the Woosung Railway, 1877," *Modern Asian Studies* (1973), 7(4):647–676; Saundra Sturdevant, "Imperialism, Sovereignty, and Self-Strengthening: A Reassessment of the 1870s," in Cohen and Schrecker, *Reform in Nineteenth-Century China,* pp. 63–70. A number of other examples of patriotically motivated resistance to Western technological innovation are discussed by Sturdevant.

45. Esherick, *Reform and Revolution in China: The 1911 Revolution in Hunan and Hubei* (Berkeley: University of California Press, 1976), pp. 106–142 (the quotation is from p. 118). The same point is made by Ernest P. Young in *The Presidency of Yuan Shih-k'ai: Liberalism and Dictatorship in Early Republican China* (Ann Arbor: University of Michigan Press, 1977), pp. 18–19.

46. See Fairbank, Reischauer, and Craig, *East Asia: The Modern Transformation,* ch. 5, especially, pp. 313–315, 404–407; also John K. Fairbank, *The United States and China,* 4th ed. (Cambridge: Harvard University Press, 1979), pp. 196–201.

47. Kennedy's article, "Self-Strengthening," in its critical examination of the "what

went wrong?" approach to late nineteenth-century self-strengthening, makes essentially the same point.

48. Kennedy, for example, characterizes the changes begun by 1894 as "far more comprehensive and farsighted than earlier studies infer" (*ibid.*, p. 27). On the Chinese side, see the following pieces from the 1980 volume of *Li-shih yen-chiu* (Historical research): Li Shih-yueh, "Ts'ung yang-wu, wei-hsin tao tzu-ch'an chieh-chi ko-ming" (From Westernization and reform to bourgeois revolution), no. 1, pp. 31–40; Hsu T'ai-lai, "Yeh p'ing yang-wu yun-tung" (A further appraisal of the Westernization movement), no. 4, pp. 19–36; Ch'en Hsu-lu, "Chung-kuo chin-tai-shih shang te ko-ming yü kai-liang" (Revolution and reform in modern Chinese history), no. 6, pp. 3–19.

49. See, e.g., Fairbank, Reischauer and Craig, *East Asia: The Modern Transformation,* pp. 81, 313–315, 404–407.

50. The phrase is Cyril E. Black's. In his book, *The Dynamics of Modernization: A Study in Comparative History* (New York: Harper & Row, 1966), Black, adopting a worldwide perspective, argues for the existence of seven distinct patterns of political modernization. Significantly, he views China and Japan as belonging to the same pattern (along with Russia, Iran, Turkey, Afghanistan, Ethiopia, and Thailand).

51. The assault on Hsu and the devastating effect it had on his official career are discussed in Fred W. Drake, *China Charts the World: Hsu Chi-yü and His Geography of 1848* (Cambridge: East Asian Research Center, Harvard University, 1975), pp. 44–51.

52. Cited in Immanuel C. Y. Hsü, *China's Entrance into the Family of Nations: The Diplomatic Phase, 1858–1880* (Cambridge: Harvard University Press, 1960), p. 183.

53. Schwartz, *In Search of Wealth and Power,* pp. 15–16. The resonance with the strain of Maoism that stresses popular support over modern weaponry will not be lost on the reader. Indeed, there is much in the *ch'ing-i* style that seems to be echoed in Chinese political behavior in the Maoist era.

54. Eastman, *Throne and Mandarins: China's Search for a Policy During the Sino–French Controversy, 1880–1885* (Cambridge: Harvard University Press, 1967), p. 18. Our understanding of *ch'ing-i* as a political phenomenon has been greatly advanced by James Polachek's "Literati Groups and Literati Politics in Early Nineteenth-Century China," Ph.D. dissertation, University of California, Berkeley, 1974.

55. Schrecker, "The Reform Movement of 1898 and the *Ch'ing-i:* Reform as Opposition," in Cohen and Schrecker, *Reform in Nineteenth-Century China,* pp. 289–305; Rankin, " 'Public Opinion' and Political Power," pp. 453–454, 467–468. The about-face in *ch'ing-i* attitudes toward the West in the 1890s was paralleled by an equally spectacular reversal of previous *ch'ing-i* attitudes on collaborating with the foreign "enemy" in 1861. See Polachek, "Literati Groups and Literati Politics," pp. 381–382.

56. The ensuing discussion is partly based on Paul A. Cohen, *China and Christianity: The Missionary Movement and the Growth of Chinese Antiforeignism, 1860–1870* (Cambridge: Harvard University Press, 1963).

57. Griffith John, cited in *ibid.,* p. 85.

58. Edward Friedman suggests the intriguing thesis that Chinese mythology "for millennia located the source of pollution in foreigners," so that "to defeat the foreigners was to restore nature's harmony." Certainly this thesis is borne out by the popular anti-Christian literature and pictorial matter that I have seen. See Friedman's

Backward Toward Revolution: The Chinese Revolutionary Party (Berkeley: University of California Press, 1974), p. 130.

59. See Marianne Bastid-Bruguière, "Currents of Social Change," in John K. Fairbank and Kwang-Ching Liu, eds., *The Cambridge History of China,* vol. 11, *Late Ch'ing, 1800–1911, Part 2* (Cambridge: Cambridge University Press, 1980), pp. 535–602, esp. pp. 576–602 (quoted portions from pp. 586, 596); Chou Hsi-jui [Joseph Esherick], "Lun I-ho-ch'üan yun-tung te she-hui ch'eng-yin" (Social factors in the formation of the Boxer movement), *Wen-shih-che* (Literature, history, and philosophy) (January 1981), 1:22–31.

60. This is clearly seen in some of the more influential writings of John Fairbank. See, especially, *China's Response to the West* and the portions of *The United States and China,* 4th ed., dealing with the nineteenth century. It also figures prominently in Joseph Levenson's work.

61. For a devastating attack on the seesaw or teeter-totter theory of historical process, see J. H. Hexter, *Reappraisals in History* (New York: Harper & Row, 1963), pp. 40–43. The parallel example of the tradition–modernity polarity is discussed in chapter 2.

2. MOVING BEYOND "TRADITION AND MODERNITY"

1. A notable exception is the recent volume, edited by Gilbert Rozman, *The Modernization of China* (New York: Free Press, 1981). The authors of this book, several of them historians, attempt a systematic application of modernization theory to post-1700 China.

2. One critic of modernization theory, Dean C. Tipps, has argued compellingly that "modernization" is an illusion and that the entire idea should be discarded in favor of some alternative approach. See his "Modernization Theory and the Comparative Study of Societies: A Critical Perspective," *Comparative Studies in Society and History* (March 1973), 15:199–226. Far more typical is the attitude of Raymond Grew, who, while acknowledging all of the criticisms that can be leveled at modernization theory, still feels that it can be used without harmful consequences and should be retained. See his "Modernization and Its Discontents," *American Behavioral Scientist* (November–December 1977), 21(2):289–312.

3. Wilbert E. Moore and Neil J. Smelser, foreword, in S. N. Eisenstadt, *Modernization: Protest and Change* (Englewood Cliffs, N.J.: Prentice-Hall, 1966), p. iii.

4. See, e.g., Tipps, "Modernization Theory and the Comparative Study of Societies," pp. 200–201 and passim.

5. Herder's views are summarized in R. G. Collingwood, *The Idea of History* (Oxford: Oxford University Press, 1961), p. 90; the quotations are from Raymond Dawson, "Western Conceptions of Chinese Civilization," in Raymond Dawson, ed., *The Legacy of China* (Oxford: Clarendon Press, 1964), pp. 14–15.

6. Quoted in Stuart Creighton Miller, *The Unwelcome Immigrant: The American Image of the Chinese, 1785–1882* (Berkeley: University of California Press, 1969), p. 16. An explanation of Chinese stagnation was offered by the American clergyman, Josiah Strong (1893): "In Asia there have been vast organizations of society, but the development of the individual was early arrested, hence the stagnation of everything.

Oriental civilization manifests unity with but little diversity, hence the dead uniformity of many centuries." Cited in Alexander Saxton, *The Indispensable Enemy: Labor and the Anti-Chinese Movement in California* (Berkeley: University of California Press, 1971), p. 279.

7. Quoted in Dawson, "Western Conceptions of Chinese Civilization," p. 14.

8. In Karl Marx, *Capital and Other Writings,* Max Eastman, ed. (New York: Modern Library, 1932), p. 325.

9. Cited in Shlomo Avineri, ed., *Karl Marx on Colonialism and Modernization* (Garden City, N.Y.: Doubleday, 1968), p. 45.

10. Levenson's major completed works were *Liang Ch'i-ch'ao and the Mind of Modern China* (Cambridge: Harvard University Press, 1953); and the individually published volumes of the trilogy, *Confucian China and Its Modern Fate:* vol. 1, *The Problem of Intellectual Continuity* (Berkeley: University of California Press, 1958); vol. 2, *The Problem of Monarchical Decay* (Berkeley: University of California Press, 1964); vol. 3, *The Problem of Historical Significance* (Berkeley: University of California Press, 1965). For a full bibliography of Levenson's writings, see Maurice Meisner and Rhoads Murphey, eds., *The Mozartian Historian: Essays on the Works of Joseph R. Levenson* (Berkeley: University of California Press, 1976), pp. 197–203.

11. See Vera Schwarcz's long review of *The Mozartian Historian,* in *History and Theory: Studies in the Philosophy of History* (1978), 17(3):349–367.

12. Tipps, in "Modernization Theory and the Comparative Study of Societies," would take issue with this, arguing that "though the terminology of contemporary modernization theory has been cleaned up some to give a more neutral impression—it speaks of 'modernity' rather than 'civilization,' 'tradition' rather than 'barbarism'—it continues to evaluate the progress of nations, like its nineteenth-century forebears, by their proximity to the institutions and values of Western, and particularly Anglo-Saxon societies" (p. 206).

13. The reader is referred to two interesting pieces that appeared in the *New York Times* shortly after the release of the American hostages. One, by Bayly Winder, discusses the intensification of cultural stereotyping in conflict situations; the other, a confidential cable sent on August 13, 1979 (just before the hostage crisis began) from L. Bruce Laingen, the American chargé d'affaires in Teheran, to Secretary of State Vance, is a perfect example of such stereotyping (*New York Times,* January 27, 1981, p. A19; January 30, 1981, p. A27).

14. Carr, *What is History?* (New York: Vintage Books, 1961), p. 26.

15. Edwin O. Reischauer and John K. Fairbank, *East Asia: The Great Tradition* (Boston: Houghton Mifflin, 1960).

16. Fairbank, Reischauer and Craig, *East Asia: The Modern Transformation* (Boston: Houghton Mifflin, 1965), p. 5. The "change within tradition" formula was, I believe, first used by E. A. Kracke in "Sung Society: Change Within Tradition," *Far Eastern Quarterly* (August 1955), 14(4):479–488. It is reiterated by Fairbank in the introductory chapter of John K. Fairbank, ed. *The Cambridge History of China,* vol. 10, *Late Ch'ing, 1800–1911, Part 1* (Cambridge: Cambridge University Press, 1978), pp. 6–8. It also finds support in Albert Feuerwerker, *State and Society in Eighteenth-Century China: The Ch'ing Empire in Its Glory* (Ann Arbor: Center for Chinese Studies, University of Michigan, 1976), p. 113; and in Richard Smith, "An Approach to the Study of Traditional Chinese Culture," *Chinese Culture* (June 1978), 19(2):75.

17. Or, as Tipps puts it: " 'Traditional societies' appeared changeless only because

they were defined in a manner that . . . recognized no significant change save that in the direction of the Western experience" ("Modernization Theory and the Comparative Study of Societies," p. 213). See also Lloyd I. Rudolph and Susanne Hoeber Rudolph, *The Modernity of Tradition: Political Development in India* (Chicago: University of Chicago Press, 1972), p. 5.

18. As confirmation of this, Fairbank's account of Chinese society in the nineteenth century (mainly in chs. 2 and 5) is liberally peppered with such words as "inertia," "equilibrium," "stability." Fairbank's early views concerning the Chinese economy on the eve of the Western intrusion reflect much the same sort of thinking. In a well-known article, written in collaboration with Alexander Eckstein and Lien-sheng Yang, he portrayed the Chinese economy in the early nineteenth century as being in a stage of "traditional equilibrium," a stage in which "minor growth, innovation and technological change may occur but . . . not sufficient to break the rigid and inhibiting bonds of the traditional framework of social and economic institutions." "Economic Change in Early Modern China: An Analytic Framework," *Economic Development and Cultural Change* (October 1960), 9(1):1.

19. Immanuel C. Y. Hsü, *The Rise of Modern China* (New York: Oxford University Press, 1970), p. 6; the same passage appears in the 2d ed. (1975), p. 6, and 3d ed. (1983), p. 6, of Hsü's text.

20. Wittfogel, *Oriental Despotism: A Comparative Study of Total Power* (New Haven, Conn.: Yale University Press, 1957), p. 420 (emphasis in original).

21. Levenson, *Confucian China and Its Modern Fate,* 1:14.

22. For Levenson's discussion of the difference between vocabulary change and language change, see *ibid.,* 1:156–163, also, 3:113.

23. *Ibid.,* 1:161 (emphasis supplied).

24. *Ibid.*

25. See, e.g., Levenson, "The Genesis of *Confucian China and Its Modern Fate,*" in L. P. Curtis, Jr., ed., *The Historian's Workshop* (New York: Knopf, 1970), p. 282, where Levenson alludes to the variability of Confucianism over the centuries.

26. Or, as Benjamin Schwartz put it in his analysis of Levenson: "We have something like the vital wholeness of a total culture which is able to maintain itself for centuries as a kind of durable entity. Chinese culture was not outside of history, but it was powerful enough to freeze its flow." See his "History and Culture in the Thought of Joseph Levenson," in Meisner and Murphey, *The Mozartian Historian,* p. 105.

27. As Arthur H. Smith, a major missionary publicist of the late nineteenth century, put it: "To attempt to reform China without 'some force from without' is like trying to build a ship in the sea; all the laws of air and water conspire to make it impossible." *Chinese Characteristics,* reprint ed. (Port Washington, N.Y.: Kennikat Press, 1970), p. 324. For comparable statements, see Jerry Israel, *Progressivism and the Open Door: America and China, 1905–1921* (Pittsburgh, Penn.: University of Pittsburgh Press, 1971), p. 16; Robert McClellan, *The Heathen Chinee: A Study of American Attitudes Toward China, 1890–1905* (Columbus: Ohio State University Press, 1971), pp. 180–181.

28. Dona Torr, ed., *Marx on China, 1853–1860: Articles from the New York Daily Tribune* (London: Lawrence and Wishart, 1951), p. 4.

29. Fairbank, Reischauer, and Craig, *East Asia: The Modern Transformation,* pp. 6–7.

30. Kuhn, *Rebellion and Its Enemies in Late Imperial China: Militarization and*

Social Structure, 1796–1864 (Cambridge: Harvard University Press, 1970), pp. 1–2, 5–6. While the monetization of the Chinese economy was to a considerable extent due to the inflow of foreign silver and was thus of partly exogenous origin, Kuhn suggests that population explosion alone might have spelled "disaster of a new sort for traditional Chinese society" (*ibid.*, p. 51). Although here, too, exogenous factors were at work, recent studies appear to place more weight on internal causation (see n. 59 this chapter).

31. Levenson, *Confucian China and Its Modern Fate*, 1:3.

32. See Joseph R. Levenson, ed., *European Expansion and the Counter-Example of Asia, 1300–1600* (Englewood Cliffs, N.J.: Prentice-Hall, 1967). The same sort of question underlies Levenson's discussion of the amateur–specialist dichotomy in *Confucian China and Its Modern Fate*, 1:15–43.

33. Levenson, *Confucian China and Its Modern Fate*, 1:xix.

34. *Ibid.*, 3:48 ff. A report on a conference on the sprouts of capitalism question, convened in 1980 at Shantung University, observed that Chinese historians have been virtually unanimous in their belief that capitalist sprouts emerged in China *prior* to the Opium War (*Jen-min jih-pao*, February 25, 1980, p. 5). For a recent assertion of this point of view, see Liu Yao, "Ts'ung Ch'ang-chiang chung-hsia-yu ti-ch'ü nung-ts'un ching-chi te pien-hua k'an T'ai-p'ing t'ien-kuo ko-ming te li-shih tso-yung" (The historical role of the Taiping revolution seen from the perspective of changes in the rural economy in the middle and lower reaches of the Yangtze River), *Li-shih yen-chiu* (Historical research) (June 1979), 6:47–48. The authority on which discussions of this topic have centered is Mao's assertion in 1939: "As China's feudal society had developed a commodity economy, and so carried within itself the seeds of capitalism, China would of herself have developed slowly into a capitalist society even without the impact of foreign capitalism." *The Chinese Revolution and the Chinese Communist Party*, in *Selected Works of Mao Tse-tung*, vol. 2 (Peking: Foreign Languages Press, 1965), p. 309. See also Albert Feuerwerker, "From 'Feudalism' to 'Capitalism' in Recent Historical Writing from Mainland China," *Journal of Asian Studies* (November 1958), 18(1):107–115; the same author's "China's History in Marxian Dress," *American Historical Review* (January 1961), 66(2):327–330; and more recently, Arif Dirlik, "Chinese Historians and the Marxist Concept of Capitalism: A Critical Examination," *Modern China* (January 1982), 8(1):105–132, esp. p. 106. The whole "sprouts" question is considerably complicated by the impact of the importation of foreign silver on the monetization of the Chinese economy beginning in the late Ming. For a recent discussion, see William S. Atwell, "Notes on Silver, Foreign Trade, and the Late Ming Economy," *Ch'ing-shih wen-t'i* (December 1977), 3(8):1–33.

35. The parameters of the unfinished trilogy are outlined by Frederic Wakeman in his foreword to Joseph R. Levenson, *Revolution and Cosmopolitanism: The Western Stage and the Chinese Stages* (Berkeley: University of California Press, 1971).

36. Levenson, "The Genesis of *Confucian China and Its Modern Fate*," p. 280.

37. Levenson, *Liang Ch'i-ch'ao*, p. 198.

38. Levenson, *Confucian China and Its Modern Fate*, 1:xvi, xix, 50, 58.

39. See Arthur Waley, *The Opium War Through Chinese Eyes* (London: Allen and Unwin, 1958).

40. Levenson, *Confucian China and Its Modern Fate*, 1:54, 57.

41. See the careful study by Han-yin Chen Shen, "Tseng Kuo-fan in Peking,

1840–1852: His Ideas on Statecraft and Reform," *Journal of Asian Studies* (November 1967), 27(1):61–80, esp. pp. 62–64, 69.

42. Hao Chang, *Liang Ch'i-ch'ao and Intellectual Transition in China, 1890–1907* (Cambridge: Harvard University Press, 1971), pp. 3–5; Guy S. Alitto, *The Last Confucian: Liang Shu-ming and the Chinese Dilemma of Modernity* (Berkeley: University of California Press, 1979).

43. Levenson, *Liang Ch'i-ch'ao,* pp. 84–85.

44. Levenson, *Confucian China and Its Modern Fate,* 1:158–159. See also *ibid.,* 3:113: "Europe and pre-modern China, reaching each other only through intellectual diffusion, had only broadened each other's cultural vocabulary . . . the Chinese cultural language changed in the nineteenth and twentieth centuries, when social subversion, not just intellectual diffusion, was set off by the West."

45. *Ibid.,* 1:145, 162–163 (emphasis supplied).

46. To use Levenson's own metaphor (*ibid.,* 3:104). For a late nineteenth-century formulation of the same idea, see n. 27. In the same vein, see James T. C. Liu's remark: "It seems that no force—social, political, or economic—could possibly emerge from within that society itself to cause radical changes, let alone to tear apart the integration . . . formed over many centuries. The only force capable of causing a disintegration had to come from the outside: an overpowering assault that brought drastic changes in the economy and economic geography, an intellectual revolution, and an institutional breakdown." "Integrative Factors Through Chinese History: Their Interaction," in James T. C. Liu and Wei-ming Tu, eds., *Traditional China* (Englewood Cliffs, N.J.: Prentice-Hall, 1970), pp. 22–23.

47. Eisenstadt, "Convergence and Divergence of Modern and Modernizing Societies: Indications from the Analysis of the Structuring of Social Hierarchies in Middle Eastern Societies," *International Journal of Middle East Studies* (January 1977), 8(1):1; also pp. 3–4.

48. Levenson, *Liang Ch'i-ch'ao,* p. 8. Here, as well as in *Confucian China and Its Modern Fate,* 1:187 n.12, Levenson cited Marion Levy's *The Family Revolution in Modern China* (Cambridge: Harvard University Press, 1949) in support of his views on convergence.

49. Wright, *The Last Stand of Chinese Conservatism: The T'ung-chih Restoration, 1862–1874,* rev. ed. (New York: Atheneum, 1965), pp. 9–10; see also p. 300, where the author states: "The failure of the T'ung-chih Restoration demonstrated with a rare clarity that even in the most favorable circumstances there is no way in which an effective modern state can be grafted onto a Confucian society."

50. Feuerwerker, *China's Early Industrialization: Sheng Hsuan-huai (1844–1916) and Mandarin Enterprise* (Cambridge: Harvard University Press, 1958).

51. Schwartz, "History and Culture in the Thought of Joseph Levenson," pp. 108–109. Schwartz raises further questions concerning the tradition–modernity contrast in "The Limits of 'Tradition Versus Modernity' as Categories of Explanation: The Case of the Chinese Intellectuals," *Daedalus* (Spring 1972), 101(2):71–88; see also his "Notes on Conservatism in General and in China in Particular," in Charlotte Furth, ed., *The Limits of Change: Essays on Conservative Alternatives in Republican China* (Cambridge: Harvard University Press, 1976), pp. 18–21.

52. Rudolph and Rudolph, *The Modernity of Tradition,* pp. 4–6.

53. See, e.g., Tipps, "Modernization Theory and the Comparative Study of So-

cieties," passim; Reinhard Bendix, "Tradition and Modernity Reconsidered," *Comparative Studies in Society and History* (April 1967), 9:326, 345–346; Joseph R. Gusfield, "Tradition and Modernity: Misplaced Polarities in the Study of Social Change," *American Journal of Sociology* (January 1967), 72:351–362; C. S. Whitaker, Jr., "A Dysrhythmic Process of Political Change," *World Politics* (1967), 19(2):190–217.

54. Rozman, *The Modernization of China,* passim; Stuart Schram, *Mao Tse-tung* (New York: Simon & Schuster, 1966), p. 14; Dwight H. Perkins, "Introduction: The Persistence of the Past," in Dwight H. Perkins, ed., *China's Modern Economy in Historical Perspective* (Stanford, Calif.: Stanford University Press, 1975), p. 3; Thomas L. Kennedy, "Self-Strengthening: An Analysis Based on Some Recent Writings," *Ch'ing-shih wen-t'i* (November 1974), 3(1):9–10; Evelyn Sakakida Rawski, *Education and Popular Literacy in Ch'ing China* (Ann Arbor: University of Michigan Press, 1979), pp. 140, 149–154. Rawski's thesis is summarized in chapter 4 of this book.

55. Friedman, *Backward Toward Revolution: The Chinese Revolutionary Party* (Berkeley: University of California Press, 1974), p. 224.

56. *Ibid.,* pp. 4, 120–121; see also pp. 118, 130–131, 136–137, 146–147, 158–159, 220–222.

57. Schram, *Mao Tse-tung,* pp. 60, 322.

58. Stuart Schram, "Introduction: The Cultural Revolution in Historical Perspective," in Stuart Schram, ed., *Authority, Participation, and Cultural Change in China* (Cambridge: Cambridge University Press, 1973), pp. 6–7.

59. To the extent that it resulted from the introduction of new food crops from the Americas, the tripling of the Chinese population between 1600 and 1850 was, of course, only partly endogenous. Overall, however, the role of new foods was probably less crucial than other, basically internal factors. See Dwight H. Perkins, *Agricultural Development in China, 1368–1968* (Chicago: Aldine, 1969), pp. 13, 47–51, 184–185, and passim; Albert Feuerwerker, *Rebellion in Nineteenth-Century China* (Ann Arbor: Center for Chinese Studies, University of Michigan, 1975), pp. 47–48.

60. Kuhn, "Local Self-Government Under the Republic: Problems of Control, Autonomy, and Mobilization," in Frederic Wakeman, Jr., and Carolyn Grant, eds., *Conflict and Control in Late Imperial China* (Berkeley: University of California Press, 1975), pp. 257–298.

61. Feng, as we saw in chapter 1, spent time in Shanghai in the 1860s and seems to have learned something about the tradition and practice of representative government in the West. While Kuhn acknowledges that this information might have "excited resonances with [Feng's] own *feng-chien* inheritance," he does not feel that there is sufficient evidence at present to warrant the conclusion that Western ideas in this area exerted a shaping influence on Feng's thought (see *ibid.,* p. 265).

62. One aspect of this analysis that I have omitted from my summary is Kuhn's discussion of local elites in the late imperial and republican eras. These elites formed a vital part of the contextual framework both for the problems of local government and for the periodic efforts to resolve these problems.

63. Yü-sheng Lin, *The Crisis of Chinese Consciousness: Radical Antitraditionalism in the May Fourth Era* (Madison: University of Wisconsin Press, 1979); see also Lin's earlier essay, "Radical Iconoclasm in the May Fourth Period and the Future of Chinese Liberalism," in Benjamin Schwartz, ed., *Reflections on the May Fourth Movement: A Symposium* (Cambridge: East Asian Research Center, Harvard University, 1972), pp. 23–58. The earlier piece, in terms of the argument advanced in this

chapter, seems somewhat contradictory in nature. While accepting in general terms the proposition that modernization need not imply the total rejection of tradition and that "the establishment of a viable modern society [may be] greatly helped rather than impaired by some elements from a cultural tradition" (pp. 26–27), with respect to China in particular it appears to embody the spirit at least of the older position: "The corrosion of the traditional political and cultural order was . . . a long and complex process that covered the whole history of Western intrusion and was affected by the lack of viable indigenous forces in traditional Chinese society which could cope with the Western challenge" (p. 28).

64. Jerome B. Grieder, "The Question of 'Politics' in the May Fourth Era," in Schwartz, *Reflections on the May Fourth Movement*, p. 99.

65. Merle Goldman, introduction, in Merle Goldman, ed., *Modern Chinese Literature in the May Fourth Era* (Cambridge: Harvard University Press, 1977), p. 5. Guy Alitto, commenting on the motives underlying Liang Shu-ming's behavior in 1917, makes the same point: "Responsibility for the spiritual and material welfare of the people was what he had been born to. It was also natural that he should call on the educated to come forth and fulfill their responsibility to society" (*The Last Confucian*, p. 61).

66. Hao Chang, *Liang Ch'i-ch'ao and Intellectual Transition in China*, p. 3.

67. *Ibid.*, passim. I-fan Ch'eng's "*Kung* as an Ethos in Late Nineteenth-Century China: The Case of Wang Hsien-ch'ien (1842–1918)," in Paul A. Cohen and John E. Schrecker, eds., *Reform in Nineteenth-Century China* (Cambridge: East Asian Research Center, Harvard University, 1976), pp. 170–180. Don Price's book is entitled *Russia and the Roots of the Chinese Revolution, 1896–1911* (Cambridge: Harvard University Press, 1974).

68. See de Bary's introduction in Wm. Theodore de Bary et al., eds., *The Unfolding of Neo-Confucianism* (New York: Columbia University Press, 1975), esp. pp. 1–2, 32; also the interview with him in Paul M. Evans, "Fairbank: Intellect and Enterprise in American China Scholarship, 1936–1961," Ph.D. dissertation, Dalhousie University, Halifax, Nova Scotia, 1982, p. 381, n. 35.

69. Thomas A. Metzger, *Escape from Predicament: Neo-Confucianism and China's Evolving Political Culture* (New York: Columbia University Press, 1977), p. 197.

70. *Ibid.*, p. 17.

71. *Ibid.*, pp. 214–215.

72. See *ibid.*, pp. 3–4, 200–201; Max Weber, *The Religion of China*, trans. Hans Gerth (Glencoe, Ill.: Free Press, 1951), pp. 226–249.

73. Metzger notes the Weberian influence on S.N. Eisenstadt's picture of Confucian ideology as "stagnative" and "nontransformative" (*Escape from Predicament*, p. 4).

74. *Ibid.*, pp. 49, 160.

75. *Ibid.*, pp. 39–40.

76. Which is, of course, exactly what Weber did also. It is hard to conceive of how *any* ethical system can exist that does not center on the tension between ethical demand and human shortcoming. Two of the basic texts of Neo-Confucianism, the *Book of Mencius* and the *Analects*, develop this tension on virtually every page. (What are Confucius' assertions concerning the difficulty of attaining *jen*, if not a statement of profound human shortcoming?) Yet Weber, because he apparently *assumed* an absence of ethical tension in Confucianism, was unable to "see" what lay

before his very eyes. H.D. Harootunian, although using a very different vocabulary in his analysis, arrives at a similar concern over Metzger's emphasis on the centrality of the Neo-Confucian sense of predicament. See his "Metzger's Predicament," *Journal of Asian Studies* (February 1980), 39(2):251.

77. Metzger, *Escape from Predicament*, p. 211.

78. Elvin, *The Pattern of the Chinese Past: A Social and Economic Interpretation* (Stanford, Calif: Stanford University Press, 1973), pp. 312–315. Elvin, although British, has acknowledged his intellectual indebtedness to a number of American scholars. The influence that he, in turn, has exerted on American economists and economic historians is undeniable. See, e.g., the discussion of Robert Dernberger's ideas in chapter 3 of this book.

79. See, e.g., Nathan Sivin's review article, "Imperial China: Has Its Present Past a Future?" *Harvard Journal of Asiatic Studies* (December 1978), 38(2):449–480, esp. pp. 459–462, 477–480.

80. Mary C. Wright, "Revolution from Without?" *Comparative Studies in Society and History* (1962), 4:247.

81. This has been especially true of studies in the subfield of intellectual history. My own book, *Between Tradition and Modernity: Wang T'ao and Reform in Late Ch'ing China* (Cambridge: Harvard University Press, 1974), may be cited as one example. Another is Alitto's *The Last Confucian*. Alitto's subject, Liang Shu-ming, believed that Confucianism not only was not incompatible with Chinese modernization but was the only possible basis for such modernization. Alitto himself, clearly unpersuaded by Liang, at times seems to come close to the older view of the absolute incompatibility between tradition (at least Liang's version of it) and modernity; see, e.g., pp. 274–278.

82. See, e.g., Schwartz, "History and Culture in the Thought of Joseph Levenson," passim; see also Cohen, *Between Tradition and Modernity*, pp. 88–90.

83. J.H. Hexter, *Reappraisals in History* (New York: Harper & Row, 1963), pp. 40-43.

84. See L.E. Shiner, "Tradition/Modernity: An Ideal Type Gone Astray," *Comparative Studies in Society and History* (1975), 17:252.

85. Tipps, "Modernization Theory and the Comparative Study of Societies," p. 215; see also Bendix, "Tradition and Modernity Reconsidered," pp. 316, 329.

86. *New York Times*, November 9, 1980, p. 1.

87. For an illuminating critique of the notion of "traditional society," see Tipps, "Modernization Theory and the Comparative Study of Societies," pp. 212–213. Shiner argues that, since the tradition-modernity polarity ought properly to be construed as an ideal type, any efforts to make it empirically descriptive are *in principle* wrong. The lack of congruity between the concept of "tradition" and the empirical reality of "traditional societies" is, for him, beside the point ("Tradition/Modernity," passim).

88. Joseph LaPalombara, "Bureaucracy and Political Development: Notes, Queries, and Dilemmas," in Joseph LaPalombara, ed., *Bureaucracy and Political Development* (Princeton, N.J.: Princeton University Press, 1963), pp. 38–39.

89. Tipps, "Modernization Theory and the Comparative Study of Societies," p. 216. The Western-centric bias of modernization theory has been widely noted. See, e.g., Ali A. Mazrui, "From Social Darwinism to Current Theories of Modernization," *World Politics* (October 1968), 21(1): 69–83.

90. Schrecker, "The West in Outside Perspective: An Introduction to the Inter-cultural-Historical Method" (unpublished paper), p. 2. Compare Schrecker's observation with the following three declarations by Denis de Rougement, in *The Meaning of Europe* (London: Sidgwick and Jackson, 1963), p. 12: "1. Europe discovered the whole of the earth, and nobody ever came and discovered Europe. 2. Europe has held sway on all the continents in succession, and up till now has never been ruled by any foreign power. 3. Europe has produced a civilization which is being imitated by the whole world, while the converse has never happened." See also Ruth Benedict who, in discussing the psychological consequences of the spread of the white man's culture into every corner of the world, wrote: "This world-wide cultural diffusion has protected us as man had never been protected before from having to take seriously the civilizations of other peoples; it has given to our culture and [*sic*] massive universality that we have long ceased to account for historically, and which we read off rather as necessary and inevitable." *Patterns of Culture* (New York: Mentor Books, 1952), pp. 5–6.

91. This paradox is perfectly illustrated in a statement made by Edward Shils: "At present [1961] the whole intellectual world outside the West, even the most creative parts of that world, is in a state of provinciality. It is preoccupied with Western achievements, it is fascinated and drawn to the intellectual output of the West. Even Japan, the Soviet Union and China, which in their different ways have many greatly creative intellectuals, are concerned with the West, and not just for reasons of state or for military and strategic reasons. They are transfixed by its shining light. They lack intellectual self-confidence and intellectual self-esteem." On one level, Shils is quite correct (and needlessly defensive) in characterizing the West as the world's intellectual center and everything outside the West as the provinces. What he fails to see is that on another level it is the West that exists "in a state of provinciality" by virtue of the fact that of all the cultures of the modern world it alone has not had the experience of having a center outside itself by which *it* is, in some sense, "transfixed." See Edward Shils, *The Intellectual Between Tradition and Modernity: The Indian Situation* (The Hague: Mouton, 1961), p. 13.

3. IMPERIALISM: REALITY OR MYTH?

1. *On New Democracy*, in *Selected Works of Mao Tse-tung*, vol. 2 (Peking: Foreign Languages Press, 1965), p. 354.

2. Peck, "The Roots of Rhetoric: The Professional Ideology of America's China Watchers," *Bulletin of Concerned Asian Scholars* (October 1969), 2(1):59–69. Peck's article, with minor changes and additions, is reprinted in Edward Friedman and Mark Selden, eds., *America's Asia: Dissenting Essays on Asian–American Relations* (New York: Vintage Books, 1971), pp. 40–66.

3. John K. Fairbank, Edwin O. Reischauer and Albert M. Craig, *East Asia: The Modern Transformation* (Boston: Houghton Mifflin, 1965), pp. 5, 9–10.

4. Marion Levy, "Contrasting Factors in the Modernization of China and Japan," *Economic Development and Cultural Change* (1953), 2:163–164.

5. John K. Fairbank, "The Great Wall," *New York Review of Books*, March 28, 1968, p. 28.

6. Fairbank, Reischauer and Craig, *East Asia: The Modern Transformation*, p. 404.

7. Jack Belden, *China Shakes the World* (New York: Harper, 1949), p. 3.

8. Reischauer, *Wanted: An Asian Policy* (New York: Knopf, 1955), pp. 101–102.

9. The internal quote is from Gunnar Myrdal, "International Inequalities," in Richard S. Weckstein, ed., *Expansion of World Trade and the Growth of National Economies* (New York: Harper, 1968), p. 63.

10. This long summation of Peck's position is drawn from "The Roots of Rhetoric," pp. 60–65.

11. Fairbank and Peck, "An Exchange," *Bulletin of Concerned Asian Scholars* (April–July 1970), 2(3):51–54.

12. *Ibid.*, pp. 54, 57, 66.

13. For the Wittfogel–Schwartz controversy, see Karl A. Wittfogel, "The Legend of 'Maoism,'" *China Quarterly* (January–March 1960), 1:72–86, and (April–June 1960), 2:16–31; Benjamin Schwartz, "The Legend of the 'Legend of "Maoism,"'" *ibid.*, 2:35–42; Karl A. Wittfogel, Benjamin Schwartz, and Henryk Sjaardema, "'Maoism'—'Legend' or 'Legend of a "Legend"'?" *ibid.* (October–December 1960), 4:88–101. The issue between Levenson and Hummel was over Levenson's treatment of Liang Ch'i-ch'ao in his book, *Liang Ch'i-ch'ao and the Mind of Modern China* (Cambridge: Harvard University Press, 1953). Hummel's attack on the book is in *Far Eastern Quarterly* (November 1954), 14(1):110–112. Levenson's rejoinder and Donald L. Keene's defense of Levenson are in *ibid.* (May 1955), 14(3):435–439.

14. "Symposium on Chinese Studies and the Disciplines," *Journal of Asian Studies* (August 1964), 23(4):505.

15. White's complaint, voiced in 1966, is cited in Michael Kammen, "Introduction: The Historian's Vocation and the State of the Discipline in the United States," in Michael Kammen, ed., *The Past Before Us: Contemporary Historical Writing in the United States* (Ithaca, N.Y.: Cornell University Press, 1980), p. 33.

16. Fairbank and Peck, "An Exchange," p. 54; John K. Fairbank, letter to editor, August 4, 1970, *Bulletin of Concerned Asian Scholars* (Fall 1970), 2(4):117–118.

17. James Peck, "Revolution Versus Modernization and Revisionism: A Two-Front Struggle," in Victor Nee and James Peck, eds., *China's Uninterrupted Revolution: From 1840 to the Present* (New York: Pantheon, 1975), pp. 88, 90.

18. Nee and Peck, "Introduction: Why Uninterrupted Revolution?" in *ibid.*, p. 6.

19. *Ibid.*, pp. 3–4; see also Peck, "Revolution Versus Modernization and Revisionism," p. 91.

20. Nee and Peck, "Introduction," pp. 10–11, 14, 34; also Peck, "Revolution Versus Modernization and Revisionism," p. 91.

21. Nee and Peck, "Introduction," pp. 14, 33.

22. Peck, "Revolution Versus Modernization and Revisionism," pp. 90–93.

23. Nee and Peck, "Introduction," p. 3.

24. Peck, "Revolution Versus Modernization and Revisionism," p. 93.

25. The emergence of embryonic capitalism is an ambiguous indicator of endogenous change for two reasons: first, it is not clear that it was entirely endogenous (see chapter 2, n. 34); and second, it is argued by at least some Chinese economic historians that not much change really resulted. See, e.g., Fu Zhufu, "The Economic History of China: Some Special Problems," *Modern China* (January 1981), 7(1):29–30.

26. The Opium War, Nee and Peck write, "marked the beginning of modern Chi-

nese history, the first important struggle against the imperialist onslaught" ("Introduction," p. 5). See also Peck, "Revolution Versus Modernization and Revisionism," p. 91.

27. Although mainland Chinese historiography has undergone significant changes since Mao's death, characterizations of the long "feudal" period as stagnant are still pervasive. See, e.g., Fu Zhufu, "The Economic History of China," p. 17 ("Throughout the era of feudalism . . . the social economy stagnated because it went through no qualitative change in more than two millenia"); Li Shih-yueh, "Ts'ung yang-wu, wei-hsin tao tzu-ch'an chieh-chi ko-ming" (From Westernization and reform to bourgeois revolution), *Li-shih yen-chiu* (1980), no. 1, p. 31 ("When the first light of capitalism appeared in Europe, China was still fast asleep in the endless night of feudalism").

28. See, in particular, Joseph Esherick, "Harvard on China: The Apologetics of Imperialism," *Bulletin of Concerned Asian Scholars* (December 1972), 4(4):9–16.

29. Moulder's book, *Japan, China, and the Modern World Economy: Toward a Reinterpretation of East Asian Development, ca. 1600 to ca. 1918* (Cambridge: Cambridge University Press, 1979), was the focus of a panel discussion at the March 1980 meeting of the Association for Asian Studies. "Wallersteinism," described as "a major academic growth industry," is discussed with specific reference to its potential applicability to Chinese history in Angus McDonald, Jr., "Wallerstein's World-Economy: How Seriously Should We Take It?" *Journal of Asian Studies* (May 1979), 38(3):535–540.

30. Quoted in Moulder, *Japan, China, and the Modern World Economy,* p. 1, from Edwin O. Reischauer and John K. Fairbank, *East Asia: The Great Tradition* (Boston: Houghton Mifflin, 1960), p. 670.

31. Moulder, *Japan, China, and the Modern World Economy*, pp. 3–4.

32. *Ibid.*, p. 25.

33. *Ibid.*, pp. 25–44, 87–90, esp. pp. 25–28, 87, 90.

34. In her preface, Moulder acknowledges that "some may feel that [she has] unduly neglected important differences in traditional Japanese and Chinese values, ethics," etc. This omission, she insists, is not because of a conviction on her part that such differences among non-Western societies "are irrelevant to understanding their transformation under the Western impact." The burden of her study is, rather, that "these differences are perhaps not as decisive as has been claimed" (*ibid.*, p. viii).

35. See, for example, her discussion of the increasing monetization of the relationship of the "mercantile lower stratum of the landed upper class" to the peasantry from Sung times on (*ibid.*, p. 41), a discussion based on Mark Elvin's controversial study, *The Pattern of the Chinese Past: A Social and Economic Interpretation* (Stanford, Calif.: Stanford University Press, 1973).

36. Moulder, *Japan, China, and the Modern World Economy*, p. 85.

37. See Brown's review of Moulder's book in *Modern Asian Studies* (April 1979), 13(2):334–335.

38. Moulder, *Japan, China, and the Modern World Economy*, pp. 95–96.

39. Hunt, *Frontier Defense and the Open Door: Manchuria in Chinese–American Relations, 1895–1911* (New Haven, Conn.: Yale University Press, 1973).

40. Moulder, *Japan, China, and the Modern World Economy,* pp. 95, 97.

41. Paul A. Cohen, *China and Christianity: The Missionary Movement and the Growth of Chinese Antiforeignism, 1860–1870* (Cambridge: Harvard University Press, 1963), pp. 186–228 (quotation from p. 195). On the policy of Hudson Taylor, see *ibid.*,

p. 321 n. 63. The China Inland Mission seems to have adhered to this policy faithfully. See Cohen, "Missionary Approaches: Hudson Taylor and Timothy Richard," *Papers on China* (1957), 11:43–44.

42. The reader will be interested to learn, for example, that Thailand (Siam) "came under French control" in the nineteenth century and that by 1896 Paris had established 30,000 consulates in the country to protect French and other foreign nationals (Moulder, *Japan, China, and the Modern World Economy*, p. 122).

43. *Ibid.*, pp. 147–150.

44. *Ibid.*, p. 152.

45. *Ibid.*, pp. 151–152, 158–159, 167–169.

46. *Ibid.*, p. ix.

47. The phrase—and something of the sentiment—is from Arif Dirlik's "Republican China: Chaos, Process, and Revolution," *Chinese Republican Studies Newsletter* (October 1977), 3(1):8. In this brief but provocative piece, Dirlik argues forcefully (1) that the dominant feature of the republican period in China was not chaos and disorder but deep-seated structural change, and (2) that the primary cause of such change was the Western intrusion. Dirlik, like Moulder, reflects the influence of the world systems approach. His argument is, however, far more sophisticated than Moulder's. It is not dealt with here only because it consists of a set of preliminary propositions to be tested rather than conclusions based on completed research.

Another recent contribution to Dirlik's empirical vacuum is Victor Lippit's "The Development of Underdevelopment in China," *Modern China* (July 1978), 4(3):251–328; also by Lippit, "The Development of Underdevelopment in China: An Afterword," *ibid.* (January 1980), 6(1):86–93. Lippit, although apparently sympathetic to the world systems approach, argues (in contrast to Moulder) that internal factors (such as class structure) were more significant than external factors (imperialism) in accounting for China's economic "underdevelopment." Lippit's study, like Moulder's, is based almost entirely on secondary sources. For a monograph with strong empirical underpinnings that in its conclusion expressly challenges the Moulder thesis, see Lillian Li, *China's Silk Trade: Traditional Industry in the Modern World, 1842–1937* (Cambridge: Council on East Asian Studies, Harvard University, 1981). See also the recent article by Elizabeth Lasek, "Imperialism in China: A Methodological Critique," *Bulletin of Concerned Asian Scholars* (January–February 1983), 15(1):50–64. Lasek, although operating from a world systems base, makes a real effort to cut across the more simplistic dualisms that have shaped much of the discussion of imperialism's role in China and to cast the problem of the relationship between imperialism and Chinese development in more complex methodological terms.

48. For an exception, see Ramon H. Myers and Thomas A. Metzger, "Sinological Shadows: The State of Modern China Studies in the United States," *Washington Quarterly* (Spring 1980), 3(2):98–100. This article, written for frankly political ends, is an odd mélange of useful scholarly insight, contorted logic, and highly charged rhetoric. It has already appeared in two other journals besides the *Washington Quarterly: Australian Journal of Chinese Affairs* (Spring 1980), 4:1–34; *Shih-huo yueh-k'an* (Shih-huo monthly) (January 1981), 10(10):444–457, (February 1981), 10(11):505–519 (in Chinese). The article was the subject of a panel discussion at the March 1983 meeting of the Association for Asian Studies in San Francisco; panel papers are scheduled to be published in a special issue of *Republican China* (the successor to *Chinese Republican Studies Newsletter*) in October 1983.

49. Moulder, *Japan, China, and the Modern World Economy*, p. ix.

50. Hou, *Foreign Investment and Economic Development in China, 1840–1937* (Cambridge: Harvard University Press, 1965), pp. 1, 130.

51. Review by Payer in *Bulletin of Concerned Asian Scholars* (April–August 1974), 6(2):67.

52. Dernberger, "The Role of the Foreigner in China's Economic Development, 1840–1949," in Dwight H. Perkins, ed., *China's Modern Economy in Historical Perspective* (Stanford, Calif.: Stanford University Press, 1975), pp. 23–24, 306 n. 6. Dernberger levels the same charge against Jack M. Potter's *Capitalism and the Chinese Peasant* (Berkeley: University of California Press, 1968).

53. Ramon H. Myers, *The Chinese Peasant Economy: Agricultural Development in Hopei and Shantung, 1890–1949* (Cambridge: Harvard University Press, 1970), pp. 213, 288, 294–295.

54. Thomas B. Wiens' review of Myers' book, *Modern Asian Studies* (April 1975), 9(2):279–288 (quoted passages from p. 283). Biases in the Mantetsu data in particular have also been pointed out by two of the scholars—Andō Shizumasa and Hatada Takashi—who took part in the original survey. See their review of *The Chinese Peasant Economy*, written together with Fukushima Masao, in *Ajia keizai* (Asian economics) (October 1971), 12(10):81–93. I am indebted to Prasenjit Duara for calling this reference to my attention.

55. Murphey, *The Outsiders: The Western Experience in India and China* (Ann Arbor: University of Michigan Press, 1977), pp. 34–35, 65–66, 73.

56. *Ibid.*, pp. 104–105, 108, 128–129, 159, 204.

57. *Ibid.*, p. 132. Again "The very size of this vast economy . . . was of course an important reason why it was so difficult for the foreign impact to have any substantial effect. The stimulus necessary to move such a mass would have had to be immense. The increase in foreign trade which looked impressive to the Westerners remained proportionately tiny when compared to the bulk of the Chinese economy as a whole" (*ibid.*, p. 167).

58. *Ibid.*, pp. 133–134, 145–146. See Lucian Pye, *The Spirit of Chinese Politics: A Psychocultural Study of the Authority Crisis in Political Development* (Cambridge, Mass.: MIT Press, 1968).

59. Murphey, *The Outsiders*, p. 125.

60. *Ibid.*, pp. 135, 206.

61. *Ibid.*, p. 135.

62. *Ibid.*, p. 133.

63. *Ibid.*, pp. 136–137.

64. *Ibid.*, p. 206.

65. *Ibid.*, pp. 9–10, 129, 155, 232–233.

66. Feuerwerker, *The Chinese Economy, ca. 1870–1911* (Ann Arbor: Center for Chinese Studies, University of Michigan, 1969), p. 17; see also his "Handicraft and Manufactured Cotton Textiles in China, 1871–1910," *Journal of Economic History* (June 1970), 30(2):338–378, esp. 377–378.

67. Rawski, "Notes on China's Republican Economy," *Chinese Republican Studies Newsletter* (April 1976), 1(3):25. (The omission of Rawski's name as the author of this article is noted with apology in the next issue.)

68. See, e.g., Dernberger, "The Role of the Foreigner in China's Economic Development," p. 36.

69. Rawski, "Notes on China's Republican Economy," pp. 23–24. The same point is reiterated in Rawski's *China's Republican Economy: An Introduction* (Toronto: Joint Centre on Modern East Asia, University of Toronto–York University, 1978), pp. 2–13.

70. Brown, "The Partially Opened Door: Limitations on Economic Change in China in the 1860s," *Modern Asian Studies* (April 1978), 12(2):177–192.

71. Dernberger, "The Role of the Foreigner in China's Economic Development," p. 47.

72. According to Rawski, the fact that Carl Riskin and even Dernberger himself find substantial economic surpluses in the 1930s, together with the fact that the People's Republic of China in the 1950s was able to raise investment rates from their prewar level of about 5 percent to 20 percent or more of total output, "cast considerable doubt upon the equilibrium trap approach" ("Notes on China's Republican Economy," p.26). Riskin's views are found in his "Surplus and Stagnation in Modern China," in Perkins, *China's Modern Economy in Historical Perspective,* pp. 49–84, esp. pp. 62–64. Other reservations concerning the trap's applicability to China are voiced by Ramon Myers, "Transformation and Continuity in Chinese Economic and Social History," *Journal of Asian Studies* (February 1974), 33(2):275–276, and by Nathan Sivin, "Imperial China: Has Its Present Past a Future?" *Harvard Journal of Asiatic Studies* (December 1978), 38(2):458–463.

73. That scholars diverge widely in their reading of the factual record is suggested by the fact that Elvin places the point at which the Chinese economy experienced sharply diminishing returns (the onset of the high-level equilibrium trap) in the late eighteenth century, Dernberger locates this point toward the close of the nineteenth century, and Dwight Perkins places it in the middle of the twentieth century. See Dernberger, "The Role of the Foreigner in China's Economic Development," pp. 24–26; Riskin, "Surplus and Stagnation in Modern China," p. 62.

74. See, e.g., Andrew J. Nathan, "Imperialism's Effects on China," *Bulletin of Concerned Asian Scholars* (December 1972), 4(4):6; Albert Feuerwerker, *The Foreign Establishment in China in the Early Twentieth Century* (Ann Arbor: Center for Chinese Studies, University of Michigan, 1976), p. 111.

75. Esherick, *Reform and Revolution in China: The 1911 Revolution in Hunan and Hubei* (Berkeley: University of California Press, 1976), esp. ch. 4; Wright, "Introduction: The Rising Tide of Change," in Mary C. Wright, ed., *China in Revolution: The First Phase, 1900–1913* (New Haven, Conn.: Yale University Press, 1968), pp. 54–55; Rhoads, *China's Republican Revolution: The Case of Kwangtung, 1895–1913* (Cambridge: Harvard University Press, 1975), pp. 268–269; Friedman, *Backward Toward Revolution: The Chinese Revolutionary Party* (Berkeley: University of California Press, 1974), esp. ch. 10; Young, *The Presidency of Yuan Shih-k'ai: Liberalism and Dictatorship in Early Republican China* (Ann Arbor: University of Michigan Press, 1977), pp. 188–192.

76. Murphey, *The Outsiders,* p. 126; Dernberger, "The Role of the Foreigner in China's Economic Development," p. 47. See also John K. Fairbank, Alexander Eckstein and Lien-sheng Yang, "Economic Change in Early Modern China: An Analytic Framework," *Economic Development and Cultural Change* (October 1960), 9(1):22. The authors, while noting the possibility that "the bark of imperialism was worse than its bite," assert that "from 1896 until the Second World War China's payments

abroad on loans and indemnities constituted a sizable and constant financial drain which inevitably impaired her capacity for domestic capital formation, both governmental and private."

77. Feuerwerker, "Handicraft and Manufactured Cotton Textiles in China," p. 378; Brown, "The Partially Opened Door," p. 184. On the consequences for Fukien tea growers and Hunan antimony producers of the vagaries of the foreign market, see Robert P. Gardella, "Reform and the Tea Industry and Trade in Late Ch'ing China: The Fukien Case," in Paul A. Cohen and John E. Schrecker, eds., *Reform in Nineteenth-Century China* (Cambridge: East Asian Research Center, Harvard University, 1976), pp. 71–79; Angus W. McDonald, Jr., *The Urban Origins of Rural Revolution: Elites and the Masses in Hunan Province, China, 1911–1927* (Berkeley: University of California Press, 1978), pp. 77–78. Linda Grove, pursuing a subregional approach, finds a substantial imperialist impact on the economy of the central Hopei plains in the period from 1900 to the early 1940s. See her "Treaty Port and Hinterland: Revolution in a Semicolonial Society," paper presented at workshop on Rebellion and Revolution in North China, Harvard University, July–August 1979.

78. See also Young, *The Presidency of Yuan Shih-k'ai,* p. 253.

79. Sun labeled China a "hypocolony," borrowing the prefix "hypo" from chemistry, where it is used to refer to a low-grade compound. See his *San Min Chu I: The Three Principles of the People,* trans. Frank W. Price (Shanghai: China Committee, Institute of Pacific Relations, 1927), p. 39.

80. Cochran, *Big Business in China: Sino–Foreign Rivalry in the Cigarette Industry, 1890–1930* (Cambridge: Harvard University Press, 1980), pp. 202–207.

4. TOWARD A CHINA-CENTERED HISTORY OF CHINA

1. Naipaul, *A Bend in the River* (New York: Vintage Books, 1980), p. 17.

2. Said, *Orientalism* (New York: Vintage Books, 1979), p. 272. For a review symposium on Said's book focused on its relevance to the specific fields of Chinese, Japanese, and Indian studies, see *Journal of Asian Studies* (May 1980), 39(3):481–517. Joseph R. Levenson adumbrates some of Said's views on "Orientalism" in his comments on "Sinology" in "The Humanistic Disciplines: Will Sinology Do?" *ibid.* (August 1964), 23(4):507–512.

3. Two partial exceptions, which identify some of the new tendencies in American historical scholarship on China, are Ramon H. Myers and Thomas A. Metzger, "Sinological Shadows: The State of Modern China Studies in the United States," *Washington Quarterly* (Spring 1980), 3(2):87–114; and Mary B. Rankin, "A Ch'ing Perspective on Republican Studies," *Chinese Republican Studies Newsletter* (October 1976), 2(1):1–6. On the Myers-Metzger article, see chapter 3, n. 48.

4. I hope it is superfluous to add here that striving empathetically to reconstruct the Chinese past as the Chinese themselves experienced it carries no implication of moral approval, on the part of the historian, of Chinese behavior or values. Americans, to take an example from very recent history, have a responsibility, as historians, to try to understand from a Chinese perspective why the Chinese government chose to prosecute human rights activist Wei Ching-sheng in 1979; we are not obliged to condone the government's action or its logic.

5. Paul A. Cohen and John E. Schrecker, eds., *Reform in Nineteenth-Century China* (Cambridge: East Asian Research Center, Harvard University, 1976), p. x. For further discussion of nineteenth-century reform, see chapter 1.

6. Jones and Kuhn, "Dynastic Decline and the Roots of Rebellion," in John K. Fairbank, ed., *The Cambridge History of China,* vol. 10, *Late Ch'ing, 1800–1911, Part 1* (Cambridge: Cambridge University Press, 1978), p. 160. A comparable call for a forward- rather than backward-looking perspective on high Ch'ing is found in Frederic Wakeman, Jr., "High Ch'ing: 1683–1839," in James B. Crowley, ed., *Modern East Asia: Essays in Interpretation* (New York: Harcourt, Brace, and World, 1970), pp. 1–27.

7. On Kung Tzu-chen, see Dorothy V. Borei, "Eccentricity and Dissent: The Case of Kung Tzu-chen," *Ch'ing-shih wen-t'i* (December 1975), 3(4):50–62; Judith Whitbeck, "The Historical Vision of Kung Tzu-chen (1792–1841)," Ph.D. dissertation, University of California, Berkeley, 1980. Wei Yuan is treated in Jones and Kuhn, "Dynastic Decline and the Roots of Rebellion," pp. 148–156; Jane Kate Leonard, "Chinese Overlordship and Western Penetration in Maritime Asia: A Late Ch'ing Reappraisal of Chinese Maritime Relations," *Modern Asian Studies* (April 1972), 6(2):151–174; and in Leonard's forthcoming book on Wei and China's rediscovery of the maritime world (to be published by the Council on East Asian Studies, Harvard University).

8. On Wang, see Paul A. Cohen, *Between Tradition and Modernity: Wang T'ao and Reform in Late Ch'ing China* (Cambridge: Harvard University Press, 1974), pp. 39–44; on Wo-jen, see John E. Schrecker, "The Reform Movement of 1898 and the *Ch'ing-i:* Reform as Opposition," in Cohen and Schrecker, *Reform in Nineteenth-Century China,* p. 290.

9. Ropp, "The Seeds of Change: Reflections on the Condition of Women in the Early and Mid Ch'ing," *Signs: Journal of Women in Culture and Society* (Autumn 1976), 2(1):5.

10. Hao Chang, *Liang Ch'i-ch'ao and Intellectual Transition in China, 1890–1907* (Cambridge: Harvard University Press, 1971), passim.

11. Schrecker, "The Reform Movement of 1898 and the *Ch'ing-i,*" pp. 289–305 (quoted phrase from p. 289).

12. James M. Polachek, "Rural Community, Career Opportunities, and Intellectual Radicalism in Late Nineteenth-Century Kwangtung," paper presented at Columbia University Seminar on Modern China, January 10, 1980.

13. The best example of Sun scholarship is Harold Z. Schiffrin's *Sun Yat-sen and the Origins of the Chinese Revolution* (Berkeley: University of California Press, 1968). Schiffrin takes the story up to the founding of the T'ung-meng-hui in 1905.

14. Chün-tu Hsüeh, *Huang Hsing and the Chinese Revolution* (Stanford, Calif.: Stanford University Press, 1961).

15. Mary C. Wright, ed. *China in Revolution: The First Phase, 1900–1913* (New Haven, Conn.: Yale University Press, 1968).

16. The distinction is emphasized by Joseph W. Esherick in his superb critical review of American (or at least largely American) writing on 1911: "1911: A Review," *Modern China* (April 1976), 2(2): 162–163.

17. Esherick, *Reform and Revolution in China: The 1911 Revolution in Hunan and Hubei* (Berkeley: University of California Press, 1976), pp. 199, 215, and passim. Esherick's analysis is much more multidimensional than indicated here, dealing not

only with the relationship of the elite to the revolution but also that of the populace and of foreign imperialism. See also his discussion of the gentry controversy in "1911: A Review," pp. 162–168.

18. Frederic Wakeman, Jr., *The Fall of Imperial China* (New York: Free Press, 1975), p. 31; Yoshinobu Shiba, "Ningpo and Its Hinterland," in G. William Skinner, ed., *The City in Late Imperial China* (Stanford, Calif.: Stanford University Press, 1977), p. 422. The long-term "trend toward private responsibility for public functions" is neatly summarized in R. Keith Schoppa, *Chinese Elites and Political Change: Zhejiang Province in the Early Twentieth Century* (Cambridge: Harvard University Press, 1982), pp. 4–5.

19. Marianne Bastid-Bruguière, "Currents of Social Change," in John K. Fairbank and Kwang-Ching Liu, eds., *The Cambridge History of China,* vol. 11, *Late Ch'ing, 1800–1911, Part 2* (Cambridge: Cambridge University Press, 1980), pp. 557–558; see also Wellington K.K. Chan, *Merchants, Mandarins, and Modern Enterprise in Late Ch'ing China* (Cambridge: East Asian Research Center, Harvard University, 1977), part 1.

20. The following discussion of the littoral and hinterland cultural contrast is based on my article, "The New Coastal Reformers," in Cohen and Schrecker, *Reform in Nineteenth-Century China,* pp. 255–257.

21. See Skinner, "Regional Urbanization in Nineteenth-Century China," in Skinner, *The City in Late Imperial China,* pp. 211–249.

22. Skinner made a statement to this effect at the workshop on Food and Famine in Chinese History, Harvard University, August 8, 1980. James A. Henretta's critique of the structuralism of the *Annales* school of historiography (as represented by Fernand Braudel) makes the same point for essentially the same reason: "[The] failure to specify causal relationships is neither accidental nor peculiar to Braudel's scholarship; rather, it proceeds directly from the method. To interpret the world in structuralist terms is to contest the philosophical primacy of nineteenth-century notions of unilineal causation. The understanding of an event depends less on a comprehension of its antecedents than on an understanding of its position or function within an existing system. Structuralists adopt a 'holistic' perspective, stressing the internal relationships among elements of a self-contained institution or world view." See Henretta's "Social History as Lived and Written," *American Historical Review* (December 1979), 84(5): 1299.

23. Skinner's distinction between "traditional change" (quantitative proliferation) and "modern change" (qualitative transformation) in the second of his articles on marketing systems reinforces this impression. See his "Marketing and Social Structure in Rural China," part 2, *Journal of Asian Studies* (February 1965), 24(2): 195–228.

24. John E. Schrecker, *Imperialism and Chinese Nationalism: Germany in Shantung* (Cambridge: Harvard University Press, 1971); Frederic Wakeman, Jr., *Strangers at the Gate: Social Disorder in South China, 1839–1861* (Berkeley: University of California Press, 1966); Angus W. McDonald, Jr., *The Urban Origins of Rural Revolution: Elites and the Masses in Hunan Province, China, 1911–1927* (Berkeley: University of California Press, 1978).

25. Sutton, *Provincial Militarism and the Chinese Republic: The Yunnan Army, 1905–1925* (Ann Arbor: University of Michigan Press, 1979).

26. See Edward J. M. Rhoads, *China's Republican Revolution: The Case of*

Kwangtung, 1895–1913 (Cambridge: Harvard University Press, 1975); Esherick, *Reform and Revolution in China;* Mary Backus Rankin, *Early Chinese Revolutionaries: Radical Intellectuals in Shanghai and Chekiang, 1902–1911* (Cambridge: Harvard University Press, 1971). Several province-centered dissertations on 1911 are noted in Esherick, "1911: A Review," p. 162.

27. Diana Lary, "Warlord Studies," *Modern China* (October 1980), 6(4): 456–460. Lary provides a full listing of authors and titles.

28. Liew, *Struggle for Democracy: Sung Chiao-jen and the 1911 Chinese Revolution* (Berkeley: University of California Press, 1971), p. 159.

29. Rhoads, *China's Republican Revolution,* p. 273; Esherick, *Reform and Revolution in China,* pp. 8, 257–259, and passim; Esherick, "1911: A Review," pp. 154 ff.; Rankin, *Early Chinese Revolutionaries,* pp. 2–4 and passim.

30. Schoppa, untitled comment, *Chinese Republican Studies Newsletter* (October 1976), 2(1):7. See also the same author's "Local Self-Government in Zhejiang, 1909–1927," *Modern China* (October 1976), 2(4): 526. In his recent book, *Chinese Elites and Political Change,* Schoppa explores more fully the key proposition that the warlord period, seen from a Chekiang perspective, was far from constituting a simple interruption in China's nation-building effort (see esp. ch. 1).

31. Cole, "The Shaoxing Connection: A Vertical Administrative Clique in Late Qing China," *Modern China* (July 1980), 6(3): 317–326.

32. Chung-li Chang, *The Chinese Gentry: Studies on Their Role in Nineteenth-Century Chinese Society* (Seattle: University of Washington Press, 1955); Ping-ti Ho, *The Ladder of Success in Imperial China: Aspects of Social Mobility, 1368–1911* (New York: Columbia University Press, 1962).

33. See Beattie, *Land and Lineage in China: A Study of T'ung-ch'eng County, Anhwei, in the Ming and Ch'ing Dynasties* (Cambridge: Cambridge University Press, 1979).

34. This is an extension of a point made by Evelyn Rawski in her thoughtful review of Beattie's book. Rawski also notes that there is an important distinction to be made between individual or household mobility and lineage mobility. There can be considerable *intra*lineage mobility at the same time that the lineage as a whole retains its elite standing. Even for T'ung-ch'eng, therefore, Beattie's study does not necessarily disprove Ping-ti Ho's contention that there was extensive individual mobility in late imperial China. Rawski's review is in *Journal of Asian Studies* (August 1980), 39(4): 793–795. Several recent studies that support Beattie's portrayal of the local elite in late imperial times are noted in a book review by Wellington Chan in *ibid.* (November 1981), 41(1): 128–129.

35. Johnson, *Peasant Nationalism and Communist Power: The Emergence of Revolutionary China, 1937–1945* (Stanford, Cal.: Stanford University Press, 1962). There had, of course, been earlier American work on the Communist movement. Johnson's book, however, serves as the point of departure for the main historiographical controversies of the past two decades. American scholarship of the 1950s, stressing the organizational role of the party and the "Soviet connection," is reviewed by Steven M. Goldstein in an unpublished essay, "The Blind Men and the Elephant: American Perspectives on the Chinese Communist Movement, 1921–1980."

36. Johnson, *Peasant Nationalism and Communist Power;* Donald G. Gillin, "'Peasant Nationalism' in the History of Chinese Communism," *Journal of Asian Studies* (February 1964), 23(2): 269–289; Mark Selden, *The Yenan Way in Revolutionary China* (Cambridge: Harvard University Press, 1971); Tetsuya Kataoka, *Resistance*

and Revolution in China: The Communists and the Second United Front (Berkeley: University of California Press, 1974) (quoted phrases are from p. 301); Roy Hofheinz, Jr., "The Ecology of Chinese Communist Success: Rural Influence Patterns, 1923–45," in A. Doak Barnett, ed., *Chinese Communist Politics in Action* (Seattle: University of Washington Press, 1969), pp. 3–77 (quoted phrases from p. 77).

37. Yung-fa Ch'en, "The Making of a Revolution: The Communist Movement in Eastern and Central China," 2 vols., Ph.D. dissertation, Stanford University, 1980; Kathleen J. Hartford, "Step-by-Step: Reform, Resistance, and Revolution in the Chin-Ch'a-Chi Border Region, 1937–1945," Ph.D. dissertation, Stanford University, 1979; David Paulson, "War and Revolution in North China: The Shandong Base Area, 1937–1945," Ph.D. dissertation, Stanford University, 1982; Elizabeth J. Perry, *Rebels and Revolutionaries in North China, 1845–1945* (Stanford, Calif: Stanford University Press, 1980), pp. 208–262. See also a forthcoming collection of essays on the revolutionary base areas (drawn mainly from papers originally presented at a workshop held at Harvard in August 1978), edited by Kathleen J. Hartford and Steven M. Goldstein.

38. Lyman P. Van Slyke, "New Light on Chinese Communist Base Areas During the Sino-Japanese War, 1937–1945," paper presented at Conference on the History of the Republic of China, Taipei, August 23–28, 1981, pp. 12–13. Although I have profited enormously from Van Slyke's piece and have relied on it for a number of points of detail, the basic themes of my discussion of base area historiography were formulated independently.

39. Paulson, "War and Revolution in North China," passim.

40. Van Slyke, "New Light on Chinese Communist Base Areas," pp. 13–14, 29. Unfortunately, not all new base area scholarship follows this pattern. Ralph Thaxton's recent study of the emergence of rural revolution in the T'ai-hang Mountain area (at the juncture of Shansi, Hopei, and Honan provinces) advances the bold argument that the CCP won the allegiance of the peasantry not by means of this or that externally generated appeal but by incorporating into its policies the peasants' own demands for a return to traditional patterns of justice. Thaxton's thesis is an intriguing one. However, the evidence with which he supports it is scandalously inadequate, and, with complete disregard for the issue of representativeness, he extends the conclusions reached for one small region (the T'ai-hang) to the Chinese Communist movement as a whole. *China Turned Rightside Up: Revolutionary Legitimacy in the Peasant World* (New Haven, Conn.: Yale University Press, 1983).

41. One of the exceptions was Wakeman's *Strangers at the Gate,* which came out in 1966.

42. G. William Skinner, "Chinese Peasants and the Closed Community: An Open and Shut Case," *Comparative Studies in Society and History* (July 1971), 13(3): 272–273.

43. *The United States and China,* 4th ed. (Cambridge: Harvard University Press, 1979), p. 43.

44. Evelyn Rawski, *Education and Popular Literacy in Ch'ing China* (Ann Arbor: University of Michigan Press, 1979), pp. 22, 140, and passim.

45. In addition to my own review of Rawski's book, in *Journal of Asian Studies* (February 1980), 39(2): 331–333, see also Chang P'eng-yuan's in *Chung-yang yen-chiu-yuan chin-tai-shih yen-chiu-so chi-k'an* (Bulletin of the Institute of Modern History, Academia Sinica) (Taipei) (July 1980), 9:455–462.

46. Another example is Rudolf G. Wagner's provocative monograph (forthcoming)

on the role of religion in the Taiping movement. Wagner, a German historian, reconstructs the inner logic of the Taiping world and hypothesizes that the Taipings, from their own perspective, were reenacting verbatim a divine scenario given them by God.

47. Daniel L. Overmyer, *Folk Buddhist Religion: Dissenting Sects in Late Traditional China* (Cambridge: Harvard University Press, 1976), pp. 16, 19, 70–71, 199, and passim. For further discussion of the nonrebellious side of popular religious sects in China, see the same author's "Alternatives: Popular Religious Sects in Chinese Society," *Modern China* (April 1981), 7(2): 153–190.

48. Overmyer, *Folk Buddhist Religion,* p. 73.

49. Susan Naquin, *Millenarian Rebellion in China: The Eight Trigrams Uprising of 1813* (New Haven, Conn.: Yale University Press, 1976), pp. 2–3, 7, 90, 314 n. 69, and passim. Naquin also stresses the overriding importance of internal, religious causation in *Shantung Rebellion: The Wang Lun Uprising of 1774* (New Haven, Conn.: Yale University Press, 1981), pp. 50–51, 61, 153, 158.

50. Naquin, *Millenarian Rebellion in China,* p. 72.

51. Roxann Prazniak, "Tax Protest at Laiyang, Shandong, 1910: Commoner Organization Versus the County Political Elite," *Modern China* (January 1980), 6(1): 41–71; Rhoads, *China's Republican Revolution,* pp. 175–179. For a quite different approach, relating popular uprisings in the Canton delta region in the immediate aftermath of the Wuchang revolt of October 10, 1911, to the hierarchy of marketing communities, see Winston Hsieh, "Peasant Insurrection and the Marketing Hierarchy in the Canton Delta, 1911," in Mark Elvin and G. William Skinner, eds., *The Chinese City Between Two Worlds* (Stanford, Calif.: Stanford University Press, 1974), pp. 119–141.

52. Mei, "Socioeconomic Origins of Emigration: Guangdong to California, 1850–1882," *Modern China* (October 1979), 5(4):463–501.

53. See, e.g., Philip C. C. Huang, "Analyzing the Twentieth-Century Chinese Countryside: Revolutionaries Versus Western Scholarship," *Modern China* (April 1975), 1(2): 132–160; Ramon H. Myers, "North China Villages During the Republican Period: Socioeconomic Relationships," *ibid.* (July 1980), 6(3): 243–266; Joseph W. Esherick, "Number Games: A Note on Land Distribution in Prerevolutionary China," *ibid.* (October 1981), 7(4): 387–411.

54. For an interesting, theoretically oriented discussion of the "new social history," see Henretta, "Social History as Lived and Written," pp. 1293–1322; the interaction between history and the social sciences is viewed in broader historical perspective in Lawrence Stone, "History and the Social Sciences in the Twentieth Century," in the same author's *The Past and the Present* (Boston: Routledge & Kegan Paul, 1981), pp. 3–44.

55. Stone speaks of "a more general shift in the 1960s and 1970s from sociology to anthropology as the dominant source of new ideas in the historical profession in general" ("Introduction," in Stone, *The Past and the Present,* p. xi).

56. Philip A. Kuhn, *Rebellion and Its Enemies in Late Imperial China: Militarization and Social Structure, 1796–1864* (Cambridge: Harvard University Press, 1970), pp. 67, 77–82; Maurice Freedman, *Lineage Organization in Southeastern China,* Monographs on Social Anthropology, no. 18 (London: London School of Economics, 1958); Maurice Freedman, *Chinese Lineage and Society* (London: Athlone Press, 1966).

57. Kuhn, *Rebellion and Its Enemies in Late Imperial China,* pp. 69–76, 82–87, 93–104, and passim (quotation from p. 76). Skinner's distinction between "natural" (economic) and "artificial" (administrative) modes of organization and his model (derived from central place theory) of progressively higher levels of societal integration ("nested hierarchies") are introduced in his "Marketing and Social Structure in Rural China," part 1, *Journal of Asian Studies* (November 1964), 24(1):5–10, 32–43; they are fully elaborated in his essay, "Cities and the Hierarchy of Local Systems," in Skinner, *The City in Late Imperial China,* pp. 275–351. Kuhn, in the preface to the paperback edition of *Rebellion and Its Enemies in Late Imperial China* (1980), demonstrates even more explicitly his indebtedness to anthropology in general and Skinner in particular.

58. Perry, *Rebels and Revolutionaries in North China,* passim (quoted phrases from pp. 95, 246, 257). Why Perry periodically modifies "rebellion" with "traditional" and "revolution" with "modern" is not clear, as she defines "rebellion" and "revolution" (on p. 2) without reference to the tradition–modernity dyad and her analysis throughout is in no way dependent on it.

59. Lary, "Warlord Studies," pp. 461-462; Andrew J. Nathan, *Peking Politics, 1918–1923: Factionalism and the Failure of Constitutionalism* (Berkeley: University of California Press, 1976); Gavan McCormack, *Chang Tso-lin in Northeast China, 1911–1928: China, Japan, and the Manchurian Idea* (Stanford, Calif.: Stanford University Press, 1977). Nathan's book is criticized in much the same terms by Marie-Claire Bergère in her review in *China Quarterly* (June 1980), 82:354, and by Hsi-sheng Ch'i in his review in *Journal of Asian Studies* (August 1977), 36(4): 724.

60. Hsi-sheng Ch'i, *Warlord Politics in China, 1916–1928* (Stanford, Calif.: Stanford University Press, 1976); Odoric Y. K. Wou, *Militarism in Modern China: The Career of Wu P'ei-fu, 1916–39* (Folkestone, Kent: Dawson and Sons/Australian National University Press, 1978).

61. See, e.g., Lary, "Warlord Studies," pp. 460–462 (Ch'i and Wou); Donald S. Sutton's review of Wou in *Journal of Asian Studies* (February 1979), 38(2): 339; Donald G. Gillin's review of Ch'i in *ibid.* (May 1977), 36(3): 548.

62. Marc Bloch, *The Historian's Craft,* Peter Putnam, trans. (New York: Vintage Books, 1953), pp. 68–69.

63. In order of publication: John Wilson Lewis, ed., *The City in Communist China* (Stanford, Calif.: Stanford University Press, 1971); Elvin and Skinner, *The Chinese City Between Two Worlds;* and Skinner, *The City in Late Imperial China.*

64. Lillian M. Li, "Workshop on Food and Famine in Chinese History," *Ch'ing-shih wen-ti* (December 1980), 4(4):90–100 (quotation from p. 98). Essays by three participants in the workshop (James Lee, Peter C. Perdue, and R. Bin Wong), along with an introduction by Li and a comment by Paul R. Greenough, appear in "Food, Famine, and the Chinese State—A Symposium," *Journal of Asian Studies* (August 1982), 41(4):685–801.

65. Esherick discusses Kuhn's ideas in "1911: A Review," pp. 166–168.

66. Young, *The Presidency of Yuan Shih-k'ai: Liberalism and Dictatorship in Early Republican China* (Ann Arbor: University of Michigan Press, 1977), pp. 3–4 and passim.

67. See the interesting discussion of this issue in Bradley K. Geisert, "Toward a Pluralist Model of KMT Rule," *Chinese Republican Studies Newsletter* (February 1982), 7(2):1-10.

68. Fairbank begins his book by placing China's response to the Westerner in the context of prior Chinese experience with and attitudes toward barbarians. *Trade and Diplomacy on the China Coast: The Opening of the Treaty Ports, 1842–1854* (Cambridge: Harvard University Press, 1953), ch. 1. Similarly, the long first chapter of my book is entitled "The Anti-Christian Tradition in Chinese Thought" and attempts to locate this tradition in the context of earlier Chinese attitudes toward heterodox teachings. In the final chapter, I explicitly characterize the political problem created for Chinese officialdom by the missionary movement as "derivative in nature. Underlying it was the much larger issue of Sino–Western cultural conflict, as concretized . . . in the mutual misunderstanding that existed between the foreign missionary and the Chinese intellectual." *China and Christianity: The Missionary Movement and the Growth of Chinese Antiforeignism, 1860–1870* (Cambridge: Harvard University Press, 1963), p. 264. For a critique of cultural conflict interpretations of the Opium War, see Tan Chung, "Interpretations of the Opium War (1840–1842): A Critical Appraisal," *Ch'ing-shih wen-t'i* (December 1977), 3(Supp. 1): 32–46.

69. The emphasis here is more on "practicing" than on "historians." The fact that Peck and Moulder were both trained in sociology is less important than the fact that neither appears to have been through the chastening experience of doing extended research in Chinese sources.

70. This assertion is based on extended conversations with some seventy-five Chinese historians in the winter of 1979–1980. Only one of these historians, a member of the Fudan History Department, was willing to break away from the conventional periodization model. He argued that the beginning of modern Chinese history should be located not in 1840 but in 1911, for it was only with the revolution of that year that real structural change occurred in Chinese society. See Paul A. Cohen and Merle Goldman, "Modern History," in Anne F. Thurston and Jason H. Parker, eds., *Humanistic and Social Science Research in China: Recent History and Future Prospects* (New York: Social Science Research Council, 1980), p. 50.

71. Rawski, *Education and Popular Literacy in Ch'ing China,* p. 140.

72. Immanuel C. Y. Hsü, *The Rise of Modern China* (New York: Oxford University Press, 1970), pp. 4–6; Hsü's discussion of this question remains unchanged in the latest edition of his text (3d ed., 1983), pp. 4–6.

73. Frederic Wakeman, Jr., "Introduction: The Evolution of Local Control in Late Imperial China," in Frederic Wakeman, Jr. and Carolyn Grant, eds., *Conflict and Control in Late Imperial China* (Berkeley: University of California Press, 1975), p. 2.

74. Ramon H. Myers, "Transformation and Continuity in Chinese Economic and Social History," *Journal of Asian Studies* (February 1974), 33(2):274; and Ramon H. Myers, "On the Future of Ch'ing Studies," *Ch'ing-shih wen-t'i* (June 1979), 4(1): 107–109.

75. Fletcher, "Ch'ing Inner Asia c. 1800," in Fairbank, *The Cambridge History of China,* 10:35.

76. Jonathan D. Spence and John E. Wills, Jr., eds., *From Ming to Ch'ing: Conquest, Region, and Continuity in Seventeenth-Century China* (New Haven, Conn.: Yale University Press, 1979), preface, p. xii. Two essays in the volume that lay particular stress on continuities from late Ming to high Ch'ing are Hilary J. Beattie, "The Alternative to Resistance: The Case of T'ung-ch'eng, Anhwei," pp. 239–276, and Lynn A. Struve, "Ambivalence and Action: Some Frustrated Scholars of the K'ang-hsi Period," pp. 321–365.

77. See the preface in Spence and Wills, *From Ming to Ch'ing,* pp. xviii–xix.

78. Tsing Yuan, "Urban Riots and Disturbances," in *ibid.,* p. 311.

79. Hsü, *The Rise of Modern China,* 3d. ed., p. 49; see also Pei Huang, "Aspects of Ch'ing Autocracy: An Institutional Study, 1644–1735," *Tsing Hua Journal of Chinese Studies* (December 1967), n.s. 6 (1–2): 116–133.

80. Beatrice S. Bartlett, "Ch'ing Palace Memorials in the Archives of the National Palace Museum," *National Palace Museum Bulletin* (January–February 1979), 13(6):1–21; Silas H.L. Wu, *Communication and Imperial Control in China: Evolution of the Palace Memorial System, 1693–1735* (Cambridge: Harvard University Press, 1970); Jonathan D. Spence, *Ts'ao Yin and the K'ang-hsi Emperor: Bondservant and Master* (New Haven, Conn.: Yale University Press, 1966), ch. 6.

81. Mote and other contributors to Gilbert Rozman, ed., *The Modernization of China* (New York: Free Press, 1981), see the impact of Ch'ing administrative centralization as having been on balance negative (see pp. 56, 63–64, 206, 483, 499–500).

82. The alert reader will note an apparent inconsistency between my characterization of the Manchus as an "internal" determinant here and an external determinant in chapter 3 (in my discussion of "layered" colonialism). Both characterizations are valid in my view. "Internal" and "external," whether considered spatially or temporally, are relative terms only. Spatially, the Manchus may be viewed as external to China when the point of reference is exclusively East Asia, but internal when the West, which is outside Asia altogether, is brought in. Temporally, the Manchus are relatively external during the early part of their rule over China but become increasingly internal with the passage of time.

83. Fischer, *Historians' Fallacies: Toward a Logic of Historical Thought* (New York: Harper & Row, 1970), p. 146.

84. One of the more notable features of Jane Leonard's forthcoming book on Wei Yuan, earlier mentioned in this chapter, is that it applies the internalist approach to problems in Chinese foreign relations and in so doing places China's perception of the Western threat in the 1840s in an entirely new light.

Index

Studies of the East Asian Institute

THE LADDER OF SUCCESS IN IMPERIAL CHINA, by Ping-ti Ho. New York: Columbia University Press, 1962.

THE CHINESE INFLATION, 1937–1949, by Shun-hsin Chou. New York: Columbia University Press, 1963.

REFORMER IN MODERN CHINA: CHANG CHIEN, 1853–1926, by Samuel Chu. New York: Columbia University Press, 1965.

RESEARCH IN JAPANESE SOURCES: A GUIDE, by Herschel Webb with the assistance of Marleigh Ryan. New York: Columbia University Press, 1965.

SOCIETY AND EDUCATION IN JAPAN, by Herbert Passin. New York: Teachers College Press, 1965.

AGRICULTURAL PRODUCTION AND ECONOMIC DEVELOPMENT IN JAPAN, 1873–1922, by James I. Nakamura. Princeton: Princeton University Press, 1966.

JAPAN'S FIRST MODERN NOVEL: UKIGUMO OF FUTABATEI SHIMEI, by Marleigh Ryan. New York: Columbia University Press, 1967.

THE KOREAN COMMUNIST MOVEMENT, 1918–1948, by Dae-Sook Suh. Princeton: Princeton University Press, 1967.

THE FIRST VIETNAM CRISIS, by Melvin Gurtov. New York: Columbia University Press, 1967.

CADRES, BUREAUCRACY, AND POLITICAL POWER IN COMMUNIST CHINA, by A. Doak Barnett. New York: Columbia University Press, 1968.

THE JAPANESE IMPERIAL INSTITUTION IN THE TOKUGAWA PERIOD, by Herschel Webb. New York: Columbia University Press, 1968.

HIGHER EDUCATION AND BUSINESS RECRUITMENT IN JAPAN, by Koya Azumi. New York: Teachers College Press, 1969.

THE COMMUNISTS AND PEASANT REBELLIONS: A STUDY IN THE REWRITING OF CHINESE HISTORY, by James P. Harrison, Jr. New York: Atheneum, 1969.

HOW THE CONSERVATIVES RULE JAPAN, by Nathaniel B. Thayer. Princeton: Princeton University Press, 1969.

ASPECTS OF CHINESE EDUCATION, edited by C. T. Hu. New York: Teachers College Press, 1970.

DOCUMENTS OF KOREAN COMMUNISM, 1918–1948, by Dae-Sook Suh. Princeton: Princeton University Press, 1970.

JAPANESE EDUCATION: A BIBLIOGRAPHY OF MATERIALS IN THE ENGLISH LANGUAGE, by Herbert Passin. New York: Teachers College Press, 1970.

ECONOMIC DEVELOPMENT AND THE LABOR MARKET IN JAPAN, by Koji Taira. New York: Columbia University Press, 1970.

THE JAPANESE OLIGARCHY AND THE RUSSO-JAPANESE WAR, by Shumpei Okamoto. New York: Columbia University Press, 1970.

IMPERIAL RESTORATION IN MEDIEVAL JAPAN, by H. Paul Varley. New York: Columbia University Press, 1971.

JAPAN'S POSTWAR DEFENSE POLICY, 1947–1968, by Martin E. Weinstein. New York: Columbia University Press, 1971.

ELECTION CAMPAIGNING JAPANESE STYLE, by Gerald L. Curtis. New York: Columbia University Press, 1971.

CHINA AND RUSSIA: THE "GREAT GAME," by O. Edmund Clubb. New York: Columbia University Press, 1971.

MONEY AND MONETARY POLICY IN COMMUNIST CHINA, by Katharine Huang Hsiao. New York: Columbia University Press, 1971.

THE DISTRICT MAGISTRATE IN LATE IMPERIAL CHINA, by John R. Watt. New York: Columbia University Press, 1972.

LAW AND POLICY IN CHINA'S FOREIGN RELATIONS: A STUDY OF ATTITUDES AND PRACTICE, by James C. Hsiung. New York: Columbia University Press, 1972.

PEARL HARBOR AS HISTORY: JAPANESE-AMERICAN RELATIONS, 1931–1941, edited by Dorothy Borg and Shumpei Okamoto, with the assistance of Dale K. A. Finlayson. New York: Columbia University Press, 1973.

JAPANESE CULTURE: A SHORT HISTORY, by H. Paul Varley, New York: Praeger, 1973.

DOCTORS IN POLITICS: THE POLITICAL LIFE OF THE JAPAN MEDICAL ASSOCIATION, by William E. Steslicke. New York: Praeger, 1973.

THE JAPAN TEACHERS UNION: A RADICAL INTEREST GROUP IN JAPANESE POLITICS, by Donald Ray Thurston. Princeton: Princeton University Press, 1973.

JAPAN'S FOREIGN POLICY, 1868–1941: A RESEARCH GUIDE, edited by James William Morley. New York: Columbia University Press, 1974.

PALACE AND POLITICS IN PREWAR JAPAN, by David Anson Titus. New York: Columbia University Press, 1974.

THE IDEA OF CHINA: ESSAYS IN GEOGRAPHIC MYTH AND THEORY, by Andrew March. Devon, England: David and Charles, 1974.

ORIGINS OF THE CULTURAL REVOLUTION: I, CONTRADICTIONS AMONG THE PEOPLE, 1956–1957, by Roderick MacFarquhar. New York: Columbia University Press, 1974.

SHIBA KOKAN: ARTIST, INNOVATOR, AND PIONEER IN THE WESTERNIZATION OF JAPAN, by Calvin L. French. Tokyo: Weatherhill, 1974.

INSEI: ABDICATED SOVEREIGNS IN THE POLITICS OF LATE HEIAN JAPAN, by G. Cameron Hurst. New York: Columbia University Press, 1975.

EMBASSY AT WAR, by Harold Joyce Noble. Edited with an introduction by Frank Baldwin, Jr. Seattle: University of Washington Press, 1975.

REBELS AND BUREAUCRATS: CHINA'S DECEMBER 9ERS, by John Israel and Donald W. Klein. Berkeley: University of California Press, 1975.

DETERRENT DIPLOMACY, edited by James William Morley. New York: Columbia University Press, 1976.

HOUSE UNITED, HOUSE DIVIDED: THE CHINESE FAMILY IN TAIWAN, by Myron L. Cohen. New York: Columbia University Press, 1976.

ESCAPE FROM PREDICAMENT: NEO-CONFUCIANISM AND CHINA'S EVOLVING POLITICAL CULTURE, by Thomas A. Metzger. New York: Columbia University Press, 1976.

CADRES, COMMANDERS, AND COMMISSARS: THE TRAINING OF THE CHINESE COMMUNIST LEADERSHIP, 1920–45, by Jane L. Price. Boulder, Colo.: Westview Press, 1976.

SUN YAT-SEN: FRUSTRATED PATRIOT, by C. Martin Wilbur. New York: Columbia University Press, 1977.

JAPANESE INTERNATIONAL NEGOTIATING STYLE, by Michael Blaker. New York: Columbia University Press, 1977.

CONTEMPORARY JAPANESE BUDGET POLITICS, by John Creighton Campbell. Berkeley: University of California Press, 1977.

THE MEDIEVAL CHINESE OLIGARCHY, by David Johnson. Boulder, Colo.: Westview Press, 1977.

THE ARMS OF KIANGNAN: MODERNIZATION IN THE CHINESE ORDNANCE INDUSTRY, 1860–1895, by Thomas L. Kennedy. Boulder, Colo.: Westview Press, 1978.

PATTERNS OF JAPANESE POLICYMAKING: EXPERIENCES FROM HIGHER EDUCATION, by T. J. Pempel. Boulder, Colo.: Westview Press, 1978.

THE CHINESE CONNECTION: ROGER S. GREENE, THOMAS W. LAMONT, GEORGE E. SOKOLSKY, AND AMERICAN-EAST ASIAN RELATIONS, by Warren I. Cohen. New York: Columbia University Press, 1978.

MILITARISM IN MODERN CHINA: THE CAREER OF WU P'EI-FU, 1916–1939, by Odoric Y. K. Wou. Folkestone, England: Dawson, 1978.

A CHINESE PIONEER FAMILY: THE LINS OF WU-FENG, by Johanna Meskill. Princeton: Princeton University Press, 1979.

PERSPECTIVES ON A CHANGING CHINA, edited by Joshua A. Fogel and William T. Rowe. Boulder, Colo.: Westview Press, 1979.

THE MEMOIRS OF LI TSUNG-JEN, by T. K. Tong and Li Tsung-jen. Boulder, Colo.: Westview Press, 1979.

UNWELCOME MUSE: CHINESE LITERATURE IN SHANGHAI AND PEKING, 1937–1945, by Edward Gunn. New York: Columbia University Press, 1979.

YENAN AND THE GREAT POWERS: THE ORIGINS OF CHINESE COMMUNIST FOREIGN POLICY, by James Reardon-Anderson. New York: Columbia University Press, 1980.

UNCERTAIN YEARS: CHINESE-AMERICAN RELATIONS, 1947–1950, edited by Dorothy Borg and Waldo Heinrichs. New York: Columbia University Press, 1980.

THE FATEFUL CHOICE: JAPAN'S ADVANCE INTO SOUTHEAST ASIA, edited by James William Morley. New York: Columbia University Press, 1980.

TANAKA GIICHI AND JAPAN'S CHINA POLICY, by William F. Morton. Folkestone, England: Dawson, 1980; New York: St. Martin's Press, 1980.

THE ORIGINS OF THE KOREAN WAR: LIBERATION AND THE EMERGENCE OF SEPARATE REGIMES, 1945–1947, by Bruce Cumings. Princeton: Princeton University Press, 1981.

CLASS CONFLICT IN CHINESE SOCIALISM, by Richard Curt Kraus. New York: Columbia University Press, 1981.

EDUCATION UNDER MAO: CLASS AND COMPETITION IN CANTON SCHOOLS, by Jonathan Unger. New York: Columbia University Press, 1982.

PRIVATE ACADEMIES OF TOKUGAWA JAPAN, by Richard Rubinger. Princeton: Princeton University Press, 1982.

JAPAN AND THE SAN FRANCISCO PEACE SETTLEMENT, by Michael M. Yoshitsu. New York: Columbia University Press, 1982.

NEW FRONTIERS IN AMERICAN-EAST ASIAN RELATIONS: ESSAYS PRESENTED TO DOROTHY BORG, edited by Warren I. Cohen. New York: Columbia University Press, 1983.

THE ORIGINS OF THE CULTURAL REVOLUTION: II, THE GREAT LEAP FORWARD, 1958–1960, by Roderick MacFarquhar. New York: Columbia University Press, 1983.

THE CHINA QUAGMIRE: JAPAN'S EXPANSION ON THE ASIAN CONTINENT, 1933–1941, edited by James William Morley. New York: Columbia University Press, 1983.

FRAGMENTS OF RAINBOWS: THE LIFE AND POETRY OF SAITO MOKICHI, 1882–1953, by Amy Vladeck Heinrich. New York: Columbia University Press, 1983.

THE U.S.–SOUTH KOREAN ALLIANCE: EVOLVING PATTERNS OF SECURITY RELATIONS, edited by Gerald L. Curtis and Sungjoo Han. Lexington, Mass.: Lexington Books, 1983.

DISCOVERING HISTORY IN CHINA: AMERICAN HISTORICAL WRITING ON THE RECENT CHINESE PAST, by Paul A. Cohen. New York: Columbia University Press, 1984.